Direct from the Disciplines

Writing Across the Curriculum

edited by

MARY T. SEGALL & ROBERT A. SMART

Foreword by

HANS BERGMANN

Boynton/Cook
HEINEMANN
Portsmouth, NH

Boynton/Cook Publishers, Inc.
A subsidiary of Reed Elsevier Inc.
361 Hanover Street
Portsmouth, NH 03801–3912
www.boyntoncook.com

Offices and agents throughout the world

© 2005 by Mary T. Segall and Robert A. Smart

Library of Congress Cataloging-in-Publication Data
    Direct from the disciplines : writing across the curriculum / edited by Mary T. Segall and Robert Smart ; foreword by Hans Bergmann.
        p. cm.
    Includes bibliographical references.
    Contents: Theoretical, institutional, and organizational contexts / Robert Smart, Mary Segall—Rewriting business as usual / William Keep—Building a scaffolding for student writing across the disciplines in communication studies / Liam O'Brien—The use of peer evaluations to foster critical analysis of writing in biology / Deborah J. Clark—Protracted peer-reviewed writing assignments in biology : confessions of an apostate cynic of writing across the curriculum / Dennis J. Richardson—The "just right" challenge / Signian McGeary—Aiding and abetting : WAC support for legal writers / Susan R. Dailey—Blogging across the curriculum / Pattie Belle Hastings, Valerie Smith—Writing assignments in computer programming classes / David S. Herscovici—Linked writing to learn assignments in a computer science general education course / Mark E. Hoffman—Writing to learn across the personal essay : the art of digital pastiche / Timothy Dansdill—Writing in political science / Sean P. Duffy—Evaluating writing across the curriculum programs / Suzanne S. Hudd—A cognitive psychologist's rationale for experimenting with WAC / Shar Walbaum—WAC and mathematics / Cornelius Nelan—Building the WAC culture at Quinnipiac / Kathleen M. McCourt—Supporting the WAC initiative : a learning center's perspective / Andrew Delohery—Decolonizing the academy : WAC and institutional recognition and reward systems / Robert A. Smart, Mary T. Segall.
    ISBN 0-86709-582-2 (alk. paper)
    1. English language—Rhetoric—Study and teaching. 2. Interdisciplinary approach in education. 3. Academic writing—Study and teaching. I. Segall, Mary T. II. Smart, Robert (Robert A.). III. Title.

PE1404.D565 2005
808'.042'071—dc22   2004030962

Editors: Lois Bridges and Gloria Pipkin
Production service: Lisa S. Garboski/bookworks
Production coordination: Vicki Kasabian
Cover design: Jenny Jensen Greenleaf
Typesetter: TechBooks
Manufacturing: Louise Richardson

Printed in the United States of America on acid-free paper
09 08 07 06 05 VP 1 2 3 4 5

Contents

Contents by Application

Broad WAC Applications

Critical Thinking: Chapters 3 (Clark; Richardson), 4 (McGeary), 5 (Dailey), 6 (Herscovici), 8 (Duffy), 9 (Hudd), 10 (Walbaum)

Writing in the Disciplines: Chapters 1 (Keep), 2 (O'Brien), 3 (Clark; Richardson), 5 (Dailey), 11 (Nelan)

Writing to Learn: Chapters 3 (Clark; Richardson), 4 (McGeary), 5 (Dailey), 6 (Hastings and Smith; Herscovici; Hoffman) 7 (Dansdill), 8 (Duffy), 9 (Hudd), 10 (Walbaum), 11 (Nelan)

Specific WAC Tools and Strategies

Peer Critique: Chapters 3 (Clark; Richardson), 4 (McGeary), 5 (Dailey), 6 (Hastings and Smith; Hoffman), 7 (Dansdill), 8 (Duffy)

Drafting/Revision: Chapters 1 (Keep), 2 (O'Brien), 3 (Richardson), 6 (Herscovici), 9 (Hudd), 10 (Walbaum)

Journals: Chapters 2 (O'Brien), 4 (ESL, McGeary), 5 (Dailey), 6 (ejournals, Hastings and Smith), 7 (ejournals, Dansdill)

Linking Writing Assignments: Chapters 2 (O'Brien), 3 (Richardson, Clark), 5 (Dailey), 6 (Hoffman), 7 (Dansdill), 8 (Duffy), 10 (Walbaum)

Brief In-Class Writing Activities: Chapters 4 (McGeary), 6 (Hoffman), 8 (Duffy)

Reader Response: Chapters 5 (Dailey), 6 (Hastings and Smith), 7 (Dansdill), 8 (Duffy)

Beyond the Classroom

Academic Support: Chapter 12 (Delohery)

Assessment: Chapters 3 (Clark) and 9 (Hudd)

Academic Integrity: Chapters 6 (Hoffman) and 7 (Dansdill), 10 (Walbaum)

Certification Requirements: Chapter 4 (McGeary)

Institutional Recognition: Chapter 13 (Smart and Segall)

Student Portfolio: Chapters 2 (O'Brien), 5 (Dailey), 6 (Hastings and Smith), 10 (Walbaum)

Foreword

Any dean likes having the foreword. Like Chanticleer, he can announce the morning of the day in which Quinnipiac University faculty members show, in chapter after chapter of the book you hold, how much they have done to make teaching better at Quinnipiac University. I could boast that the book will help all those who care about writing and learning in an undergraduate institution. I could crow, ruffle my feathers, and suggest that the administration enabled the change, just as the rooster thinks he created the sunrise. But I, a more modest bird, bring you instead glad tidings of a faculty that has generously, and in astonishing numbers, taken up the ideas and methods of Writing Across the Curriculum. They have demonstrated not just its practical applications in improving the individual piece of undergraduate writing but also demonstrated, and in part enacted, WAC's more radical potential to change almost everything about undergraduate learning. I am sure that Robert Smart and Mary Segall's claims in the last chapter of this collection for a "revolution" are not too bold.

The successful Writing Across the Curriculum efforts at universities across the country begin with the ambition of (usually) one English professor who is a full believer in the movement but crafty enough to understand that the movement must spread itself slowly, from faculty member to faculty member. Nothing about WAC can be mandated, precisely because it itself is not about learning by mandate. Professor of English Robert Smart is the Quinnipiac director, a man smart enough to know he must, like a good parent, plan for his own obsolescence. He must even pretend he didn't have all the good ideas first. He must encourage participation in workshops with (false) promises of lobster tails for lunch, and then, at the celebratory dinner for winning the Davis Foundation grant, which served real lobster tails, the pathfinder must don a funny floppy lobster hat and be photographed with his new peers. He must, as he and Mary Segall explain, continually transfer responsibility away from himself and even watch that responsibility take up residence outside the English department, nesting inside other disciplines. Writing Across the Curriculum insists that all disciplines ask "in what ways will graduates of our institution use language?"

The faculty members who joined Professor Smart in the Quinnipiac Writing Across the Curriculum program all shared the courage of knowing that their teaching needed something new. Good teachers always start over and over again, beginning in the acknowledgment of defeat, or at least of insufficient victory. We teachers despair because our undergraduate students seem not to know enough *and* not to care enough about knowing. We despair that, in the main, they do not have the exciting experience that we often have. We have a tremendous sense of the excitement of learning, of epiphanies at looking through a microscope at genetic material, at reading a Virginia Woolf paragraph, at understanding a theorem, at *writing it down*. Teachers also know, I think, that learning things does not simply stack up our knowledge like corn in a grain elevator. Learning is another element entirely, a fire that creates the ability to learn further, that makes for abilities and freedoms, that reduces privation and the private. More than that, even, learning is exciting and important just in itself. That learning is hardest of all to describe, as Thoreau admits in his book about learning through writing, his *Walden*:

> The true harvest of my daily life is somewhat as intangible and indescribable as the tints of morning or evening. It is a little star-dust caught, a segment of the rainbow which I have clutched.

To hope for "a little star-dust caught" is not too bold, even in the introductory college classroom, I think. The explicit goal of the many writing-to-learn techniques described "direct from the disciplines" in this book is better writing. The essays show professors from all the disciplines taking up the tools they learned and adapting and readapting them to work in their own classrooms. The implicit revolution these faculty members nurture is a new idea of undergraduate education. They feed the idea that the student is a learner, creating knowledge, creating *texts* of knowledge, not simply a grain elevator of information. The student must become, like the expert, a learner who knows he or she is learning, a self-monitoring learner thinking through prose.

Direct from the Disciplines: Writing Across the Curriculum is valuable in all its chapters, in its individual accounts of teaching in many of the disciplines. The story it tells about our whole institution is more important still. I crow after all—for the faculty.

Hans Bergmann
Dean, College of Liberal Arts
Quinnipiac University

Preface

While the Writing Across the Curriculum (WAC) movement has an inspiring history, most of the WAC literature focuses on program development and research from the WAC director's point of view, describing implementation of writing across the disciplines. Since WAC directors tend to have a background in English, or more specifically rhetoric and composition, their perceptions will, quite naturally, be shaped by the theories and paradigms that shape literary and composition studies.

Our text differs significantly in that we offer a perspective directly from the discipline faculty, the support staff, and the administrators themselves who are involved with the program. In this way, we hope to contribute to the field by offering an unfiltered view of WAC from participants within their own disciplines. We are excited about their views and believe that sharing their concerns and successes will broaden the literature available to engage further research. In describing their experiences, the contributors provide revealing commentary that reinforces some conventional wisdom about WAC, while provoking pragmatic and theoretical questions as well. We believe that these fresh voices from the disciplines will enable other WAC programs to revisit their own assumptions and will offer administrators and faculty alike an invigorating look at WAC from their peers' point of view.

Acknowledgments

We wish to thank all our colleagues and administrators at Quinnipiac University whose steady support of our WAC Program inspired us to compile their stories. We also wish to thank the staff at Heinemann, especially Lois Bridges and Gloria Pipkin for their stalwart guidance and extraordinary effort, even during Hurricane Ivan, for making the publication of this book possible. Our family and friends endured loyally during the project, especially our spouses Elizabeth and Seth, our children (Matthew, Adam, Micah, and Jamie, Josh and his wife Mondeep, and Jessica), and Paula Rogovin (dear lifelong friend). To all of them we are grateful. And finally, thanks to the Davis Educational Foundation for their financial support of Quinnipiac University's writing-across-the-curriculum program.

Introduction

Theoretical, Institutional, and Organizational Contexts

Robert A. Smart and Mary T. Segall

"Whew! Now that I've passed English 101 and 102, I can get on with the *real* courses for my future." Such expressions by students are pervasive and can cause premature graying of writing faculty. Unfortunately, faculty may inadvertently reinforce these students' perceptions when their pedagogy does not support writing to learn or does not include the scaffolding necessary to promote writing in the disciplines. Often, these attitudes result in the perception that students cannot write or that the first-year composition faculty are not doing their job.[1] How to change such perceptions is one of the challenges that many nascent Writing Across the Curriculum (WAC) programs face, and we are no exception. In this introduction, we would like to explain the theoretical and historical context in which our contributors joined the WAC movement at Quinnipiac and from which they describe their motivation, application, and assessment of writing from within their various disciplines.

Theoretical Context

We believe that the growth and success of our WAC program is due to acceptance of two major premises by the faculty outside the English department, whose voices you will hear in the following chapters. The first premise is that growth in writing necessarily occurs beyond the student's first-year composition course(s). Based on the literature about writing development and on the fact that academic discourse is not a single discourse that can be taught in only one semester (Elbow 1991, 153), attention to writing must continue during the student's entire four years. Furthermore, discipline-specific discourse remains in flux, even as we continue to redefine the epistemology relevant to each field (Thaiss 1999, 315; see Dailey [Chapter 5]). As more faculty outside of English attend to their students' writing, the more we know about the complex nexus between writing instruction and content area learning. Helping students to make the transition to discipline-specific discourse, then, becomes the responsibility of all faculty. If we accept this premise, it follows that WAC is more than grammar-across-the-disciplines; it encompasses all writing in the disciplines in all its various forms. Writing becomes not just an "add-on" (McLeod and Maimon 2000, 575; see also Duffy [Chapter 8]), a formalistic acculturation; rather, it requires pedagogical reorientation to provide an environment for cognitive understanding (see Walbaum [Chapter 10]). Expressive writing becomes a tool to nurture more transactional writing (Young and Weiss 1999, 63), and consequently broadens our definition of what constitutes a "text" (see Hoffman; Hastings and Smith [Chapter 6], and Dansdill [Chapter 7]). In this way, false dichotomies, represented by the example of the student who thinks there is little connection between writing and learning about his major, can be recognized and dispelled more readily.

In their article, "Clearing the Air: WAC Myths and Realities," Susan McLeod and Elaine Maimon, while debunking several myths about WAC, offer the following definition as more representative of sustained WAC program characteristics:

> WAC is a pedagogical reform movement that presents an alternative to the "delivery of information" model of teaching in higher education, to lecture classes and to multiple choice, true/false testing. In place of this model, WAC presents two ways of using writing in the classroom and in the curriculum: writing to learn and learning to write in the disciplines (this later may also be thought of as "writing to communicate"). (579)

They see little distinction between WAC and WID because, in their view, one can as easily use writing to learn in the disciplines as is typically assumed in WAC. Similarly, Christopher Thaiss sees a false dichotomy in polarizing expressive writing (writing to learn) and transactional writing (learning to write) (Thaiss 1999, 302). As our Quinnipiac WAC committee struggled to stipulate our own definition of WAC, we wanted to ground this working definition on several key principles:

- Writing is integrally related to reading and speaking.
- There are at least two kinds of writing in the academy, both appropriate to the learning and assessment of learning that takes place in the classroom (writing to learn and writing to measure learning, "expressive" and "transactional," respectively).
- Plans for implementation of a WAC program should take their scope from the curriculum as a whole.
- The cumulative effect of a WAC approach like this one on the community would be to enhance both the teaching and the learning that takes place in our classes, without dramatically altering what we already do.

We also wanted to apply these essential WAC principles to our work with the Core Curriculum and with the rest of the undergraduate curriculum via WAC workshops focused on the needs of the four schools on campus.[2] These principles in turn shaped our second premise, that WAC has complex, interconnected parts. We came to appreciate the truth of the second "reality" that McLeod and Maimon (2000) identify: "WAC is a programmatic entity made up of several elements, all of them intertwined: faculty development, curricular components, student support, assessment, and an administrative structure and budget" (580). Thus, the intimate involvement of our Learning Center (see Delohery [Chapter 12]), our administrators (see McCourt [Chapter 12]), our core curriculum committee (see Duffy [Chapter 8]), our assessment committee (see Hudd [Chapter 9]), and faculty development were all crucial to our success.

We found as well that the factors identified by Eric Miraglia and Susan McLeod in their article, "Wither WAC? Interpreting the Stories/Histories of Enduring WAC Programs," also characterized our program: "Administrative support (including funding) . . . Grassroots/faculty support . . . [and] Strong, consistent program leadership" (1997, 48). The last factor requires some explanation. Not only has our WAC program director exhibited the strong leadership necessary for program consistency and growth, but he has also led in a democratic, even Socratic, way as well. Our faculty unanimously describe his leadership as *inductive*, an approach that involves "stakeholders" (Condon 2001, 46) in the process. Indeed, we have been fortunate in a director who fits Miraglia and McLeod's description: "The best WAC directors we know . . . have a collaborative, collegial leadership style, one that encourages faculty to take credit for the success of WAC" (56).

In this book, we would like to have our faculty not only "take credit for the success of WAC," as Miraglia and McLeod suggest, but also to share their unique voices and motivations for bringing to fruition our WAC vision. In keeping with the collaboration that has characterized our work from the beginning, you will hear from the faculty in various disciplines precisely how WAC has shaped their teaching. When we organized the first WAC committee on campus in spring 2001, we drew from faculty who had expressed some previous interest in writing across the curriculum. Supplemented by new faculty at Quinnipiac who arrived with an interest in fostering better writing in their courses, this charter group—called QUWAC, the Quinnipiac University Writing Committee—grappled with some of the key elements of a writing across the curriculum pedagogy: the difference between WAC and WID, the role of writing to learn assignments (WTL) in any campuswide initiative, and the optimum saturation percentages that should become our target numbers for full implementation of the university's WAC program. For many of the committee members, these concepts and distinctions were new territory, and they might have seemed at times a little beside the point. Nevertheless, using well-circulated and accepted articulations of the various concepts as our discussion signposts, we worked to develop a set of distinctions that would be appropriate for Quinnipiac University.

As a lowest common denominator, we decided that our goal would be to have nearly all faculty, full- and part-time, use WTL assignments in their classes, based on the belief that WTL assignments in any classroom enhance critical thinking and prepare students to do better writing. From this basic objective, the difference between courses—in terms of how much attention the teacher would pay to formal writing—would be governed by class size and by the willingness of faculty to require drafts, to craft linked assignments, and to use peer editing and workshop techniques. We knew that this would be burdensome to teachers in large sectioned classes, and might also be onerous for faculty who saw writing instruction in their courses as competing for valuable class time normally used to teach "content." Over a five-year implementation calendar, beginning with fall semester 2001, we determined that a 70 percent participation rate for full- and part-time faculty would be optimum, even if a bit optimistic.

Nearly all these discussions during that first semester were surprisingly practical; it was as though everyone tried to ask the same questions that their colleagues would ask. The success of a particular approach at another campus was not automatically accepted as proof that the same ideas or techniques would be successful at Quinnipiac. Quinnipiac University is a multifaceted institution, with a mission that clearly points students towards professional employment after graduation. For many faculty, interest in new approaches to teaching writing and learning is directly tied to writing in the disciplines, and the key to our success with them depends in large part on our ability to translate the general benefits of WTL into specific improvement in student writing in their upper-level courses or in professional roles after university.

All these issues were raised by the faculty serving on QUWAC. The most striking part of these early conversations, as we look back, was the near absence of nay-saying among the members of the committee. When committee members had tough questions about the logistical feasibility of a particular idea, they asked them, and then everyone set out to find ways to make it work. Almost never did we get sidetracked by discussions about why a particular idea or a particular approach to teaching writing across the curriculum wouldn't—or shouldn't—work. In this, we were particularly blessed, so much so that at moments when we genuinely disagreed—about whether to implement writing intensive classes, for example—it took all of us a day or two to recognize that we had come to fruitful consensus and not to a programmatic or philosophical impasse. Incidentally, we decided against establishing writing intensive courses, as a guard against institutionalizing WAC into a select number of courses, instead of striving to include attention to writing performance in all classes.

The second most notable moment in this process occurred when the committee approved a decentralization plan for its workshop activities. Between spring 2001 and spring 2003, QUWAC hosted nine campuswide workshops (some focused on the particular issues of one of the four undergraduate schools on campus), all of them successful. We drew wide participation, we disseminated WAC materials broadly at all the meetings, and the meetings were hosted by faculty from all the various schools. By spring 2003, however, we had reached the saturation point for these workshops, marked by the fact that the same people began to turn up at all the workshops. At this point, we changed the charter for QUWAC to make it primarily a strategic planning committee, and devolved the general workshop function to the various schools of the university. The key benefit from this change is the direct input we receive from the individual schools about the workshops that would be the most useful and attractive for their faculty. General instruction about how to include WTL in all classes, for example, is handled in paid summer workshops for faculty. In summer 2003, the first team of WAC committee members completed their training to lead individual faculty workshops in Summer 2004 through 2006.[3]

The key success factors in this process are clear: the purposeful organization of willing faculty into a steering committee, the willingness of the group to solve problems using local campus realities, and an implementation plan that involved everyone on the committee, as well as sympathetic faculty from the various schools. Without any one of these factors in play, Quinnipiac University's WAC program would have languished as an English department initiative, viewed by many faculty as an attempt to impose the English department's work on non-English faculty. To be sure, administrative support has been crucial to the success of this effort, but the willing and full participation of faculty from all the university's constituencies has been and remains decisive.

The many essays in this volume suggest several groupings, from the fairly predictable arrangement by discipline (see the table of contents) and school, to more dynamic alignments that might suggest intertextual discourses that none of the individual contributors would have conceived in the drafting process. Another useful arrangement of all this good work, however, might be by scope, ranging from broadly framed applications of WAC principles and pedagogies within courses, to applications of specific tools (such as peer editing) to a variety of already established courses, to a final grouping which spans the territory outside the classroom, essays that consider logistical and/or administrative questions. In this way, a reader wishing to learn about how a faculty member from the same discipline adapted WAC principles to his or her class might peruse the primary table of contents. Another reader who is more interested in particular techniques and approaches might skip directly to the Contents by Application. Yet a third reader—probably a new WAC campus coordinator—might find solace and advice in Chapter 12, the administrative section. Our fond hope, however, is that these chapters not appear exclusive, and that reading one essay might suggest other threads of the discussion, which are developed in other essays from different perspectives. We should also note that in all cases, the particular philosophical and/or pedagogical "fit" between specific techniques or practices and disciplines or hierarchical perspectives has been left to the authors to describe. In this way, many of the essays reflect not only the practical concerns of the authors, but also the peculiarities and differences that develop as WAC theory is put into practice by varied professionals at all levels of the institutional community.

In the table of contents, eleven specific disciplines are represented: Biology, Business, Law, Interactive Digital Design, Mass Communications, Mathematics, Occupational Therapy, Political Science, Psychology, Sociology, and English. Some of these essays describe fairly modest implementations of WAC, and these descriptions of WAC techniques augment, rather than radically change disciplinary curricula: Business (Keep), Psychology (Walbaum),

IDD (Hoffman and Herscovici), and Occupational Therapy (McGeary) would fall into this category. In all these essays, the implementation of WAC techniques and philosophy was purposeful, and the uses to which the in-class writing and revision were put represent value added to existing syllabi and course designs. Some other faculty, however, implemented more radical WAC pedagogies, with the aim of improving overall student writing and thinking performance by dramatically changing the way that the courses were taught. The essays from Political Science (Duffy), Law (Dailey), and English (Dansdill) exemplify this more radical approach.

Other chapters (see "Specific Tools" in Contents by Application) focus primarily on the uses of particular WAC techniques, such as peer-editing (Biology—Clark and Richardson) and weblogs (Hastings and Smith) in classes to foster better writing from students. For classes that do not require heavy reliance on technology access, peer-editing represents one of the most fruitful applications of an expanded writing pedagogy. Peer-editing allows students to review their drafted work and to comment meaningfully on these drafts from rubrics that are particularly focused on the writing objectives of the course, all without dramatically increasing faculty review and evaluation time. In the Clark, Hudd, and Richardson essays, readers will also find some assessment data that measure the immediate response of students to the perceived improvement of their writing from the peer-editing exercises. Weblogs represent one of the hottest and most accessible writing environments that can augment what happens in the classroom. Smith and Hastings' essay reviews not only the most current uses of weblogs (along with relevant resources for interested readers), but also samples extensively from weblogs that their students have kept for a number of years.

The last group of essays, Chapters 12 and 13 ("Beyond the Classroom" in the Contents by Application), looks beyond the beginning implementation of WAC in the classroom to issues concerning administrative support (McCourt and Delohery), assessment of programmatic outcomes (Hudd, Chapter 9), and institutional questions about faculty rewards and professional valuation (Smart and Segall). While these essays come at the end of the volume (thereby suggesting an additional, evolutionary logic to the arrangement of the essays), they raise critical, sometimes crucial questions about WAC in the post start-up phase: How can (should?) institutional support of WAC move effectively beyond start-up and through implementation without diverting a disproportional share of its resources to this one effort? How should an institution support both its faculty and its students once increased attention is paid to student writing across the curriculum? How can we determine accurately the effectiveness of what we are doing and what we are asking our colleagues to do about writing in class? It should be clear that our authors have addressed these questions slightly differently, and it seems to us that these subtle but significant distinctions are not contradictory or exclusive, but rather they form key parts in a larger, almost global picture of the future of WAC at Quinnipiac University.

The final essay is perhaps the most speculative one in the collection, in which we consider the issue of faculty research and professional development within a WAC institutional environment. In what is surely a recapitulation of the English department "wars" of recent decades, between traditional litera-ture pedagogies and the new crop of compositionists who arrived in the late 1960s to address writing within and outside of the discipline, non-English fac-ulty are likely to run into critical questions about how their WAC work is to be valued in the department's decisions about promotion, tenure, and review. While many faculty who are initially involved in our WAC workshops receive a small stipend, as do their trained faculty leaders, the issue goes far beyond the issue of money and stipends. The small sums of money that all the faculty receive are nominal, and largely represent our recognition as an institution that this faculty development work takes place outside the contracted nine months for full-time faculty and outside the course-by-course obligations of our part-time faculty.[4] The money we pay faculty for their time in the summer is not a substitute for institutional rewards and recognition, and, we would suggest, a WAC program that hopes in the long term to interest faculty in WAC and maintain their participation via stipends will likely discover that individual faculty participation in WAC training and activities falls off once the faculty member is promoted or tenured. The usual designation for WAC participation in a faculty member's professional portfolio is as part of "Community Service," along with service on student judicial boards and advising the stu-dent newspaper. If we have any hope of institutionalizing the hard work that these faculty do, we need to shift that work into teaching and scholarly activ-ity, which at most institutions like ours, form the most valued part of the pro-fessional triangle. We hope that our speculations about these crucial issues will prove helpful to every reader.

Notes

1. Even this common issue is not always easy to deal with, since many of the faculty who complain bitterly about how the English faculty are not doing their jobs very well are convinced that the most obvious signs of poor writing are spelling and common punctuation errors, problems that rarely have any connection to more im-portant writing issues like logical development, the student's ability to articulate and sustain an argument and to present credible evidence for it. This common and sad misunderstanding also diminishes, we have found, as more and more faculty participate in the WAC conversations that we provide across campus.

2. The School of Liberal Arts, The School of Business, The School of Health Sci-ences, and The School of Communication. Quinnipiac University also has a School of Law whose faculty participate regularly in our WAC workshops, but to date there are no plans to formally include The School of Law in the plans for the un-dergraduate school.

3. All these workshops are supported by a generous grant from the Davis Educational Foundation for support of faculty development in WAC.

4.   It should probably be noted that Quinnipiac University has a faculty union that ne-
     gotiates and oversees the implementation of all full-time faculty contracts.

References

Condon, William. 2001. "Accommodating Complexity: WAC Program Evaluation." In
     *WAC for the New Millennium: Strategies for Continuing Writing-Across-the Cur-
     riculum Programs*, eds. Susan H. McLeod, Eric Miraglia, Margot Soven, and
     Christopher Thaiss, 28-51. Urbana, IL: NCTE.

Elbow, Peter. 1991. "Reflections on Academic Discourse: How It Relates to Freshmen
     and Colleagues." *College English* 53 (February): 135–55.

McLeod, Susan, and Elaine Maimon. 2000. "Clearing the Air: WAC Myths and Reali-
     ties." *College English* 62 (May): 573–83.

Miraglia, Eric, and Susan McLeod. 1997. "Wither WAC? Interpreting the Stories/His-
     tories of Enduring WAC Programs." *Writing Program Administration* 20 (Spring):
     46–65.

Thaiss, Christopher. 1999. "Theory in WAC: Where Have We Been, Where Are We
     Going?" In *WAC for the New Millennium: Strategies for Continuing Writing-
     Across-the-Curriculum Programs*, eds. Susan H. McLeod, Eric Miraglia, Margot
     Soven, and Christopher Thaiss, 299–325. Urbana, IL: NCTE.

Young, Art, and Donna Weiss. 1999. "WAC Wired: Electronic Communication Across
     the Curriculum." In *WAC for the New Millennium: Strategies for Continuing
     Writing-Across-the-Curriculum Programs*, eds. Susan H. McLeod, Eric Miraglia,
     Margot Soven, and Christopher Thaiss, 52–85. Urbana,: IL NCTE.

1

Rewriting Business as Usual

William Keep
Professor of Marketing and Advertising

I remember clearly the story told by a senior faculty member when I was a Ph.D. student at a large land grant university. A political battle brewed—which school would house the new major in advertising, the School of Communications or the School of Business? Faculty in both schools knew advertising would be a "hot" major bringing many new students and proportional budgetary support. The School of Business would either get to offer courses comprising the new major, or keep current courses labeled "business writing," but not both. The business school lost the new major and, much to their collective disappointment, continued to be responsible for writing courses.

So began my exposure to the ironic, if not contradictory, consideration of writing in business schools. Virtually all business faculty members agree that good writing is a fundamental business skill and most, in my experience, express disappointment in the writing skills displayed by a typical undergraduate business student. Still, the notion of keeping "business writing" in the business school curriculum at the cost of losing "advertising" was by all accounts a poor trade-off. This was true even though business writing was taught by only a few writing specialists, not the entire business faculty. Why?

I will hazard a guess. No doubt those writing specialists within the business school carried their message of sound writing not just to the students but to their faculty colleagues as well. No doubt the message to their colleagues included some encouragement to including writing exercises with substantial feedback. And, no doubt their colleagues emitted an unheard but collective groan. Quite possibly, teaching good writing seemed to require more effort, more frustration, and more individual student contact than many business professors want to put forth.

This doesn't mean that business faculty lack the conviction of their claim that writing well is important in business. Rather, factors ranging from class

size to teaching loads to an absence of effective teaching techniques contributed to the result. Perhaps, just like their own students, business professors
drew away from a task they felt they could not handle effectively given the time
available. Place that business faculty member in a large university with introductory courses populated by no fewer than five hundred students per section,
and the question of embedding writing assignments appears prohibitive.

Advertising, on the other hand, brings to mind creativity, jingles, and
snappy copy that may go against grammar rules to surprise or shock the reader.
Aborting writing conventions can sometimes be a key aspect of the copy strategy. Fewer "rules" mean greater flexibility. Alternatively, critiquing a business
writing sample can remind both faculty and student of similar negative feedback
received in other courses that focused on structure, flow, and word use. To business faculty, teaching writing lay in the realm of a different discipline, not in the
realm of creative copy and the more empirically driven income statement.

If the above picture captures the mood, the basic problem remains. How
will undergraduate business students progressively learn to become good writers? Interestingly, some time after the decision to assign advertising to the
School of Communication, the School of Business at the above university discontinued the business writing courses. For the next twenty years, student
writing was addressed according to the interest and time available to individual
faculty—if it was addressed at all.

With this background, I decided that representing the School of Business
on the Quinnipiac University Writing Across the Curriculum (QUWAC)
Committee made good sense. Despite the small classroom size (somewhere between twenty and thirty) and relatively frequent student contact in our business
school, writing problems among students persist. The most encouraging message from the very first meeting of QUWAC was that some earlier presump-
tions I held about teaching writing might not have been true. Helping students
become better writers need not require significantly more effort, time, frustration, or uncertainty and the skill set is achievable by faculty in any discipline.

In the following sections I outline what I have come to view as the most
significant issues that need to be addressed as we move to implement writing
across the curriculum in the business school. I do not see these as insurmount-
able issues, and I have experienced a modest amount of success in my own
classroom.

Writing Within the Discipline

Good writing is accomplished within a context. In fact, unlike creating a standard income statement, an author's writing style can be altered to fit the context, thereby making it more palatable for the audience and ultimately more
effective. Any faculty member in business who has published in a professional
journal, written a consulting report, or written a newspaper or magazine piece
for the general public has experienced the impact of context. Thus both the

variety of writing situations and the discipline-specific context within which business students write are critical. As a result, I quickly realized that we cannot just talk about good business writing. In the School of Business at Quinnipiac University, we need to talk specifically about writing for students in finance, accounting, management, marketing, international business, and computer information systems. While all these students will face certain common writing situations (for example, writing a business memo), there will also be some important differences.

For example, a marketing major can easily find him or herself writing for a very broad audience, such as when creating an advertisement for a popular magazine. Writing in marketing can range from lengthy internal documents such as strategic plans, to marketing content used in trifold support pieces given to salespeople for distribution to industrial customers, to direct mail (commonly called "junk" mail) sent directly to consumers, to multimedia advertising campaigns using voice and visuals in a variety of formats (such as radio, billboards, newspapers, etc.), to technical marketing research reports.

Management majors will typically write documents for internal consumption. These can range from policy statements coming out of the Human Resources office, to "how to" instructions for line workers, to descriptive and technical reports. Finance majors and accounting majors will tend to use text that describes quantitative results, relying less heavily on writing than, for example, international business majors. And of course, papers written by majors in computer information systems will be riddled with technical jargon.

Just as the writings of political science majors may differ from those in psychology, differences within the business school need to be explicitly recognized. Any attempt to roll out writing-across-the-curriculum to business school faculty necessarily means adjustments at the discipline level. At times, these differences may be an artifact of the departmental silos we are so fond of. The fact that some differences, certainly not all, may be more perceived than real creates what may be the first challenge. Just as a tailor can make from the same whole cloth an attractive suit for a variety of customers, the comfort will be in the style and customized fit for each customer.

The formation of the first QUWAC committee addressed this issue by being truly multidisciplinary. Though logically chaired by a professor of English, committee meetings were open forums for discussing writing issues. In one early meeting, I listened with amazement as a political science professor described passive voice as a valued writing style. I began fighting against passive voice with my very first student, yet here was a respected colleague valuing a style I sought to dramatically reduce. In the back of my mind, I immediately saw every passive voice–intensive paper I ever received as the residual effect of a previously completed course in political science. Not true of course, but I now had someone to blame. I also learned that professors in the hard sciences often teach report writing that is strong on information and weak on style. There were culprits everywhere!

Within just a few meetings, we began to share both concern for and appreciation of the different approaches to writing found on a college campus. Passive writing has a history and tradition in some contexts and, of course, can be very effective when strategically mixed with active voice. Market research reports can closely resemble the results of a chemical laboratory experiment, and the executive summary of a business plan can include all the drama and believability of a good short story. In short, we learned to see the skill of writing as separate yet embedded within our respective disciplines. This lesson was important as the committee considered issues of implementation.

The Vocabulary Hurdle

Teaching the language of writing also varies across disciplines. English professors describe writing according to dynamic yet fairly well established labels (for example, argumentative essay, descriptive essay, etc.). Students first use the vocabulary of English in elementary school where they work hard on grammar and structure. High school follows with more of the same, generally embedded within a strong dose of literature. Literature and composition provide opportunities for students to explore the nuances of specific writing situations and styles. English courses in college provide yet again further opportunities to learn the language of English. Even the least competent student is on somewhat familiar ground.

The first discipline-specific course for many non-English majors quickly departs from years of reinforcing the vocabulary used in English. If the student is very lucky, her non-English faculty member will help demonstrate how what was taught in English is relevant to the student's new discipline. Based on conversations with faculty, however, I suspect that rarely takes place. More commonly, non-English faculty either implicitly convey the message that writing in this discipline is different, without saying how, or convey the more simplistic and often negatively tinged message that writing is an important skill that most students lack. Even the most helpful first course in the discipline generally comes without a grammar book, a handout, or even an agreed-upon format. Not surprisingly, students may conclude that they have passed, successfully or otherwise, through their "English" stage and are now onto their chosen careers. The unspoken message is clear: studying and writing in their discipline is different from studying "English."

The business disciplines offer a vocabulary steeped in ambiguity. Unlike some fields that choose and use labels carefully, business disciplines offer clearly defined terms whose applications vary with situations. Thus "gross margin" can mean "gross profit," "operating profit," "contribution margin," and even "profit"—or not. Market segments may or may not be described simply as "markets," "segments," and "target markets," depending on one's perspective. Marketing appears to be particularly susceptible to new language that presumably fits an increasingly clear and specific understanding of market phenomena. But no one in the discipline seems inclined to clarify the differences between old and new, and even the glossaries and indices among textbooks vary in definition and word use.

The implications for teaching writing are not encouraging. If academics in business are not careful with their own language, will they carefully observe the language of other disciplines? Further, and perhaps more important, have attempts been made to bridge the language of "English" to other disciplines? One can easily imagine a book or paper describing the application of various writing tasks within each discipline, yet no such book or paper circulates in business. Therefore, the student never really learns the similarity between an argumentative essay, on the one hand, and a product positioning paper in marketing on the other.

To appreciate the impact of this vocabulary gap, consider the language of mathematics. Often I find myself reminding students of one or two simple algebraic approaches to solving numeric problems in marketing. Even more importantly, on occasion a student will approach me after class to defend an alternative mathematical approach, citing a lesson learned in an earlier math course. Never in fifteen years has one of my students offered an alternative writing approach based on lessons learned in an English class. This is not to suggest that lessons weren't learned, but rather that the student could not see the relevance or application. Long ago in business, we adopted the vocabulary of mathematics, but not that of English.

The absence of a clear transition between the vocabulary of English and that used within non-English disciplines creates a learning chasm that few faculty members on their own seem interested in bridging. Whether at a large state university or small private school, business faculty invariably laid responsibility for teaching writing on the English faculty. According to this thinking, if a student cannot see the relevance between a lesson learned in English and a writing assignment in business, the fault lies with the English faculty.

The logical approach would be to link vocabulary used in English courses with the fundamental writing tasks found in business. To make such a linkage requires a dialogue between English faculty and those in business disciplines. Writing Across the Curriculum can establish such a dialogue. This effort at Quinnipiac University is apparent in two formats. First, the QUWAC committee provides school-specific seminars that bring together faculty from the English department with those in various disciplines. In business this allows finance and marketing faculty to hear about doable writing assignments purposely designed to summarize, describe, or argue. Generally, school-specific seminars include at least one faculty member who has already experienced some success in the classroom using one or two new approaches to writing.

A second effort provides one-on-one training in the form of a three-day summer faculty development program. Here a QUWAC trainer works with a dozen faculty members from a wide range of disciplines. Each faculty member brings a syllabus that can be revised with new writing assignments. The session combines candid descriptions of a wide variety of writing situations with well-established methods for increasing writing effectiveness without simply increasing writing volume. The end result is a shared appreciation for the variety of writing situations and a shared vocabulary.

The Troubles with Teams

In many business disciplines students often work in groups. At times, all student work in a business course, with the exception of exams, will be completed in groups. And the class size in a business course is often double that of a composition course. Student groups work on cases, simulations, business plans, research projects, and presentations. While such work can be supportive and enhance student learning, group work does not easily accommodate the improvement of individual student's writing skills. In fact, group work often inhibits this goal. When left to their own devices, students will often self-select according to their strengths. The student who already writes well becomes the group's author; the student with strong math skills analyzes the numbers, and so on. And in the end faculty rereward students according to their individual strengths.

The problem is compounded in schools with high average class size. I have taught MBA classes with as many as 45 students. A class of 45 students taught using the case method will generate 405 individual analyses if nine cases are assigned throughout the semester. At five pages per analysis, grading cases involves correcting 2,025 pages of text, and this does not include exams. The prospect of providing feedback on both the analysis and writing becomes daunting. No wonder faculty resort to either group write-ups or comments quickly written in the margin, such as "vague" and "weak organization," with little direction for improvement. Compare this to the thoughtfully constructed approach sometimes found in an English class where revision is the focus and students are given examples in advance.

A desire to move to the next case or discipline topic may also undermine an emphasis on revision and feedback. Unlike English, where even in literature classes good composition and approaches to writing are discussed, in non-English disciplines writing is not generally considered part of the course content. Writing is moved to the back burner. In team-based courses, writing can easily be further diminished by providing limited feedback, no individual accountability and, above all, by returning major written works at the conclusion of the semester (or worse yet, the beginning of the next). Yet each of these tactics can be found time and time again.

Some Personal Reflections on QUWAC

The goal of QUWAC is no less than restructuring how writing is treated by non-English faculty. Ironically, English faculty have for many years realized the benefits of short written assignments, self-critique, revision, and peer feedback. Logs and journals give students the opportunity to show improvement over time without requiring that each entry be graded. Examples of revision and good writing abound, but not so in business.

In larger sections, I now address the team issue by making each individual solely responsible for writing one or more case analyses. The team discusses the content and arguments to be presented, and one person composes the answer. The paper receives two grades, one for analysis shared by all team members and one for writing recorded only for the author. One of the immediate positive benefits of this approach is that students quickly realize that writing and thinking are interconnected. As soon as I implemented this approach, a few students openly worried that the author might fail to adequately convey the team's thinking. They realized good ideas can be lost in poor writing. I allow those students concerned with a possible thinking/writing disconnect to provide supplementary evidence at the time the case is submitted. Thus far, I have found that even poor writers try hard to include all major points and arguments discussed by the group.

I have also begun using short reflective assignments that are peer reviewed. These assignments serve three purposes. First, when reading multiple samples aloud to the class, I demonstrate how a single subject can be understood differently by an audience of students. Second, the assignment encourages students to reflect on what is being said in the classroom by me and their classmates. Third, students are forced to recognize that in the work environment they are always speaking and writing to an audience. What peers think they said becomes tangible evidence of their ability to communicate.

During the next few years, QUWAC will build a database of success stories and examples from various disciplines. My goal is to help ensure that all business disciplines are represented and that business faculty members understand that helping students write better can be achieved even in a team-oriented teaching environment.

Revision, Reflection, Respect

National Public Radio stations offer a weekly program entitled *Whad' Ya Know?* In it contestants vie for prizes by demonstrating knowledge in a given subject area. It is this theme that seems to permeate undergraduate education. We have multiple tools for measuring what our students know. We use a variety of descriptive statistics to measure everything from knowledge of concepts to how often they access a course webpage. We can check vocabulary, math skills, and theory applications. We can give assignments that require integration and creativity, and nationally normed tests allow us to compare our students with others studying the same discipline.

Despite their importance, however, we appear less prepared and have fewer tools for evaluating the verbal and written communications of individual students. On the writing side, we are challenged to adopt efficient processes that reveal writing skills and lapses, and provide opportunities for improvement. Ironically, improvement in the evaluation of written work with the opportunity to revise will likely help students better understand and retain content.

To my best understanding, revision is the only way to avoid simply rere-warding strong writers and repunishing weak ones. In the case context, revi-sion means giving students an opportunity to improve their writing by having them rewrite in light of my comments on the current case. In this way, I pre-serve my timetable yet give students the opportunity to demonstrate improve-ment. In some cases, this means sending students—even graduate students—to the Learning Center for assistance. In courses that involve lengthy projects, I grade successive sections with writing comments intended to improve the final product.

By providing such opportunities, we encourage students to view the im-provement of their writing to be an ongoing and important goal. The vocabulary issue I raised earlier in some ways limits my effectiveness, as students and I struggle to establish a shared vocabulary that provides meaningful feedback. A successful writing across the curriculum rollout can help remedy this situation.

Reflection also helps students as they self-assess their ability to communi-cate. Again, consider the case analysis approach. Student, usually in groups, read and analyze a business case, generally selecting one or more remedies. The case is then discussed during the class period when the assignment is turned in to the professor. Points off follow because the student has failed to recognize and use relevant information, or failed to successfully communicate the application of that information. In short, something is missing.

I have adopted a case log to encourage students to think reflectively about their work. After the class discusses the case, each student writes a case log. The purpose of the log is to answer two questions: (1) what are the theories and ideas that underlie a successful case analysis? and (2) if given the opportunity, how would the student communicate his or her analysis differently? In this way, I hope students will reflect on both what they didn't know and how they would have communicated differently. Here I am looking less at style issues than issues of emphasis and argument.

Student reactions to writing feedback range from affirmation, to surprise, to denial, to resignation. In most classes, students seem surprised that a mar-keting professor wants to aggressively evaluate and help improve their writing. I reject the notion that any student, even a graduate student who has been writ-ing for years, has exhausted his or her capacity to improve. To me it is a matter of respect. If I can convey confidence in the potential for all students to become strong writers, and an equal confidence in my ability to be helpful, I may be able change how they feel about themselves. Once they see that is possible, stu-dents become less defensive and more open to comments.

Conclusion

My involvement in writing across the curriculum has altered my view of what is possible in my classroom. From the very beginning, the approach for implementing QUWAC has been inclusive, extending well beyond the English faculty. We still have a long way to go, particularly in the School of Business, where there is significant momentum for "business as usual."

Since my initial participation in QUWAC, I have moved from a full-time faculty position to become a full-time administrator with some teaching responsibilities (i.e., one course per semester). As the primary administrative representative on the QUWAC Committee, I continue to be impressed by the sustained positive attitude of the committee. From the beginning, the program director outlined a multiyear process with identifiable sign posts. Achieving anticipated progress has sustained morale and encouraged committee members to press on.

We are now about to move deeper into the respective disciplines. Like me, most faculty members have yet to fully appreciate the tools available to support good writing. Two tasks lie ahead: increasing faculty awareness of what is possible, and building faculty confidence using tools specific to their discipline and teaching style. The patient yet persistent hands-on approach adopted thus far will likely take us to a point in the near future where faculty members will openly discuss among their peers successful approaches to improve writing in the classroom.

2

Building a Scaffolding for Student Writing Across the Disciplines in Communication Studies

Liam O'Brien
Associate Professor, School of Communications

Every department or school of Communication is a department or school of storytelling. Effective communication demands mastery in the presentation of story through the organized delivery of the written word, whether the final form is a print article, a radio or broadcast news segment, a theatrical perform- ance, an academic paper, a film, or even a class lecture based on notes. Writ- ing fosters critical thinking. As students distill their thoughts into words, writing becomes a fundamental component of the learning process. With writing the story at the heart of what we teach, is there a framework, a scaffolding for writ- ing across our disciplines in communication that can unite all our efforts to graduate effective communicators?

When I first offered a Senior Seminar in Docudrama, I was amazed at the range of critical thinking and organized argument (or lack thereof) and the mishmash of styles present in my students' research papers: Modern Language Association style, Chicago style, "It's my own" style, and no discernable style. My twenty-one fourth-year students in the course were drawn from all the dis- ciplines in our school: Media Studies, Journalism, Public Relations, and Media Production. Some of the papers were insightful and well organized, a very few were brilliantly argued and flawlessly cited. Others were devoid of any dis- cernable thesis and peppered with obviously "Googled" citations, demonstrat- ing only an ability to regurgitate the opinions of others.

My first thought was that this must be a reflection of how writing to de- velop critical thinking was taught in the different disciplines inside our school. Certainly, I thought, the best papers were coming from Media Studies students, but this wasn't the case. Journalism and Public Relations majors were just as likely—or unlikely—to submit the best papers. So what could account for such a wide range of skills in thesis framing, argument, and style? One of my colleagues pointed a finger at the English department: "Who knows what they're teaching in ENG 101 and 102?" Discussing this with an instructor in English, I was met with an all-knowing and all-encompassing sigh.

The reality is that English professors have their hands full with damage control, helping many students catch up with the basics, developing what should have already been mastered. It is clearly beyond the capacity of any English department to beat a clear path through thesis, argument, research methodology, style, attribution, and citation in English 101 or 102 in such a way that three years on, senior-year students across the university will suddenly burst forth and deliver the well-wrought paper in their discipline. Could it be that the development and honing of these critical skills actually occurs through a process of academic osmosis?

Should a student be persistent or lucky enough to get a seat in the classroom and flourish under the demanding tutelage of Professor X in History, or Professor Y in Political Science, or Professor Z in Media Studies (just a few of the possible combinations of sophomore- and junior-year experiences that demand critical thinking and the well-crafted paper), will that Communication major flourish in a research paper–heavy senior seminar? Yes, I expect so. But what happens to the student who did not encounter professors X or Y or Z and has had little to no contact with professors and courses where the fostering of critical thinking through substantive writing is expected and clarity in the presentation of thesis argument and defense is demanded?

Some institutions have adopted a "Library 101" model where writing to foster critical thinking and in-depth exploration in the requirements of the well-wrought research paper are required. Other institutions have adopted a universitywide series of seminars delivered over the first three years of a student's education. Each of these seminars presents an array of increasingly demanding "writing to learn how" critical thinking and writing-across-the-discipline experiences to facilitate a student's growing mastery of thesis framing, argument, and defense. Even if one's institution has either or both of these programs or something similar in place, and certainly if it does not, what can a department or school of Communication do, across the four-year undergraduate experience, to expand and unify all its "writing to learn how" critical thinking and writing-across-the-disciplines offerings in order to foster excellence in both thesis work and in discipline-specific storytelling?

I suggest the creation of a writing scaffolding for Communication in three parts: the foot plates, our discipline-specific courses and their modes of inquiry; the cross bracing, all required "writing for and in the media" course work and our integrative seminars; and the decking, a departmental or schoolwide annual or biannual writing and production competition. The foot plates ground the student in what we demand as professional competency; the cross bracing widens student understanding of the vibrant array of writing across all our disciplines, and the decking allows students to compete against and collaborate with other students in and outside of their disciplines to determine who among them has mastered the skills we expect from professional communicators. Reward (cash prizes or perhaps key ring data-storage devices) for this mastery should be awarded.

The Foot Plates

All Communication disciplines, from Media Studies to Journalism to Television and Film Production to Public Relations and to Theatre, offer an array of modes of inquiry that require critical thinking and clarity of expression through the use of discipline-specific writing styles. While each of these modes of inquiry requires its own and ofttimes others' mastery of presentation style, asking and answering fundamental questions drives and unites all our work:

- "What is the news here?" demands that Journalism students quickly weigh and assess the value and meaning of the information at hand.

- "How are we going to respond to these events?" demands that Public Relations students quickly weigh and assess the effects these events will have both on their organization and the wider community.

- "What basic assumptions are present here?" demands that Media Studies students deconstruct and scrutinize the message as well as the medium.

- "What is the impact of this visual metaphor?" demands that Media Production students analyze meaning, intent, and success in delivery.

- "Why does this character speak these lines?" demands that Theatre and Film Production students understand the arc of the stage or screenplay and each character's individual objectives and superobjective.

In each four-year cycle, the faculty will ask these and many other basic discipline-specific questions to each student we encounter. As each student's professional competency grows, these fundamental questions are replaced by questions of greater complexity. The shifting, doubling, and reinforcing of the foot plates for a writing scaffolding in Communication quickly becomes an increasingly more layered four-year process. This process is perhaps best reinforced by an ever more rigorous demand for personal journaling.

As students gain discipline competency, they are entertaining a wide range of increasingly sophisticated inner monologues seeking an opportunity to pour forth in written form. These inner monologues in conjunction with their myriad in- and out-of-classroom experiences can provide fertile ground for an array of empowering assigned journaling experiences, an especially rich tool for the development of critical thinking.

Journal assignments can be open-ended or guided and specific, such as contemporary issues journals and exam preparation journals. The tough questions we ask all lend themselves to journal-based responses. I believe the more our students journal in discipline-specific courses during their second and third year as undergraduates, the greater the likelihood that not only will we see leaps in their critical thinking and self-assessment skills, but we will also be presented with substantively better ideas for and clarity in the execution of their research topics. As with most WTL (writing-to-learn) assignments, these journal questions can be used in the service of improving critical reading skills or improving critical thinking skills, in anticipation of longer assignments where they would be asked to synthesize these assignments into something longer (see the following examples).

I require my third- and fourth-year Media Production students to keep a semistructured journal to track their ideas, observations, opinions, and activities throughout the preproduction, production, and postproduction phases of that semester's major production project. On the last day of class, they submit a Production Report. From one of my syllabi:

> Using your Production Journal as reference, you will deliver an up-to-ten-page, double-spaced Courier 12 pt. Production Report that explains in detail exactly what you learned in the process of creating your Production Project. You will be required to comment on exactly how well you and your production partner(s) collaborate on all tasks undertaken and on how successful your working relationships are. I am specifically interested in what you learned: challenges undertaken, surprises found, mistakes made and rectified, tasks poorly finished, visions unfulfilled—and why. I am equally interested in what you believe to be the greatest strengths of your Project—and why. Following the Report you will include your marked script, storyboards, shooting schedule, and talent and location releases. You will be graded on the sophistication of your self-criticism and your insights into the production process.

The Cross Bracing

The generally common to all disciplines courses: Introduction to Communication, Introduction to News Writing (or its broader successor course offered at many institutions, Media Writing), Media History, Media Law, and Media Ethics are verdant fields for planting any number of exploratory writing exercises in response to readings and lecture topics. For example:

- In the next ten minutes write an essay on "Should the FCC be abolished?" Pick a side and argue the merits of your case.
- You are a Hollywood director who has been "blacklisted." You have never been a member of the Communist Party. Do you testify next week before the House Un-American Activities Committee? Write the reasons for your decision in a letter to your infant child to be read when the child turns eighteen.
- Write an "as long as it takes" telephone conversation between a producer at Fox News and Michael Moore or Al Franken.

- Write a three-minute-long defense summation in support of Lenny Bruce; write a three-minute-long prosecution argument against Lenny Bruce.

- Write a jailhouse letter from John Peter Zenger to a friend.

- In the next five minutes write a summation of today's lecture on the national and international newspaper coverage of Watergate.

- At home tonight write William Shakespeare's review of the film *Shakespeare in Love*.

While foundational research papers on topics in communication are often assigned during Introduction to Communication and Media History courses, some Media Writing courses now ask students, beyond an introduction to all writing styles in the media and in-depth study of Associated Press style, to write a research paper on a topic in communication. Media History courses can provide excellent opportunities for the implementation of a Communication-specific version of "Library 101": an introduction to Nexus Lexus, an overview of the breadth and content of trade journals and academic publications, and an introduction to research tools such as Arbitron and the Nielsen ratings. Media Law and Media Ethics courses provide myriad opportunities for students to write in and out of class on the subject matter, to create thesis statements, and to write practice essay exams.

Interdisciplinary third- and fourth-year special topics courses, often offered in the form of seminars, afford students many opportunities to experience and to experiment with modes of inquiry and styles of writing beyond those regularly explored in their own discipline, to write in those other disciplines, and to write across the full breadth of "writing to learn how" assignments.

The Decking

A capstone school or departmentwide storytelling experience that builds on "writing to learn how" journaling (in response to fundamental and advanced questions posed in discipline-specific "base plate" courses) and exploratory writing (during both "cross bracing" common school or department core courses and interdisciplinary seminar courses) can provide substantive material for student eportfolios. I suggest the creation of a department- or schoolwide annual or biannual writing and production competition: a contest that allows all of our students the opportunity to "walk across" the decking of a writing scaffold, to compete for prizes offered for excellence in the mastery of the writing styles of each of our disciplines. How might such a competition, open to all students regardless of area of study, be organized? At our school, the two-part competition would begin with Journalism and Public Relations in the fall and end with Media Production, Theatre, and Media Studies in the spring.

In the spring of 2004, with the help of some of my colleagues who teach print journalism, broadcast journalism, and public relations, I carried out a small test of an idea that such a competition might center on two sets of intentionally jumbled "facts," created by the faculty, based upon an actual event but altered in ways that would make researching that actual event difficult. I asked my colleagues to hand out two jumbled sets of "facts" rewritten from the facts of an actual news story (an attack on faculty and students at Case Western Reserve University in May 2003) for their students to unscramble. The first set consisted of seven bare-bones bullets designed to provide just enough information for breaking wire copy and "first on the scene" breaking radio and broadcast news copy.

The second set of fourteen bullets was more comprehensive: "facts" drawn from print news reports two days after the actual event. These bullets were designed to serve as the basis for follow-up print and broadcast stories as well as a public relations response release from the "university." I did not want motivated students to have an advantage by researching the actual story, so I changed names, changed dates, and changed locations. Of course, I buried the lead, cracked any likely "nut graph," and sliced-and-diced key facts. Following are the first set of bulleted and scrambled "facts" handed out:

Friday, May 13, 2005, Sioux City, Iowa, 4:52 P.M.

- An eyewitness says several dozen people have been seen fleeing Patterson Hall, home of the Business School on the campus of Carlson University.
- The campus is normally quiet on a Friday, especially during Exam Week.
- Numerous gunshots have been heard inside Patterson Hall.
- Multiple police cruisers, at least one SWAT team, and several ambulances have responded to the scene.
- An eyewitness said a man wearing a bulletproof vest and "a kind of World War II Army helmet" entered the building around 4 P.M. and began opening fire with what sounded like an automatic weapon.
- Sporadic gunfire continues as police move a large crowd of onlookers back from the scene.
- At least two people have been carried to ambulances and transported to local hospitals. Their condition is unknown.

In response, as an example of breaking radio news copy, a student in Professor Edward Alwood's Journalism 263 Reporting class submitted:

Carlson University   36 seconds

JRN 263

4/14/04

This just in. Eyewitnesses say several dozen people have been seen running from the business school at Carlson University after numerous gunshots were heard. Police, paramedics, and SWAT have responded to the scene. It's believed a man wearing a bulletproof vest and a helmet entered the building around four-pm and began firing an automatic weapon. At least two people have been transported to hospitals as gunfire continues to take place. Stay tuned as we try to learn more about the situation.

Following is the second set of bulleted and scrambled "facts" handed out:

Sunday, May 15, 2005, Sioux City, Iowa, 5:30 P.M.

- Authorities stated today that the shooter arrested inside Patterson Hall at Carlson University was a graduate who had sued an employee at the school.
- Police identified the shooter as Biswanath Rai, 62, an employee of Carlson University.
- The Carlson University employee who Rai had sued was in the building but escaped during the standoff, University President Thomas Martin said. He said the lawsuit, which accused the employee of having "added and deleted things from a personal website" belonging to Rai, was dismissed and Rai had lost an appeal about a month ago.
- Rai's anger centered on university employee Seamus Lane, a school computer-lab assistant Rai believed had hacked his site, thereby destroying his life. He pursued Lane, whom he described as an evil man, through the civil courts and in numerous complaints to the university president, the campus police, the mayor of Sioux City, the FBI, and even the U.S. House and Senate Judiciary Committees. "The end result of all these outright evil actions will be that society will end up paying a severe price," Rai had warned in one such communiqué.
- Rai was a loner and believed himself a victim of discrimination and malicious interference. He had been chronically unable to hold a job (his last known one was in the late 1980s) but routinely sued companies that refused to hire him. He believed he possessed the secrets to peace and prosperity for all mankind and graciously shared these nuggets of wisdom via his website—until someone deleted its entire contents from his computer. "I try to solve mankind's problems through the Internet," Rai explained in a court deposition against Lane. "In a few seconds, the evil man wiped out everything that it took my lifetime to create," he said in an email to school officials.
- Authorities said 93 people were trapped inside the building for hours, hiding in offices, classrooms, and closets.
- Rai, who suffered a gunshot wound to the shoulder, was to be released into police custody Saturday, a spokeswoman at Riverview Hospital said. It wasn't clear if he had an attorney.
- The two people who were injured, a graduate student shot in the buttocks and a female professor of economics shot in her collarbone, were released from Riverview Hospital on Saturday, authorities said.

- Rai received a master's degree in business administration in 1999 from Carlson University.

- One graduate student was found dead inside the building. The victim, identified as Francis Smith, 30, was a graduate student from Davenport.

- Sioux City Deputy Coroner James Thompson said the preliminary cause of death was a gunshot wound.

- Gregory Rolfe, 46, an economic research director at the university, barricaded his office's door with furniture to protect him and four others inside. The female economics professor who was wounded was shot through her office door. "We saw the shadowy figure walk by the door," Rolfe said. "He was shooting down at the ground, yelling inaudible cries, sort of a high-pitched scream. We could hear the shell casings clinking on the ground."

- Sachin Kumar, 26, a master's student from India, said he was talking with two friends on the first floor outside the cafeteria when the gunman approached and shot one of his friends. "My friend said he would give me a ride home and then I heard him shouting. I heard gunshots," he said. His friend screamed as he was shot. Kumar and his other friend dove under a table and the gunman fired at them. "But he couldn't get us. And then he again shot at us and we turned the table and put it in front of us," Kumar said.

- Margaret Bourke, who works in the admissions office for the university master's degree program, said she went into the building's atrium after hearing what she thought were firecrackers and seeing students running. "The gunman was there pointing at me and two other students," she said. He fired and missed, she said. Bourke and five other people barricaded themselves in her office by putting a five-drawer file cabinet in front of the glass doors. "We kept each other calm. We kept each other company," she said.

In response, as an example of print follow-up, a student in Professor Margarita Diaz's JRN 160 class submitted:

JRN 160M

Diaz

O4/20/04

Police arrested and identified the gunman from the shooting at Patterson Hall yesterday afternoon as a graduate and employee of Carlson University. One graduate student was killed and two people were injured during the shooting.

The gunman, Biswanath Rai, 62, entered Patterson Hall wearing a bulletproof vest and "a kind of World War II helmet," according to one eyewitness, at around 4 p.m. and began firing what sounded like an automatic weapon.

Authorities said 93 people were trapped inside the building for hours, hiding in offices, classrooms, and closets.

"We saw the shadowy figure walk by the door," Gregory Rolfe, 46, an economic research director at the university, said. "He was shooting down at the ground, yelling inaudible cries, sort of a high-pitched scream. We could hear the shell casings clinking on the ground."

The two people who were injured, a graduate student shot in the buttocks and a female professor of economics shot in her collarbone, were released from Riverview Hospital today, authorities said.

Rai sued a fellow university employee for allegedly tampering with his website. The case was dismissed and Rai lost an appeal about a month ago. When the contents of his website were deleted, Rai took action and complained to civil courts, the university president, campus police, the mayor of Sioux City, the FBI, and the U.S. House and Senate Judiciary Committees.

"The end result of all these outright evil actions will be that society will end up paying a severe price," Rai had warned officials. Rai, who suffered a gunshot wound to the shoulder, was released into police custody today, according to the spokesperson for Riverview Hospital.

All students in the school or department would be presented with both sets of bulleted "facts" and would be invited to submit their best efforts in breaking news, follow-up news report, and public relations response statement. With the awarding of prizes for the best (as good as or better than the above) student submissions in these categories, the first part of the competition ends and the second (and final part) begins. The student winners in the follow-up news and public relations statement categories will meet and brief teams of screenwriting students in late October. Their winning submissions along with all the bulleted "facts" will serve as the only basis for work submitted during the second part of the competition. The screenwriting student teams, (and any group of students can form a writing team) will author seven- to ten-minute screenplays based on the events as presented.

In the spring, Media Production and Media Studies students will take up the competition challenge. Theatre students will be cast in these student-authored short screenplays. Media Production and other interested students will direct, shoot, and edit the short screenplays. Public screenings of their work will be held. Media Studies and other interested students will write and publish reviews of these short screenplays and submit research papers on the competition topic—in this case, media coverage of workplace and school violence. Prizes will be awarded for best screenplay, best short film or video, best critical review, and best research paper. The kicker is (in our case as a school) that graduate students in journalism, given the real facts of the event in January, would cap the public screening of the spring work with a short documentary film delineating and investigating the actual events.

Such a departmental or schoolwide competition with every prize category open to every undergraduate student would, I believe, not only improve the writing skills of students across all our disciplines, but also be illuminating for the faculty. What might we discover regarding our overall teaching effectiveness as students in all our disciplines approach the same "facts"?

A scaffolding scheme for writing across our disciplines that includes journaling across all "base plate" discipline-specific courses, exploratory writing across the "cross bracing" of our common core and integrative seminars, and multidisciplinary writing during a school- or departmentwide "decking" competition allows our students to create substantial individual eportfolios, both written and audiovisual, that can be shared with peers, prospective graduate schools, and potential employers. Such a scheme empowers students to gain clarity through self-criticism and to become better writers, thinkers, readers, listeners, and communicators.

3

The Use of Peer Evaluations to Foster Critical Analysis of Writing in Biology

Deborah J. Clark
Associate Professor of Biology

Introduction

Several years ago, Quinnipiac University renovated the freshman and upper-level biology lab rooms, replacing the traditional long benches with octagonal tables designed to encourage cooperative learning. With the help of funding from a National Science Foundation grant (Opheim et al. 2000), my colleagues and I in the department of Biology subsequently redesigned the first-year curriculum, replacing weekly labs that complemented a broad coverage in lecture with multiweek research units that fostered the development of critical scientific inquiry and analytical skills. Briefly, within each research unit, highly structured lab exercises that provided opportunities for foundational learning and hands-on experience in the scientific method progressed to capstone experiences with open-ended research questions. The final stages of the learning process involved critical analysis of the research in the form of a presentation to the class and/or written analysis in a lab report.

In spite of these radical changes to the curriculum, it was clear that many of my first-year General Biology students still demonstrated a poor ability to select and interpret relevant sources of information and were very superficial in their analyses of their experiments. Many students used Internet websites indiscriminately—giving equal credence to student-generated information and research reported by professional scientists—and the "copy and paste" style of plagiarism was a common problem. Furthermore, students' papers clearly indicated the need for more practice in scientific writing style. Initially, I tried to provide detailed feedback on each lab report, so students could revise and resubmit their work. This task was extremely difficult, even daunting, since the students' lack of understanding of disciplinary conventions of scientific writing often obscured the conclusions they were attempting to convey. I was spending a disproportionate amount of time suggesting improvements to grammar, sentence structure, and scientific writing style, and not enough time assessing the effectiveness of the delivery or analysis.

My third- and fourth-year students in Cell Physiology displayed some of the same problems in their writing as the first-year students. While forced by the narrow focus of their projects to use primary research rather than Internet articles, students still had difficulty understanding the significance of the research to their own experiments. Cell Physiology students, like the first-year students, were not completely cognizant of scientific writing format and styles. For example, they still used citation methods appropriate for writing in their English or history courses, first- or second-person pronouns in the Methods section, and stand-alone tables or graphs with no statements of conclusions in the Results section. On the other hand, these students were, on the whole, better versed in basic writing skills than the first-year students.

Although I saw myself as a professor of biology, I finally realized, through interactions with my Quinnipiac University Writing Across the Curriculum (QUWAC) colleagues, that requiring more writing in my classes might, in fact, better stimulate my students to learn biology. I therefore made two significant changes to both Cell Physiology and General Biology Lab courses. First, I worked with my department to adopt consistent standards for writing in all biology courses. Second, I increased the amount of writing in both of my courses, using a peer-reviewing process to provide feedback and keep my workloads manageable. At the end of the semester, I surveyed the students' perceptions of changes in their ability to write, think, and understand course material. Some of the results were encouraging, while others suggested areas that still needed improvement.

Learning for Understanding in the Sciences

The National Science Foundation (1996), the National Research Council (CUSE 1999), the Boyer Commission (1998), the BioQUEST Curriculum Consortium (2001), and others stress the value of inquiry-based courses in teaching the process and the importance of science in society. Studies contrasting the learning of experts and novices suggested specific guidelines for these courses (NRC 2000). First, in order to achieve learning for understanding, learning must facilitate the construction of knowledge or only short-term benefits can be expected. This means that pedagogical scaffolding must be included for exploration of basic concepts before students can be expected to develop sophisticated expertise. Second, the initial learning must be reconstructive, challenging and replacing imperfect preconceptions and enhancing correct ones. Thus, whether in a lab or lecture setting, a course must expose students' preconceptions and, in that context, work to add new knowledge.

Another important component of inquiry-based courses is cooperative learning and "peer persuasion" (BioQUEST 2001; NRC 2000; Allen, Duch, and Groh 1996). In the proper supportive community, students will learn from each other and increase their depth of understanding. In fact, peer persuasion is an important step in scientific research that should be experienced by students. In addition, having to persuade *peers,* rather than simply the instructor, provides strong motivation.

The final component of an inquiry-based course should be opportunities for practice and reflection to encourage the development of metacognitive skills. Presenting students with open-ended problems, such as the design and execution of their own lab experiment, allows them to test their preconceptions, entertain competing hypotheses, and finally, attempt to draw conclusions. In these studies I investigated the specific role of writing in the improvement of students' metacognitive skills.

Writing to Learn

The preparation of manuscripts has always been the standard method of "peer persuasion" (BioQUEST 2001) in the sciences. While PowerPoint presentations are the means of conveying research to a larger audience, results ultimately must be published in a written format. For students, writing a lab report requires them to write clear conclusions, create logical transitions between paragraphs, and carefully select and paraphrase their sources, since there are no animations or colorful backgrounds to distract the reader. While writing lab reports is very demanding, the writing process provides better opportunities for students to reconstruct and reflect on their understanding of biological concepts. The periodic writing required in lab courses has another benefit as well. According to the research by Richard Light (2001) on Harvard undergraduates, there was a striking "relationship between the amount of writing for a course and students' level of engagement—whether engagement is measured by time spent on the course, or the intellectual challenge it presents, or students' level of interest in it." In fact, Light found that the students' level of engagement in their courses was more strongly related to the amount of writing than to any other course characteristic. This is very good news for science faculty like myself, who have always assumed that writing lab reports is well worth the amount of time required both by the students and by the instructor for grading.

Unfortunately, even after the completion of the introduction, methods, results, and discussion sections of multiple lab reports, not all students will have grasped the meaning of their experiments and improved their understanding of the course. Why do some students fail in their analysis and writing? Frequently, students do not fully understand what is expected of them, and, according to Edward White, they have "not internalized any consistent standards to which they can hold themselves." This problem can unfortunately be exacerbated by inconsistent feedback from faculty. In White's opinion, "Teacher evaluation is so idiosyncratic and its criteria so hidden that most students see grading and commentary as merely personal reactions by this or that unique teacher, not clear or generalizable enough to be used for the writer's own purpose" (White 1998). Finally, students may fail simply because they can not become experts in analysis and writing in their discipline in one semester. These skills must be practiced repeatedly, in multiple courses throughout the undergraduate years.

Within a given course, assigning many writing projects (for example, lab reports) for the purpose of practicing skills tends to greatly increase the work load of the instructor. If the projects are better written, however, then the workload should be slightly reduced. The process of peer critiquing followed by revision can accomplish just this, and, according to research on composition courses, has the added benefit of allowing students to use their writing as an opportunity for discovery, taking risks, and making mistakes (Flynn, McCulley, and Gratz 1986). In an important preliminary study, Flynn, McCulley, and Gratz tested the value of peer critiquing in a more content-oriented biology course. Students were given instruction in peer critiquing alone, modeling alone, or both peer critiquing and modeling, and compared to the reference group that received no additional preparation guidelines. The value of the instruction was assessed by having all lab reports scored by trained external readers (graduate students). While it appeared that the peer critiquing and modeling instruction was valuable in that the lab report scores were higher in all test groups compared to the reference group, only the scores of the peer critiquing/modeling test group could be considered significant; unfortunately, there was a significant difference between the grade point averages in the other test groups compared to the reference group. In my studies, I decided to use a different approach to assessing the value of course changes, by having students rank the importance of these changes to their learning and writing skills.

Implementation of a Writing Intensive/Peer Reviewing Process

The freshman year is the natural starting point for teaching the process of scientific writing and using writing as a tool for stimulating higher-level thinking and understanding. I therefore implemented changes in the writing requirements in General Biology Lab (Bi101-102), a full-year course for first-year majors in basic (as opposed to health) sciences. Each lab section consists of up to sixteen students, working in groups of three whenever possible. The lab meets for two hours each week of the semester and is taught mostly by full-time faculty members, including myself. Students are also enrolled in one of three lecture sections, taught by two full-time instructors.

I also instigated similar changes in writing requirements in the upper-level Cell Physiology (Bi346) course. The Cell Physiology lecture/lab course is required for all biology, microbiology, and psychobiology majors, and is usually taken late in the students' undergraduate coursework. I teach all students in one large lecture section that meets for seventy-five minutes twice a week, and three lab sections that meet for three hours once a week. Whenever possible, students are assigned to groups comprised of three members.

As part of the renovation of the lab curriculum for both courses, I expanded the writing experience to include two to three formal research proposals and lab reports per semester. For the proposal assignments, students summarized relevant background information and described their planned experiments in detail. The instructor critiqued these proposals as a means of providing valuable training in the scientific method and also of steering the project (if necessary) toward a more positive research experience. For the lab reports, students reported and discussed the significance of their group's own experimental data, following the standard scientific format. The length and depth of analysis expected of the Cell Physiology students and the sophistication of their research projects was much greater than for the General Biology students.

Karen Knisely's *A Student Handbook for Writing in Biology* (2002) was selected as the standard for writing in both General Biology and Cell Physiology courses, and adopted by the faculty in the Department of Biology for other courses as well. This change was an attempt to address concerns of consistency in writing instruction in biology classes at Quinnipiac University. Knisely's book serves as a reference manual for the structure of a scientific writing report, finding good sources, revising, and all the other steps needed to complete a research project, and includes helpful appendices on using the scientific applications of Microsoft Excel and Word.

In both General Biology Lab and Cell Physiology classes, students submitted first drafts of their lab reports to a peer evaluator. Peer evaluations were completed either during (Cell Physiology) or outside (General Biology Lab) of class, using checklists adapted from Knisely (Knisely 2002). Peer evaluators were required to make specific suggestions directly on the student author's paper as well as summarize their positive and negative comments on the evaluation form. The peer evaluation was quickly graded by the instructor before being given to the student author. Some of the General Biology Lab instructors did not require peer evaluations for all lab reports.

In the upper-level Cell Physiology course, one peer evaluation was done during the seventy-five-minute lecture, when all lab sections were together. For the most part, students were "buzzing" during their in-class evaluation time, asking each other questions, summoning the instructor to clarify details, and very actively participating in the review process. The other lab reports received peer evaluations of a different sort. For one report, students received instructor feedback of short experimental methods paragraphs throughout the five weeks of experiments. Lab groups then evaluated other groups' data and results sections as directed by the instructor during one ninety-minute lab meeting. For the last lab report, the lab group cooperated to prepare a group report. Group members were encouraged to use each other as reviewers, and no drafts were submitted to the instructor.

After Bi101 and Bi346 students had revised their reports, they submitted them to the instructor. First-year students received a grade and extensive instructor comments, and then were allowed to rewrite their papers one more time. Almost every student took advantage of this opportunity. The Cell Physiology students were given a one-week period before the due date during which they could seek the instructor's suggestions for revision; about a third of the students sought this extra help for all or part of their paper before they submitted their final report.

Method of Assessment

On the last day of classes, all students were administered a survey, consisting of fifty-five multiple choice questions, that profiled their perceptions of improvement in technical and scientific reasoning skills, general and discipline-specific writing skills, and understanding of course concepts. The survey also polled the students' perceptions of the value of their specific experiments, writing and peer-reviewing exercises to their learning, writing, thinking, and general engagement in the course. All answers were selected from a scale of one to five (or sometimes four); space was also provided for anonymous, handwritten comments. Responses of students in General Biology Lab (Bi101) were compared to those of students in Cell Physiology (Bi346) using a two-sample t-Test, assuming equal variances and a two-tailed distribution.

I hoped that the enhanced writing and peer evaluation processes would make students feel they had learned to write in the scientific style required in their profession, but also learned analytical and writing skills that they could apply to other courses. Finally, although I did not directly assess students' proficiency in biology, I hoped they had been stimulated to a deeper understanding of the concepts of the course.

Results

General Biology is a full-year course that consists of approximately 80 to 90 percent freshman and 10 to 20 percent sophomore science majors. In the year of study (fall 2003), 85 percent of the students were studying for a Bachelor of Science degree in biology; the remaining students were mostly science majors (Figure 3–1). In Cell Physiology, 65 percent of the students were seniors and 35 percent juniors; biology majors constituted 75 percent and 92 percent of the student population in the fall of 2002 and 2003, respectively.

Both General Biology and Cell Physiology labs included scaffolded lab exercises, building toward unique, student-generated research proposals and experiments. Students were noticeably more engaged when given the chance to design their own research project. Two students independently wrote that the

Profile		Responses (percent)	
		General Biology	Cell Physiology
Year in school	Freshman	81	0
	Sophomore	19	0
	Junior	0	35
	Senior	0	65
Major	Biology[a]	85	75
	Microbiology	4	2
	Psychobiology	2	4
	Chemistry	0	2
	Nonscience/Other	4	17[b]
Confidence in lab report writing skills prior to this course[c]	Very confident (1)	2	9
	Pretty confident (2)	28	45
	Somewhat confident (3)	55	47
	Not at all confident (4)	15	0
	Mean Confidence	2.87	2.38[*]

Data were collected on the last day of classes in the fall 2003 semester from students in General Biology Lab ($N = 53$) and Cell Physiology ($N = 47$).
[a]Biology majors include students in biology/marketing, veterinary technology, and preprofessional biology programs.
[b]The percentage of students in the reportedly "nonscience/other" category was inaccurate, reflecting students' confusion on how to report a "premed" major (personal communications).
[c]Response scale used by Mulnix (2003).
[*]The mean confidence levels were significantly different ($p < 0.005$).

Figure 3–1 Profile of Students

"best aspect of the course was designing experiments" and "the group planning of experiments was very useful and really expands your mind too. It's good to *design and do* the experiments." The enthusiasm reflected in those comments in both General Biology and Cell Physiology lab students was readily observed. The students arrived early and most had prepared in advance to take advantage of the full lab period. All members of the group were actively engaged and self-motivated. In fact, 79 percent of the Cell Physiology students and 68 percent of the General Biology students agreed or strongly agreed that, overall, the "lab exercises were enjoyable," and they were "stimulated to think and/or want to learn more during the lab exercises."

Clear differences existed in the confidence in lab writing skills of General Biology and Cell Physiology students prior to taking the course (Figure 3–1). While 54 percent of Cell Physiology students reported that they were "very confident" or "pretty confident" in their lab report writing skills, only 30 percent of the General Biology students were similarly confident. In addition, 15 percent of the General Biology students were "not at all confident" (including two students who reported "no prior experience" in lab writing skills). The mean lab report-writing confidence level (on a scale of 1–5, with 1 being the most confident) was significantly lower ($p < 0.005$) in the upperclassmen than in the first-year students.

Consistent with their lower confidence and experience in writing lab reports, the first-year students generally wrote very poor quality research proposals and lab reports, even after receiving suggestions for revision from their peers. Deficiencies were seen in every aspect of the report, from basic writing skills and literature surveys to data display and conclusions. Many students improved their report by a full letter grade after the second revision, but some students showed only marginal improvement. In contrast, the lab reports written by the third- and fourth-year Cell Physiology students were generally consistent with the discipline-specific format, well researched and better argued after revision. Shortcomings were often seen in the discussion section, where the significance of the students' work was not put in the context of published work, or the published results were misunderstood.

At the completion of their first semester at Quinnipiac University, 54 percent of the General Biology Lab students reported that writing lab reports was a valuable learning exercise (those that reported "strongly agree" or "agree") (Question 1, Figure 3–2). Approximately half of these students agreed that using the Knisely handbook was helpful (Question 4), and an even greater number (58 percent) reported that revising their lab reports after instructor feedback was a valuable learning experience (Question 5). With regard to the peer-reviewing experience, 39 percent of the General Biology students agreed that peer suggestions helped them improve their own lab reports (Question 3), and only 30 percent agreed that reading another student's report helped them

Question	Class	(N)	Responses (percent)					Mean Response	p-value
			1	2	3	4	5		
1 Writing lab reports was a valuable learning exercise.	Bi101	(53)	8	46	27	12	8	2.65	4.40×10^{-6}*
	Bi346	(47)	49	38	9	2	2	1.70	
2 Reading and peer-evaluating other students' lab reports helped me improve my own lab report.	Bi101	(53)	13	17	47	17	6	2.70	3.79×10^{-5}*
	Bi346	(103)	33	41	17	7	2	2.02	
3 The suggestions made by my peer reviewers were valuable and helped me improve my lab report.	Bi101	(53)	13	26	42	15	4	2.70	1.07×10^{-2}*
	Bi346	(103)	19	46	23	10	2	2.29	
4 Using the Knisely handbook helped me write and/or improve my lab reports.	Bi101	(53)	17	32	25	13	13	2.74	1.12×10^{-2}*
	Bi346	(75)	31	36	25	7	1	2.12	
5 Revising my lab reports after getting instructor's feedback was a valuable learning experience.	Bi101	(53)	26	32	25	15	2	2.34	3.40×10^{-8}*
	Bi346	(47)	72	26	2	0	0	1.30	
6 The peer-reviewing process probably improved my grade.	Bi101	(53)	17	19	45	11	8	2.74	2.44×10^{-1}
	Bi346	(72)	19	35	32	11	3	2.43	

Responses to questions were Strongly agree (1), Agree (2), Neutral (3), Disagree (4), and Strongly disagree (5). Responses from two classes in Bi346 (2002, 2003) were similar and were combined. The survey was expanded in 2003 to include questions 1 and 5. Insufficient data from Bi101 was gathered in 2002; Bi101 responses represent data only from 2003.
*The mean responses were significantly different ($p < 0.05$).

Figure 3–2 Importance of Peer Reviewing

improve their own report (Question 2). Similarly, only 36 percent agreed that the peer-reviewing process probably improved their grade (Question 6). The mean responses for these three questions about the peer-reviewing process were closer to "neutral" than to "agree."

In comparison to the responses of the General Biology students, responses of the students in Cell Physiology were significantly different regarding the value of writing lab reports and the peer-reviewing process (Figure 3–2). Many more Cell Physiology students (87 percent) strongly agreed/agreed that writing lab reports in their course was a valuable learning exercise (Question 1). They almost all (98 percent) agreed that revising their lab reports after getting instructor's feedback was a valuable learning experience (Question 5). However, many students indicated that they also benefited from the peer-reviewing process. A large number (65 percent) felt that they were able to improve their lab reports after being peer-evaluated (Question 3), and an even larger number (74 percent) agreed that reading and peer-evaluating another student author's paper helped them improve their own report (Question 2). The mean responses of the Cell Physiology students to these two questions were significantly lower (more responses of "strongly agree") than those of the General Biology Lab students. Finally, the Cell Physiology students valued the Knisely handbook more than did the first-year students (67 percent versus 49 percent) (Question 4). One student commented: "My process of writing is different because I start with the methods, then results, then intro, and finally discussions." This method of approaching the process of writing the first draft of a lab report is what is recommended in the Knisely (2002) handbook.

The survey next asked questions that related to students' writing efforts, the amount of writing, and the improvement in specific writing skills (Figure 3–3).

Question	Class	Responses (percent)					Mean Response	p-value
		1	2	3	4	5		
In relation to the writing I do for my other classes, I would say that in this class . . .								
1 I worked harder on my writing.	Bi101	15	57	8	8	13	2.09	$1.77 \times 10^{-4*}$
	Bi346	60	34	4	2	0	1.49	
2 There was much more writing.	Bi101	11	43	32	6	8	2.35	$4.39 \times 10^{-6*}$
	Bi346	57	30	11	2	0	1.57	
3 I learned more about how to write.	Bi101	8	40	34	9	9	2.50	$4.24 \times 10^{-3*}$
	Bi346	26	49	13	6	6	2.00	
4 I could see improvement in my writing.	Bi101	9	43	28	8	11	2.38	6.12×10^{-2}
	Bi346	19	51	17	4	9	2.07	
5 I have been prepared for the type of writing required in my major.	Bi101	8	36	30	8	19	2.47	$4.40 \times 10^{-2*}$
	Bi346	30	43	17	11	0	2.09	
6 I am better prepared to do writing in my other classes.	Bi101	8	34	34	9	15	2.53	$1.79 \times 10^{-6*}$
	Bi346	36	47	11	0	6	1.73	

Responses to questions were Strongly agree (1), Agree (2), Disagree (3), Strongly disagree (4), and Uncertain (5). Uncertain responses were not included in the means. The responses of Bi101 (N = 53) and Bi346 (N = 47) students were compared.
*The mean responses were significantly different (p < 0.05).

Figure 3–3 Comparison of Writing

Both first-year and upper-level biology students responded that they had worked harder on their writing (Question 1) and that there was much more writing (Question 2) in these specific biology courses than in their other courses. This was surprising for the Bi101 lab students, who would have almost all been enrolled in the writing-intensive course, English 101. It was not surprising, however, for the Cell Physiology students, since past students have consistently indicated that the Cell Physiology course challenged their conceptual and analytical abilities, and also demanded a large time commitment.

Almost half of the General Biology and three-quarters of the Cell Physiology students reported that they had learned more about how to write in their courses (Question 3, Figure 3–3); again, the mean responses were significantly different between the two groups. The few handwritten remarks from the General Biology students in this section commented on the ability to "gather my information beforehand so that my thoughts are written clearly," and "after doing the lab reports, I feel like I can write better papers." Cell Physiology students were more prolific in their handwritten comments, yet some were similar to those of the freshmen: "I go through the lab, then organize what I will say and analyze. Then I write the paper"; "I spend more time revising papers and looking for ways to be more concise/accurate/specific"; "I learned how to research topics using appropriate resources and was able to use those resources to learn and better my paper and the concepts of my paper."

In separate survey questions, students pinpointed the exact ways in which they had changed their approach to a writing assignment (Figure 3–4). The Bi101 students identified improvements in their use of more than one draft, organization/flow of thoughts, and citation format as the major

Question		Class	Responses (percent)				Mean Response	p-value
			1	2	3	4		
As a result of this course, my ability to prepare papers has been affected in the following ways:								
1	Outlining/organizing before I write	Bi101	13	42	43	2	2.34	3.37×10^{-1}
		Bi346	20	41	39	0	2.20	
2	Writing more than one draft	Bi101	21	38	40	2	2.23	$4.32 \times 10^{-3*}$
		Bi346	37	48	15	0	1.78	
3	Organization/flow of thoughts	Bi101	15	49	34	2	2.23	$2.15 \times 10^{-2*}$
		Bi346	22	65	13	0	1.91	
4	Grammar and sentence structure	Bi101	8	49	42	2	2.38	9.18×10^{-1}
		Bi346	11	39	50	0	2.39	
5	Citation format	Bi101	15	51	32	2	2.20	$1.73 \times 10^{-2*}$
		Bi346	37	41	22	0	1.84	

Responses to questions were Definitely improved (1), Improved somewhat (2), Has not changed (3), and Has worsened (4). The responses of Bi101 (N = 53) and Bi346 (N = 47) students were compared.
*The mean responses were significantly different ($p < 0.05$).

Figure 3–4 Changes in Approach to Writing

changes; approximately 60 percent reported that they had "definitely improved" or "improved somewhat" in these areas (Questions 2, 3, and 5). Cell Physiology students judged their writing to have improved in these three areas significantly more than did the General Biology students. More than half of the Cell Physiology and General Biology students also felt their outlining/organizing and grammar and sentence structure had improved (Questions 1 and 4).

As a result of the changes to the General Biology Lab and Cell Physiology courses, the majority of both groups of students (52 and 70 percent, respectively) strongly agreed or agreed that "in relation to the writing I do for my other classes, I would say that in this class I could see improvement in my writing" (Question 4, Figure 3–3). Interestingly, many students felt they were not only better prepared for the type of writing required in their major (Question 5), but also in other classes (Question 6). Cell Physiology students agreed/strongly agreed that they were better prepared for discipline- (73 percent) or non-discipline-specific (83 percent) writing, while about 43 percent of the General Biology Lab students agreed/strongly agreed; the mean responses were significantly different between the two groups for both questions. Clearly, however, not all students felt their scientific writing had improved their nonscientific writing, since one Cell Physiology student wrote that "I am better prepared to do scientific style of writing, not business or English based classes. The formats are completely different." In addition, a fairly large number (15 to 19 percent) of the General Biology Lab students were uncertain about their writing improvement, in contrast to 0 to 6 percent of the upperclassmen.

The outcome of the most important goal of this study, to stimulate and encourage analytical thought processes and deepen understanding of course concepts, was assessed indirectly, using students' perceptions of their level of understanding (Figure 3–5). It was clear that students in both Bi101 (65 percent) and Bi346 classes (71 percent) were receptive to the idea that writing and thinking *were* related, as supported by their disagreement with the statement "It seemed like the writing and thinking in this class were not related" (Question 6). Cell Physiology students felt very strongly (91 percent "agreed" or "strongly agreed") that they understood course topics better as a result of their lab report writing (Question 1). The mean response was significantly different from the mean response of the General Biology students. Only about half of the Bi101 students perceived an improvement in understanding that they attributed to writing (Question 1), and reported that their writing assignments improved their thought process in a general way (Question 4). Both groups of students agreed that the writing helped them relate concepts in their course to concepts in their other courses (51 percent and 71 percent for Bi101 and Bi346 students, respectively) (Question 2), and that they got more out of their class because of the writing (52 percent and 72 percent, respectively) (Question 7).

Question	Class	Responses (percent)					Mean Response	p-value
		1	2	3	4	5		
1 I understand course topics better because of the writing.	Bi101	9	45	26	6	13	2.34	7.83×10^{-8}*
	Bi346	31	60	4	2	2	1.76	
2 The writing helped me to relate concepts in this course to concepts in other courses.	Bi101	9	42	30	6	13	2.38	1.98×10^{-3}*
	Bi346	20	51	24	0	4	2.04	
3 The writing assignments helped me to better understand the way I learn.	Bi101	4	45	40	2	9	2.44	2.28×10^{-3}*
	Bi346	18	40	29	0	13	2.13	
4 The writing assignments improved my thought process in a general way.	Bi101	8	53	25	4	11	2.28	2.22×10^{-4}*
	Bi346	20	64	13	0	2	1.93	
5 I used the writing assignments to help me organize my thinking.	Bi101	6	34	38	9	13	2.59	3.41×10^{-3}*
	Bi346	9	53	29	2	7	2.26	
6 It seemed like the writing and thinking in this class were not related.	Bi101	6	19	40	25	10	2.94	3.35×10^{-1}
	Bi346	4	16	42	29	9	3.05	
7 I got more out of this class because of the writing.	Bi101	15	37	23	12	13	2.36	1.23×10^{-2}*
	Bi346	27	45	11	9	7	2.02	

Responses to questions were Strongly agree (1), Agree (2), Disagree (3), Strongly disagree (4), and Uncertain (5). Uncertain responses were not included in the means. The responses of Bi101 (N = 53) and Bi346 (N = 45) students were compared.
*The mean responses were significantly different($p < 0.05$).

Figure 3–5 Effect of Writing on Understanding

Conclusions

The first-year General Biology Lab and upper-level Cell Physiology curricula were redesigned with the goal of enhancing learning through writing. In both classes, the number of short (research proposals) and long (lab reports) writing assignments were increased, and a process of peer evaluation and revision was established to encourage deeper analysis of experimental data and reflection on the process of writing itself. The adoption of a scientific writing handbook (Knisely 2002) made teaching the conventions of scientific writing easier and more consistent from instructor to instructor. Responses to survey questions given on the last day of classes were used to assess the value students attributed to these writing exercises.

The most conclusive findings from this project were the almost uniformly strong assessments of the value of writing by the students in Cell Physiology. They strongly agreed that the writing exercises themselves, as well as the peer reviewing process, were valuable learning experiences. Not only did they work harder on writing and learn specific writing skills, such as how to better organize ideas and write a second draft, but the vast majority also felt better prepared for writing both in and out of their discipline. These students started the course with a fairly high mean confidence level of 2.4 out of a scale of 1 to 4. This mean represented confidence ratings midway between "somewhat" and "pretty" confident. Importantly, more than 90 percent of these students felt that they understood the concepts in the Cell Physiology course better as a direct result of their writing exercises, and nearly three-quarters reported that the writing helped them relate these concepts to those in other courses.

The majority of first-year students also judged the writing done in their course as valuable, and could see improvement in their overall writing as well as in the specific ways in which they approached writing, such as writing more than one draft. This was encouraging, given that these students began the course feeling "somewhat confident" (a rating of 2.9 on a scale of 1–4) in their lab report writing skills. The first-year students also rated their understanding of course topics and their thought processes in general as improved due to assigned writing. However, the ratings by the first-year students of their improvement in writing and understanding may have been overestimated. A Cornell University study found that participants who scored in the lowest quartiles on three types of tests overestimated their performance, to a much greater extent than participants who scored higher (Kruger and Dunning 1999). This inflated sense of confidence was not seen in the more skilled participants, who were more likely to underestimate their performance. By implication from the Cornell study, the majority of the first-year biology students and a small number of the upper-level students did not have the metacognitive skills to truly assess improvement in their writing and understanding.

Another important finding from this project was the striking difference between the responses of first-year and upper-level students with regard to the peer-evaluation process. While the upper-level students agreed that evaluating a peer's paper, as well as receiving suggestions on their own paper, was a valuable experience, the majority of first-year student responses were "neutral" on these subjects. The first-year students were much more comfortable with their instructor's feedback.

The lower value placed on the peer-reviewing process by first-year students is not surprising for two reasons. First, since the freshmen and sophomores are climbing such a steep learning curve themselves, it is natural for them to distrust their peers. While first-year students had no trouble keeping their peer evaluation comments constructive, there were, however, a number of peer comments that were misleading and had to be corrected by the instructor. The earlier peer evaluations included few, and largely superficial, comments, not addressing problems of clarity, organization, or significance. In fact, this happened in the upper-level Cell Physiology course as well, illustrating the potential problem with peer reviews in any course. To quote an insightful student: "Peer review was only helpful to me when I had someone reviewing my paper that knew what to look for, and didn't just say, 'the report was great, except you misspelled . . .' Reviews like that were not helpful. I guess the review session is only as good as the reviewer."

The second reason that first-year students were close to neutral on the importance of the peer-reviewing process was that the four different Bi101 lab instructors did not give consistent messages about the importance of the peer evaluations. The requirements of the different instructors also varied, ranging from two to three lab reports and one to two peer evaluations. Consistency in requirements was not a problem in Bi346, since I taught all the students myself.

Another problem encountered with the peer-reviewing process used in General Biology and Cell Physiology was that some student authors took advantage of the system. Since they knew that a peer, not the instructor, would be reading their first draft, they submitted very incomplete drafts to their peer evaluator. These students cheated themselves and their peer, since they weren't prepared to evaluate their peer's paper thoroughly, and their peer evaluators missed the benefit of a comprehensive comparison to their own papers.

The higher level of satisfaction with learning as a result of writing in the upper-level course requires further consideration. Why was the process more successful? The National Research Council (2000) findings that experts and novices learn and process new information differently can be applied to the two groups of students: those in the introductory General Biology Lab course and those in the upper-level Cell Physiology course. In fact, the Cell Physiology students, although certainly not "experts," were much more sophisticated in their ability to analyze scientific literature and grasp the implications of open-ended experiments than were the first-year "novices." They also valued the writing exercises in their course, more than the first-year students, because they were able to make connections and comparisons between their writing in previous courses and current courses, and also between their writing and that of experts in the scientific literature.

Learning to write in a discipline-specific style, such as that used in the sciences, must be approached using scaffolded writing exercises, beginning with lab reports and other writing exercises in the first year and continuing throughout all four years of the undergraduate experience. The process of peer evaluating, followed by rewriting, and perhaps a second revision after instructor evaluation, is important. It is during this process that students derive many chances for reconstructing their knowledge of how to write—that is, losing high school habits and replacing them with appropriate skills for a college science major.

The implications of these studies strongly suggest that writing, including peer evaluating, can make a large difference in the students' assessment of the conceptual understanding they gained from their course. Writing exercises that encourage students' reflection on their successful, and not so successful, writing methods, and on what they do and do not understand, should improve students' metacognitive skills and increase the degree of transfer (NRC 2000). The receptiveness of the first-year students to these methods, however, is highly variable. For a number of reasons, including maturity, motivation, and academic preparation, some first-year students are unable to generate well-written scientific work and have only begun to develop the metacognitive skills they need to be successful in college. As a result of these studies, I realize that while my upper-level students benefited greatly from the increased focus on writing in their biology class, I need a different approach for "coaching" the first-year students. While the results of the student surveys highlight improvements in a number of areas, in order to reach more of the first-year students, I will need to more directly address the qualities of good scientific writing, comparison of those qualities to nonscientific writing styles, and guidelines for the most powerful peer evaluations.

Acknowledgments

The support and suggestions provided by the Chairman, Allan Smits, and other colleagues in the Department of Biological Sciences: Dennis Opheim, Donald Buckley, Gene Wong, Robert Martinez, Charlotte Hammond, and Emily Rodriguez were instrumental in helping to design the lab curricula and writing exercises. Invaluable assistance was also provided by Professors Andri Smith, John Jenkins, and QUWAC colleagues, Robert Smart, Suzanne Hudd, and Mary Segall. Curriculum renovations were funded in part by a National Science Foundation Grant (Opheim et al. 2000) and Quinnipiac University matching funds.

References

Allen, D. E., B. J. Duch, and S. E. Groh. 1996. "The Power of Problem-based Learning in Teaching Introductory Courses." *New Directions for Teaching and Learning* 68: 43–52.

BioQUEST Curriculum Consortium. 2001. *A 3P's Approach to Science Education: Problem-posing, Problem-solving and Peer Persuasion.* Available at *http:// bioquest.org.*

Boyer Commission on Educating Undergraduates in the Research University, The. 1998. *Reinventing Undergraduate Education: A Blueprint for America's Research Universities.* New York: State University of New York at Stony Brook.

Committee on Undergraduate Science Education (CUSE). 1999. *Transforming Undergraduate Education in Science, Mathematics, Engineering, and Technology.* Arlington, VA: National Research Council.

Flynn, E., G. McCulley, and R. Gratz. 1986. "Writing in Biology: Effects of Peer Critiquing and Analysis of Models on the Quality of Biology Laboratory Reports." In Art Young and Toby Fulwiler (eds.), *Writing Across the Disciplines: Research Into Practice.* Upper Montclair, NJ: Boynton/Cook.

Knisely, K. 2002. *A Student Handbook for Writing in Biology.* Sunderland, MA: Sinauer Associates, Inc./W. H. Freeman and Co.

Kruger, J., and D. Dunning. 1999. "Unskilled and Unaware of It: How Difficulties in Recognizing One's Own Incompetence Lead to Inflated Self-Assessments." *Journal of Personality and Social Psychology* 77(6): 1121–34.

Light, R. J. 2001. *Making the Most of College: Students Speak Their Minds.* Cambridge, MA: Harvard University Press.

Mulnix, A. B. 2003. "Investigations of Protein Structure and Function using the Scientific Literature: An Assignment for an Undergraduate Cell Physiology Course." *Cell Biology Education* 2: 248–55.

National Research Council (NRC). 2000. *How People Learn: Brain, Mind, Experience and School,* eds. J. D. Bransford, A. L. Brown, and R. R. Cocking. Washington, DC: National Academy Press.

National Science Foundation (NSF). 1996. *Shaping the Future: New Expectations for Undergraduate Education in Science, Mathematics, Engineering, and Technology (NSF 96–139).* Arlington, VA: National Science Foundation.

Opheim, D., R. Martinez, D. Borst, A. Smits, and D. Buckley. 2000. *Creating a Faculty Culture of Teaching Reform at Quinnipiac University.* National Science Foundation Grant # 9952610.

White, E. M. 1998. *Teaching and Assessing Writing, 2d ed.* Portland, Maine: Calendar Islands Publishers.

Protracted Peer-Reviewed Writing Assignments in Biology

Confessions of an Apostate Cynic of Writing Across the Curriculum

Dennis J. Richardson

Associate Professor of Biology, School of Health Sciences

Introduction: The Making of an Apostate Cynic

For years I relished lamentations shared with fellow biology teachers over the abysmal state of student writing. It's the same old story. We assign a term paper: due at the end of the semester, typed, ten pages in length, double-spaced, a minimum of five references. The students wearily trudge through the assignment and ultimately turn in a seriously deficient document, to put it graciously. Then, the excruciating process of evaluation begins. After the third glass of scotch, one encounters the challenge of reading yet another paper that appears impenetrable to constructive criticism. Finally, there are the students' moans as the papers are returned. They walk away tossing their papers at the wastebasket, contemplating yet another affirmation of their writing deficiencies, and I head off to the lounge to share my grief over the deteriorating state of western civilization due to student apathy and lack of basic English skills.

Then I met the zealots proclaiming the attributes of writing across the curriculum. I came, skeptical and cynical, to the meetings and workshops. Demurely, I listened to ideas for implementation of writing assignments and to enthusiastic testimonials regarding their success. Slowly, I acquiesced and began integrating a few of the suggested exercises into my classroom. To my amazement, the exercises worked! My students were learning more, with less effort on my part. (Better results for less work . . . not a bad deal.) I learned to my surprise that many of the perceived problems with student writing were in reality a result of pedagogical shortcomings of the assignments. Implementation of writing across the curriculum principles has resolved most of these problems, with the result of greatly improved student papers. Now I am the one proselytizing the benefits of writing across the curriculum.

Protracted Peer-Reviewed Writing Assignments:
An Introduction

I have found a fair number of practical writing exercises to be very effective and most successful when combined into a series of linked assignments. This approach enables students to appreciate writing and critical thinking as a *process*. Following is an integrated series of basic writing across the curriculum exercises collectively presented as protracted peer-reviewed writing assignments that I utilize in my junior-level Animal Parasitology course. These exercises may be adapted to an array of pedagogical applications within any discipline.

A plethora of good references provide specific information concerning the theory and application of each type of component exercise. [Bean (1996) provides an excellent overview of the array of fundamental types of writing across the curriculum exercises along with a discussion of the theory underlying each. Knisely (2002) provides good specific advice concerning scientific writing.] The purpose of this chapter is to share my experiences in the application of a few of these exercises.

Two ultimate goals underlie the following assignments: (1) to foster critical and creative thinking and (2) to improve written communication skills, both within the discipline and across the curriculum. In the series of exercises presented, an actual piece of research is conducted and findings are presented in the form of a scientific paper as it would be written for publication in a scientific journal.

Defining the Topic

The subject matter must be interesting and provocative. Nothing is more stifling to intellectual development than traditional term papers in which a boring topic is chosen from a long list of boring topics. Students are interested in their own work and ideas. Having students write about results of their original research encourages them to assume ownership of the work.

In these exercises, students conduct a group experiment in which they actually infect rats with tapeworms that they have reared in the laboratory, and then data are collected from the infections. Data are, as they say, like a box of chocolates; you never know what you're gonna get. Whatever data are generated by the experiment, good, bad, or ugly, they are the student's own to analyze and discuss. In order to maximize collaborative creativity among the students and to maximize consistency and ease in evaluation, the experiment should be a group exercise, so that everyone in the class is working with the same data. The data are still their own, at least in a corporate sense, in that they participate in generating the data.

Assignment 1: Organization of Thoughts (Prioritization)

One informal writing assignment comes before the experiment actually begins. Students delve into the scientific literature to accumulate background information. Students may conduct their own literature search or may be provided with a list of selected references. Then, students clearly state the purpose of the study they are about to undertake, briefly summarize what is known about the topic, and generate a hypothesis and predictions to direct their study. I do not collect this exercise; instead, I discuss it in class in an attempt to come to a consensus on our methodological approach and goals. In larger classes, it is helpful for students to share their ideas in small groups before class discussion. This entire exercise takes only one class period but provides students with an outline for their introduction and a conceptual framework for their investigation. This exercise ensures that the students begin their first draft with clear delineation of the conceptual basis of their topic. This discussion also allows me to assess the students' depth of understanding of the background material. I remediate any deficiencies identified through further lecture and discussion.

The scientific method provides a conceptual guideline to direct students' critical thinking. Using the scientific method nurtures the student's understanding of thinking and writing within the discipline. If students are not familiar with the scientific method and its application, it is advisable to conduct some remedial training. [See Chapter 1 of Knisely (2002) and Chapter 1 of Richardson and Richardson (2005).]

Assignment 2: Critical Analysis of Scientific Writing

Before students write their own papers, I have them conduct a critical analysis of papers from journals. This enables students to become familiar with the nature and scope of information that should be provided in each section of the paper and prepares them for the writing process. It is best for the instructor to select the papers that the students will critique. Selections should include some "good" papers and some "not-so-good" papers. I ask students to critique the success of the authors in concisely conveying requisite information in each section of the paper. Students may work in pairs and present their analysis to the class in the style of Ebert and Roper (two-thumbs up, two-thumbs down, etc.), while providing the rationale underlying their individual criticism. At the outset, it is difficult for students to assess scientific papers; however, the critical approach to this exercise provides the students with an avenue to assess their own thoughts about technical writing. It is important for the instructor to provide her personal insights concerning the strengths and weaknesses of each paper discussed in class. Such a critical approach facilitates an environment of active learning.

Assignment 3: The First Draft

Once the scope and general outline of the project is defined, experiments are designed and conducted, and data are gathered and analyzed. Students are then ready to produce the penultimate document. Even though students began the project as collaborative work, they are ultimately responsible for writing their own papers. At this juncture, writing across the curriculum meets disciplinary writing. Soon after being released from my care, my students will be professional scientists. They will be expected to convey their work and ideas within the confines prescribed by the discipline; it is important to help the student bridge the gap between academic and professional writing. This may be accomplished by requiring the students to present their work in the form of a paper to be submitted to a professional journal.

Since one of the most important aspects of scientific writing is learning to follow meticulously detailed instructions, I give the students a copy of *Guidelines* and *Instructions to Authors* for a journal with which I am familiar and comfortable. A short lecture is presented detailing pertinent information conveyed in each section of a scientific paper, while I review the guidelines to authors and provide advice on points of style. One benefit of having the students follow a highly prescribed set of instructions is that an evaluation assessment form can easily be constructed. Such a rubric makes both the student's job and my job easier. The student knows exactly what is expected, and I have detailed guidelines to provide fair and consistent evaluation.

One of the most common questions from students at this point is, "How long does the paper have to be?" My initial answer is, "Long enough but not too long." Highly prescribed length limitations (both minimum and maximum) often hinder critical thinking and expression of ideas. Frankly, some ideas require more volume for expression than do others. I tell students to completely, yet *concisely,* convey requisite information and to then stop writing.

Assignment 4: Peer Review

In a few weeks, the first draft of the paper is due. Paradigmatically, this is the one that is notoriously unpleasant to evaluate. Evaluation of first drafts is what makes many instructors avoid writing exercises altogether.

Assisting students in the transition from student to professional in the field demands a high degree of modeling professionalism in the classroom. I do this by mimicking the editorial process that is utilized in the submission, review, and ultimate publication of scientific papers. I have the students submit their first draft in triplicate along with a formal cover letter. I forward two copies to two other students for peer review. Likewise, I provide a cover letter to the student reviewers, conveying guidelines concerning my expectations of their review. Placing this assignment within the context of the writing and review process for a real scientific journal makes it more relevant and interesting for the student than "just another term paper." Furthermore, the applied nature of this approach enables students to capitalize on the skills acquired from their training in academic writing (such as English composition) by using them in disciplinary writing.

One legitimate question that arises is, "How detailed should information provided to the peer reviewer be?" I give students a letter that an actual reviewer of a scientific paper for a professional journal would receive. Providing a seemingly minimal amount of guidance at this point fosters independence that will be required as students begin to assume their place as professionals within the discipline. While it superficially appears to the student that they are receiving a minimal amount of guidance, modeling is conducted by providing the students with several examples of reviews of scientific papers that I have personally submitted for publication. Successful completion of the task with a "minimal" amount of guidance fosters self-confidence, another requisite to professional success. Although they are students today, within a mere couple of years they will be our colleagues and will be expected to assume all the "rights, privileges, and responsibilities appertaining thereto." They have to begin that transition from student to professional sometime, and that might as well be today.

Another decision that has to be made is whether or not to make the reviews double anonymous, to leave only the reviewers anonymous, or to reveal both the authors and reviewers. Once again, I defer to the most common practice actually used within the professional community, in which the author is revealed to the reviewers but the reviewers remain anonymous to the author; doing so facilitates more critical and candid reviews. I have the student reviewers submit marked-up copies of each paper reviewed to me, along with a detailed cover letter and review form. I briefly examine the review. If I find the review to be lacking in rigor, it may be returned to the student reviewer for more work.

The benefits to the student of the peer review are obvious. They get two independent assessments of their work by peers who are completing the same assignment. Likewise, the student reviewers benefit because they gain a fresh perspective on the same problem that they are addressing. And what about the benefits to the instructor? Let's take a look at what the instructor will have done thus far in terms of evaluation: a brief examination of the student reviews to determine their acceptability, and that's it. The instructor will have dodged the bullet that we call the first draft.

Assignment 5: Revision

Reviews are returned to student authors along with a cover letter in which they are directed to revise their manuscript accordingly. It is important to emphasize that the reviewer's comments are only suggestions; the authors are ultimately responsible for the content of their paper.

I also encourage my students to employ the aid of outside reviewers: roommates, tutors at the University Learning Center, or a friend who is an

English major. The more criticism they receive, the more they will be compelled to examine critically their own writing and thought processes. It should be made clear, however, that the work must ultimately be their own. This is a good time to engage students in a discussion about academic integrity, propriety in the review process, and intellectual property rights.

After ample time is given for revision, the paper is ready to be submitted for evaluation by the instructor. *(Note that this is the first time that the instructor is required to read the student's paper.)* The student has been asked to conduct a substantial amount of work by this point; thus, each student deserves a thoughtful evaluation with ample comment. However, the paper has already been revised, making initial evaluation much more palatable.

When I incorporated peer review into the writing assignments in my courses, I was amazed at the increase in quality of student manuscripts. The time that once was relegated to correcting many basic mechanical errors in writing was now available to help the students focus on substantive issues in their writing and rhetoric.

Assignment 6: The Final Draft

The assignment could end with the revised first draft and still greatly enhance the educational value of the semester's paper relative to the traditional term paper approach. However, too often students do not carefully consider comments on a paper that is the final draft. So at this juncture, the opportunity to maximize the true value of the assignment is presented. I require my students to rewrite the manuscript in view of my comments and suggestions. When substantial revisions were required, it has been constructive to arrange individual meetings with the students to discuss the manuscripts and to answer any questions they might have regarding my expectations. Then, I grade their rewrite as a separate assignment. I do not let the grade on the rewrite replace the original grade, as this would reduce the incentive to produce the best "first draft" possible. Nevertheless, a higher grade earned on the rewrite increases their overall average.

Having the students do a final revision ensures that they will thoughtfully consider my comments and apply the suggestions. Evaluation of the rewrite is easy; I simply have the students turn in a copy of my initial evaluation along with the rewrite. I have to only ensure that the students have thoughtfully considered my comments and have made a satisfactory attempt to implement them. Of all the components of this series of assignments, the final rewrite is the most powerful because it compels the student to *apply* constructive criticism provided by the teacher. This leaves the student with an affirmation of the improvement that they have exhibited in their writing and rhetorical skills, instead of an affirmation of their deficiencies. It also leaves me satisfied because I have led the students through a valuable writing exercise, instead of merely evaluating the writing skills that the students have learned in other courses.

Finally, what do I do with all the time that I save by not having to evaluate those often hideous first drafts? I do the assignment myself, incorporating the same data that the students use. When I return the evaluation of the first draft, I attach a copy of my own paper, giving them an example of how I think the paper should be written. This helps the student feel like a partner in the learning process and demonstrates to the student that I am willing to engage in the writing process with them. Providing an example models good writing (at least, I like to think so) and elucidates expectations concerning such details as formatting, proper citation, etc.; thus, students are able to interpret my comments and suggestions more readily. In reality, it doesn't require a lot of time for me to write my own paper because the assignment is conducted each year. It simply becomes a matter of modifying the paper from previous years by incorporating data from the current year. This activity also grounds my appreciation of the student's perspective and the challenges that students face.

Example of Protracted Peer-Reviewed Writing Assignments

Following, I have provided a copy of instructions that are given to my students for each component of the protracted peer-reviewed writing assignments described. They are presented to students as a series of formal cover letters. The entire series of assignments is worth 300 points, 150 points of which are based on the penultimate document turned in to me. Note that only 50 of the 300 points are given for conducting reviews of two student papers. An inadequate review is returned to the student reviewer. This is repeated until I am satisfied that the student reviewer has provided a thorough and thoughtful review. While the point value awarded for reviewing is minimal, the real reward is the reciprocal reviews received from other student reviewers. Obviously, the point values assigned to various assignments will depend on the grading structure of the class. In my Animal Parasitology course, this writing assignment constitutes 15 percent of the overall course grade. Other writing assignments linked to this process are assigned independent point values as applicable.

Initial Assignment

Dear Student:

For the past several weeks, you have been investigating the life cycle of the tapeworm *Hymenolepis diminuta* and the phenomenon known as the crowding effect. Write a manuscript reporting your findings. Your manuscript should be prepared according to the attached "*Comparative Parasitology* Policies and Instructions for Authors." Additionally, I strongly recommend reading several papers from this journal, which is available in the laboratory and the library. I will provide examples of papers I have submitted to this journal, as examples of proper format. There is no minimum or maximum number of pages required. The manuscript should be long enough to convey your research findings, without including extraneous material. The first draft of the manuscript is due on or before October 30, 2003. Please submit three hard copies and one electronic copy of your manuscript.

Cover Letter Accompanying Papers for Review

Dear Student:

Please find enclosed two manuscripts regarding the life cycle of *Hymenolepis diminuta* and the crowding effect that were submitted by your fellow students for evaluation. Please review the manuscripts for clarity, concision, scientific accuracy, and the style required by *"Comparative Parasitology* Policies and Instructions for Authors." Also refer to *A Student Handbook for Writing in Biology* by Knisely (2002) for valuable advice concerning the review process. (Chapter 5 has some particularly helpful information.) As you review the manuscripts, pay careful attention to proper spelling, grammar, and sentence structure. Make editorial remarks and suggestions directly on the manuscript. In addition, provide the authors with detailed comments summarizing specific areas for improvement on the enclosed review form. As in any professional relationship, don't forget to mention the strengths of the work. Please do not sign the review form, as the review process is anonymous. However, submit signed cover letters to me. Your careful review of this manuscript will ensure better learning for your classmates. If your reviews of your peers' papers are found to be insufficient, you will be required to rereview the manuscript. I will provide examples of reviews in the laboratory. Reviews are due on or before November 6, 2003. Each review is worth 25 points.

Cover Letter Accompanying Peer Reviews of a Manuscript

Dear Student:

Please find enclosed two peer reviews of your manuscript. Please pay careful attention to the comments of both reviewers and revise the manuscript accordingly. In addition, pay careful attention to *"Comparative Parasitology* Policies and Instructions for Authors." Please bear in mind that while the reviews may be helpful, you are in no way required to follow the reviewers' recommendations. However, you are required to provide a point-by-point response to each of the reviewer comments given on the review forms. If you do not agree with a reviewer's suggestion, please provide appropriate rebuttal in the cover letter. Ultimately, you are solely responsible for the content of your paper, which must be submitted to me for evaluation on or before November 13, 2003. The manuscript is worth a possible 150 points.

*Cover Letter Accompanying My Initial Formal Evaluation
of the Manuscript*

Dear Student:

Please find enclosed my evaluation of your manuscript. Please redraft the manuscript in accordance with my recommendations. For your reference, I am also enclosing a copy of a manuscript that I have written using the same data to serve as an example. The final revision of your manuscript is due on or before December 4, 2003. The revision is worth a possible 100 points.

Performance Assessment Guidelines

One of the most difficult parts of evaluating student papers is assigning point values to various parts of the paper, and grading rubrics become a very personal issue depending on priorities of the instructor. Nevertheless, I have included the assessment guideline that I utilize in evaluation of the penultimate paper described above at the end of this chapter. [The assessment form is based on information from Knisely (2002) and Clopton (2003).] On the copy of the assessment form given to the student, the point values indicated by italics are not included. These are for my personal use to loosely serve as general guidelines for maintaining consistency in quantitative assessment of individual student papers. The guideline presented is designed to obtain a percentage grade (of 100 points). Note that in some instances the number of points listed within a section adds up to more than the total point value given for that section. The values for the individual points reflect a maximum that I deduct for each issue addressed; I never deduct more than the total point value assigned to the section. For instance, if the running head is excessively long and appears on each page, I deduct only the maximum of 1 point assigned to the running head.

Pedagogical Merits of the Protracted
Peer-Review Format

Three hallmark characteristics of good writing-across-the-curriculum exercises are that they consist of a series of linked exercises that are recursive, reflective, and that require prioritization. The exercise described above does all three. It is recursive in the sense that the students are continually asked to reevaluate and redraft their own writing and ideas over the course of the semester. It is reflective in that the students are urged to examine their work from different perspectives or points of view. This is particularly true of the review process in which the student considers the approaches taken by two fellow students in dealing with the same data set and when considering insight provided by the student reviews of his own paper. Prioritization is required and stressed throughout the series of exercises. Concision, one of the hallmarks of scientific writing, requires keen prioritization skills. I have found this to be one of the hurdles that students have in bridging the gap from English composition to scientific writing. The initial literature review along with group classwork in defining the hypothesis and experimental design of the study facilitate prioritization skills, as do dealing with peer reviews and the instructor's comments on the final document.

Concluding Remarks

After implementation of a few suggestions given above, I found that my cynicism regarding the writing and critical thinking ability of my students was misdirected. The problem was *my* attitude and approach to student writing. I had underestimated the power of carefully crafted writing assignments as pedagogical tools, and I had underestimated the ability of my students. Thus, I like to consider myself an apostate cynic. The most important lessons I have learned are these: writing is a process and we all spend a lifetime honing our writing skills, and that contrary to my initial pessimism, my students are a group of extremely gifted and skillful individuals. I just have to find pedagogical approaches that enable my students to exercise and refine their talents.

Ultimately, the wellspring of my lamentations was the inadequacy of the traditional term paper approach to writing. Now when I converse with my colleagues about classroom writing, I find myself discussing the fine papers that my students produce. Alas, I have been converted. I find myself engaging in meaningful discussions about innovative writing exercises that will foster critical thinking.

No suite of tools will work for any one teacher, but I have presented a series of exercises that work for me. The exercises outlined above are the result of several years of trial-and-error pedagogical research on my part. It is my hope that they will also work for others. It is essential not to try too much too fast. Only one or two new writing exercises should be implemented into a curriculum at a time. Then the results (measured by student performance) may be examined and the exercises may be modified according to the desired outcome and the individual goals of the teacher. Eventually, an orchestrated series of assignments may be developed to fit the individual's teaching style. Mastery of effective writing skills is a difficult, lifelong endeavor, but leading students toward this goal doesn't have to be.

Acknowledgments

I owe a debt of gratitude to Dr. Robert Smart, the Writing Program Director, and the Writing Across the Curriculum Committee at Quinnipiac University for empowering me in my attempt to better teach writing in my classroom. I extend my appreciation to Kristen Richardson for providing excellent critical review of early drafts of this manuscript in which she clearly and willingly provided a mile marker on my personal road to mastery of effective writing skills.

References

Bean, John. 1996. *Engaging Ideas: The Professor's Guide to Integrating Writing, Critical Thinking, and Active Learning in the Classroom.* San Francisco: Jossey-Bass.

Clopton, Richard. 2003. *"Comparative Parasitology* Policies and Instructions for Authors." *Comparative Parasitology* 70: 218–25.

Knisely, Karen. 2002. *A Student Handbook for Writing in Biology.* Sunderland, MA: Sinaure Associates, Inc. W. H. Freeman and Co.

Richardson, Dennis, and Kristen Richardson. 2005. *Biology: A Laboratory Guide to the Natural World, 2nd ed.* Upper Saddle River, NJ: Prentice Hall.

Assessment Guideline for a Scientific Paper

Assessment Form

Running Head: (1 pt.)

>   Running head excessively long? (1/2 pt.)
>   Running head descriptive and appropriate? (1/2 pt.)
>   Running head appears on each page? (1 pt.)

Abstract: (5 pts.)

>   Is purpose of the investigation stated and is the investigation adequately introduced? (2 pts.)
>   Methods briefly described? (1 pt.)
>   Results briefly described? (2 pts.)
>   Conclusions briefly summarized? (1 pt.)

Introduction: (30 pts.)

>   Conceptual framework underlying the study clearly established? (15 pts.)
>   Background literature search complete and adequate? (15 pts.)
>   Purpose of the study clearly articulated? (7.5 pts.)

Materials and Methods: (7 pts.)

>   Procedures described in enough detail to enable replication? (3.5 pts.)
>   Everything indicated in past tense? (1 pt.)
>   Information presented in narrative form (not listed like steps in a set of instructions or recipe)? (5 pts.)

Results: (5 pts.)

>   Results summarized in narrative form? (5 pts.)
>   Results not interpreted in this section? (2 pts.)
>   All figures and tables cited if and where appropriate? (2 pts.)

Figures and Tables: (10 pts.)

>   Appear at the end of the manuscript? (1.5 pts.)
>   Figure captions on a separate captions page? (1.5 pts.)
>   Figures and tables formatted according to instructions? (5 pts.)
>   Captions detailed enough that tables are "stand alone"? (5 pts.)

Discussion: (30 pts.)

Results briefly reiterated? (7.5 pts.)
Implications of present findings thoroughly and adequately discussed in light of existing data? (15 pts.)
Sound rhetoric? Do the findings address the purpose of the study? Is there an attempt to explain any deviation from expected results? (7.5 pts.)

Literature Cited: (10 pts.)

References formatted properly? (5 pts.)
Literature cited properly in text? Are all references cited in the text? Do all references cited in the text appear in the Literature Cited section? (5 pts.)

Miscellaneous Considerations:

Page numbers given in the upper right-hand corner of each page? (2 pts.)
Section headings formatted properly? (1 pt. each)
Everything written in past tense from third person point of view?
All numbers written in Arabic, except when used at the beginning of a sentence?
All scientific names properly spelled, used, and written?

In addition to points deducted for specific issues outlined above, 1 point is deducted for each "major" error (run-on sentence, sentence fragment, improperly written scientific name, improper or inconsistent use of tense, major misspelling, etc.) and ½ point is deducted for each minor error (improper use of commas, minor misspelling, typographical errors, etc.)

4

The "Just Right" Challenge

Signian McGeary

Assistant Professor of Occupational Therapy,
School of Health Sciences

The word *occupation* is derived from the Latin root *occupacio*, meaning to seize or to take possession, conveying action. My role as a professor of occupational therapy has been influenced by a three-year involvement in the Quinnipiac University Writing Across the Curriculum Committee. During this time, I have undergone a transformation as a teacher and a writer because now I feel that I am really helping students to evolve from their core outward. The WAC experience has transcended my discipline because I can help students learn a process that allows for a growth that they can apply to a lifetime of learning. My work with the committee has helped me to understand in a new way the power of *occupation* clearly linked to the action of writing, specifically through writing-to-learn assignments.

Like other health care professionals, occupational therapy students must possess excellent clinical and critical thinking skills at the time of graduation. Writing-to-learn (WTL) assignments support critical thinking, a skill needed for clinical analysis. Today, a master's degree is a minimum requirement for many entry-level professional positions in health care, so the mandate for high-performance standards goes beyond basic clinical skills to include clinical scholarship. Evidence-based practice is the mantra of twenty-first century clinical practice and learning; therefore, effective education must nurture and foster excellent writing skills and improved critical thinking to support the link between research and its translation into clinical practice. As educators, we must take responsibility for the needs of the student and the demands of the society, and we can provide more effective education by employing WAC principles and practices to help students learn with understanding.

One key value of WAC that has meaning for me is the ability to meet the individual needs of the students through the variety of WAC teaching strategies based on using low-stakes writing to foster mastery of classroom material. C. R. King in 1978, in a national address at an American Occupational Therapy Association conference, stated that, "doing with meaning promotes individual adaptation." A therapy program tailored to the client and which the client understands will more successfully engage and motivate that client to participate. Similarly, a carefully designed writing-to-learn activity will stimulate students to find meaning in the course material, and if they are also engaged directly in the learning process, students will take ownership of the construction of that personal meaning. As John C. Bean states, "Students via writing to learn are able to express concepts in their own words to recognize what they do and do not know" (1996, 47). When we provide a classroom environment that allows students to reflect on their own learning process through writing, their understanding deepens in a more personal and meaningful way. In some instances, it is easy for faculty to overestimate student competency and self-efficacy. Writing-to-learn activities allow students to discover weaknesses in their comprehension without feeling penalized, thereby allowing faculty to strategically intervene in more helpful ways, while also fostering a more hopeful atmosphere for student growth. Students simply learn to trust the classroom process more as they strive to master difficult and often confusing material.

In Occupational Therapy, the phrase "just right challenge" means that the therapist is optimistic that a client can achieve success by challenging the client to struggle against pain and incapacity, but not unduly. The same applies to writing assignments in an Occupational Therapy course. The transactional writing required of students to demonstrate their mastery of course material needs to be supported by the scaffolding offered by carefully designed, informal WTL assignments in order to create the "just right challenge." One such activity is employed in our junior-level anatomy course. The ability to master the complexity of the shoulder girdle function is daunting for the novice. It requires the appreciation of the dynamic interplay of six joints working congruently. It is not enough to assume that the student can understand the force couple arrangements with axial and appendicular muscles and the movement of the humerus on the scapula (all based on lecture, model demonstrations, videos, and cadaver exposure). I am now using an in-class writing exercise (short essay), which asks the student to explain the process of scapular humeral rhythm. Their first attempt is nongraded and returned to the students with descriptive feedback that highlights excellent explanations and identifies poor analyses of the dynamic shoulder girdle structure. The assignment is announced in advance, and students can bring outlines to class or use their notes if they so desire.

The assignment is designed to reinforce student learning through writing, and it exposes what they genuinely understand as well as what is still unclear. Their failure to competently explain a complex dynamic indicates a lack of understanding. Perhaps the student is not clear on a particular muscle function or the interplay between multiple muscles. Their written work allows me to see where they are stuck; then I can provide specific feedback to pinpoint where they need further thought or a more thorough review of text material. Traditionally, I gave a quiz to review student progress or I waited until the midterm or final exam to test for this knowledge. It seems too late to wait until students expose poor understanding when the stakes are this high. Remediation can occur much earlier in the classroom and be specifically directed to individual student needs with ungraded WTL class activities.

The success of these WTL assignments becomes clear when a variation of the same shoulder complex essay question is presented on a midterm or final exam. The student then will have a "just right challenge" that has been rehearsed and refined, and the results can be rewarding for the new learner and the instructor. Student mastery of material appears more secure in the years since I have incorporated WTL tasks and observed student analysis of shoulder girdle material. The students appear to have much better overall understanding of the basic foundation that allows for ease of transition to a higher application demand. For example, after working with these ungraded assignments to master the basic physical concepts, students are better able to identify which muscle is not working when a dysfunctional shoulder case example is presented in a test format.

A second WTL assignment that works well within the same anatomy class is designed as a simulated professional role-modeling exercise. This time the students' ability to understand their audience when describing the complex brachial plexus is key. The physical structure that they need to understand involves the spinal cord nerves as they exit the spinal cord and their path under the clavicle, over the ribs, and through to the axial area, all the while changing in name as they move from roots, to trunks, to divisions, to cords, and finally to the branches. The mnemonic "real therapists drink cold beer" is frequently used to aid in memorization of the terms *root, trunks, divisions, cord*, and *branches*, but more is needed to move students from memorization to understanding. Damage to these structures at any point in the path can result in paralysis or some weakness in the particular muscle that has loss of innervation. The WTL exercise for this topic directs the student therapist to respond in writing to this scenario: Your grandfather calls to report a friend's brachial plexus injury and asks you to explain what it entails. This type of exploratory writing, according to Bean, "is messy because thought is messy—a first draft allows for that time to clarify ideas" (1996, 101). I want less rote parroting of information and more demonstration of how the student is integrating information to accurately describe a serious injury to a layperson. The exercise can become a discovery process of what students can explain, describe, reason through logically, and diagnose. Students who have difficulty with the process beyond mastery of material can be directed to our learning center for assistance in writing future drafts of the assignment. In this way, valuable student remediation can occur on many levels, including the most basic. Most students require two or three drafts of the above assignment in order to master both the descriptive element and content.

The WTL exercises in my class are informative and reveal the level of mastery the student possesses at various points in the class. An entry-level therapist must be able to grasp the implications of spinal cord injury in a clinical setting as part of the clinical reasoning therapeutic role. In the classroom, however, the individual variety of student competency levels is clear when WTL exercises are employed. Thus my role is also clarified: I can become both coach and teacher as I help each of them reach the appropriate level of understanding. Interestingly, some students did have relatives who had brachial plexus injuries, allowing them to become engaged with the writing role-play. Their final descriptive essays had the correct content, and students succeeded in presenting a sophisticated topic to a nonprofessional. Students who completed this assignment clearly demonstrated a professional collective standard of knowledge that was relevant to their future professions and necessary for their effective practice in it. Students need to be able to describe and demystify a medical condition for a client by using their own words, or "owning the material." The classroom environment supported this "real-life" context, allowing students to practice through role-play what they will soon be doing. This example indicates that WTL assignments prepare students for writing that demonstrates proficiency in a professional "field-specific" knowledge or practice (Detweiler and Peyton 2000, 51).

The Bean reference text, *Engaging Ideas: The Professor's Guide to Integrating Writing, Critical Thinking, and Active Learning in the Classroom,* has provided me with many suggestions for experimentation with WTL activities in my classroom. One such technique resulted in my changing a routinely assigned Biomechanics journal article review to include a peer review segment that my colleague, who is not involved in WAC/WTL work, and I agreed improved the quality of work students submitted. What made the difference? My assessment is that the thought of having another student read their work pushed students to spend a little more time on the assignment, and the feedback that students received from peers struggling with the same material also enhanced their understanding and performance.

There are numerous other WTL applications that can be incorporated into the classroom, each tailored to meet the particular needs of various disciplines. This variety seems also to provide for diverse student and faculty needs. For example, WTL exercises used in a classroom with ESL students proved enormously valuable for the Psychology of Pain course that I have team-taught for a number of years in the School of Health Science Physical Therapy Program. The course attracts students from India, Pakistan, Saudia Arabia, Yemen, Sweden, Australia, and the United Kingdom, as well as the United States. The double entry journal and exam question journal WTL assignments proved to be very successful in this class. Having students write more often, without the pressure of grading, acted as a rehearsal for the testing situation and provided practice opportunities to perfect the use of a second language in demonstrating comprehension, at the same time as the students used self-reflection to acquire real understanding of the material. Diffusing a tricky situation where bright, capable, international students could be unnecessarily intimidated without the opportunity to spend extra time on the writing component to prepare for testing demands was an added value. As John C. Bean suggests, "The double entry journal requires students to reflect on course material and then reflect again," a recursive exercise to reinforce mastery (1996, 108). The exam preparation journal "with strong intrinsic motivation" asks students to respond to instructor questions during the semester (Bean 1996, 109). Students brought this journal to class during testing periods and soon it became a ready-made reference, complete with models and cues for responding accurately and effectively to questions framed in a second language. This approach has been very widely applauded for the last three years by the international students.

WTL exercises provide alternative and valuable ways to help people learn. WTL assignments seem to encourage a natural way of strengthening the process of developing individual meaning of class material content. Self-expression is essential, and students understand the high value society places on communication skills. Being able to use their own words and phrasing to prepare for formal assignments can promote greater understanding and mastery of the material. Health care professionals must see writing as an everyday competency, since medical chart record-keeping is a primary job performance requirement. Documentation, for example, is an essential entry-level skill for all health care providers (McGuire 1997). This includes recording a client's status with detailed descriptions of therapeutic intervention. Third-party payment sources mandate very careful record-keeping, and adequate documentation skills also include being able to predict the client's outcome based on intervention and evaluation. Long- and short-term goals along with discharge dates and plans also need to be clearly articulated for third-party review and legal considerations. WTL exercises assist in the development of basic documentation skills for students in the health care arena by fostering step-by-step mastery throughout the professional program. Clinical reasoning skills combined with the student's capacity to articulate and demonstrate a knowledge base via the application of proficiency skills becomes evident in the process of the written documentation. These strategies truly promote a successful outcome to a professional education.

I have been delighted with evidence of a growing concern about student writing and attempts to provide support in the classroom in my own health care discipline. How faculty in other occupational therapy programs are beginning to incorporate this concept in the classroom is detailed in *Innovations in Occupational Therapy Education* (2000). Professors and their students have presented recently at the American Occupational Therapy Association national conference on strategies to assist others in creating an environment that supports writing, advocating for the "transformation of writing from a solitary activity to one of a community practice" (Cohn, Crepeau 2003).

I believe that the foundation for new learning is strengthened through using WTL assignments. The key elements are (1) fostering an interest in the subject matter, (2) breaking down the content challenges to small steps, (3) facilitating student problem solving, (4) acknowledging student diversity and tailoring assignments to their needs, and (5) following up with descriptive praise and phrases that assist learners in reflecting on how to improve their work and enhance mastery of material, thereby inviting ownership through individual meaning and perception development (Nesbit 2004).

Supporting the concept of lifelong learning and linking the enhancement of learning with writing exercises is an academic value that serves students throughout their health professional career. Developing the writing habit to learn, to express, and to respond to the needs and demands of the twenty-first century seems like a good investment of time and energy for student and teacher alike.

References

Bean, J. C. 1996. *Engaging Ideas: The Professor's Guide to Integrating Writing, Critical Thinking, and Active Learning in the Classroom.* San Francisco: Jossey-Bass.

Cohn, Ellen S., and Elizabeth B. Crepeau. 2003. "Transforming Writing from a Solitary Activity to One of Community Practice." Paper presentation handout at the American Occupational Therapy Association Annual Conference. June 6. Washington, D.C.

Detweiler, J., and Claudia Peyton. 2000. "Developing a Language for Discussing Writing: Composition in Occupational Therapy." In *Innovations in Occupational Therapy Education 2000,* ed. P. Crist, The American Occupational Therapy Association, Inc.

McGuire, M. 1997. "Documentation." *Occupational Therapy Practice.* Dec.

Nesbit, S. 2004. "Energizing the College Classroom." *Occupational Therapy Practice.* January 5.

Willingham, Daniel T. 2002. "How We Learn: Ask the Cognitive Scientist." *American Educator.* Winter.

5

Aiding and Abetting

WAC Support for Legal Writers

Susan R. Dailey
Associate Professor of Legal Writing

For many law students, their first experiences with legal writing are fairly trau-
matic. Faced with the task of writing a coherent, tightly organized memo in the
unfamiliar language of a new discipline, even experienced writers often see
their sentences deteriorate and their reasoning crumble. Students commonly
short-circuit the invention stage of the writing process in favor of focusing on
the more formulaic surface features of legal writing. The unfortunate result is
writing that is both substantively superficial and stylistically awkward. Feedback on these early assignments is humbling, and while many students are able
to move beyond this initial stage in their writing, others struggle to regain their
confidence. In my individual conferences with students, I often find myself trying to reconnect them with their critical thinking abilities while reassuring
them that their experience is not unusual for a novice writer in a new discipline.

For some years, I had been grappling with various ways of helping students build on what they already knew about writing and critical thinking to
make a more effective transition into law school. As a dedicated user of WAC
principles in my own classes, I decided to apply these principles to the design
of a series of workshops that addressed various stages of the writing process
and emphasized the critical thinking component of legal writing. This essay
tells the story of these workshops: the rationales, the experiments, the students'
reactions, and the faculty response.

The decision to focus on connections between writing and critical thinking stemmed from my positive assessment of the integration of WAC ideas into
my Law and Humanities class. Reading journals had helped students to generate creative, problem-centered paper topics in which they were often quite personally invested. The peer-editing process brought these busy night students

into dialogue (if not debate) with each other that spilled out of the classroom and into the café. The reflective pieces that introduced their portfolios at the end of the semester gave me interesting feedback on their writing processes and ideas about how I could improve the class. While there is still room for improvement, the class structure often produced the authentic sense of a community of writers that I had hoped to create when I designed the course.

During a summer course that required an exam rather than a paper, I had the opportunity to experiment with other types of writing assignments. The course, which incorporated difficult readings in Irish history and literature, presented significant challenges to the law students, and I decided to use writing assignments to help them focus their reading of texts such as Roy Foster's *Modern Ireland: 1650–1972* and James Joyce's *Ulysses*. Using a sequence of linked writing prompts, the students wrote short paragraph-length microthemes (Bean 1996, 80) about some aspect of their reading assignments.

In designing the prompts, I reflected on the questions that I planned to pose in the exam and worked backwards. I theorized that the writing assignments would give students the opportunity to rehearse their thoughts and test their ideas in a low-stress environment. Instead of collecting the paragraphs, I asked one or two students to read their responses aloud at the beginning of each class, and the readings became the initial focus for discussion. In creating the prompts, I took particular care with areas of the course with which students had had the most difficulty in the past. For the unit on Joyce, for example, the writing assignments started with a definition of a term from their historical readings and grew in complexity to a more fully developed essay that commented on Joyce's portrayal of the social and political milieu of his time. Three times during the semester, students had the additional option of writing more extended essays, similar to practice exams, which they could submit for detailed, written comments.

This experiment yielded a number of interesting results. First, the students' preparation for writing their paragraphs guided their reading so they were better able to participate actively in class discussion. Moreover, as they read their paragraphs aloud in class, I was able to learn where they had misunderstood the material or failed to connect it appropriately to some concept we had discussed earlier. The writing assignments also provided me with opportunities for self-critique and adjustment. I soon realized, for example, that poorly worded writing prompts produced weak, unfocused student paragraphs, and my responses to the practice exams helped me to articulate more clearly my own assumptions about well-written exam answers.

At the end of the semester, the final exams were much better than they had been in previous years. I was especially delighted with several beautifully written essays on James Joyce that demonstrated that students had really mastered this complex subject matter. Their decision to write about Joyce, instead of one of the other options for this exam question, reflected their confidence in tackling difficult material. I attribute much of the success of this particular unit of the course to the use of the writing prompts.

While these experiences with writing-to-learn activities in my own class had been positive, I was initially unsure about how these ideas could be applied to help first-year students as they face the significant challenges involved in writing their first assignments in law school. Reading the cases that they analyze in their written work, for example, can be difficult in itself. Expert reading of a text requires knowledge of the subject matter that first-year students have not yet attained. They are also reading a genre that is unfamiliar to them and has a structure they haven't encountered before. The vocabulary alone can be daunting to a novice. Unfortunately, "[f]ew law students attribute their difficulties to the text or the new conceptual problems that they face" (Dewitz 1996, 665). Regardless of the academic success they may have enjoyed in the past, they blame themselves for not being able to understand the texts and begin to question their own abilities.

In their writing, students' attempts to use this unfamiliar language can result in convoluted sentences and obscure paragraphs because they are not sure how they can incorporate the court's language into their analysis in a coherent way. As Joseph Williams (1991, 18) points out, first-year law students typically seize on the superficial aspects of writing models and provide information in their analyses that would be obvious to experts in the field. Novices writing in a new genre are likely to make a variety of errors in their first assignments. Nevertheless, students are often quite dismayed at their professor's evaluation of their work, especially since it has often been the product of an extremely labor intensive effort.

Students writing in any new discipline frequently face similar problems, but in law school these challenges are intensified by the importance placed on writing assessment. Most law school grades are based entirely on written exams, and first-year grades are particularly significant because law reviews automatically extend invitations to students with the highest class ranks. Other students may vie for coveted law review positions by participating in "write-on" competitions in which student judges select the best writers based on written work they produce over the course of a weekend. Employers typically view participation in law review and other extracurricular activities such as moot court, which also has a writing component, as attractive additions to a student's resumé. Moreover, employers ask for writing samples as part of the hiring process, and writing skills play a pivotal role in the assessment of a firm's new associates. All these factors can create a writing environment that produces ineffective writing habits. Faced with so many aspects of writing that are different from anything they have done before, students sometimes lose confidence in the writing skills they may have had before and have a hard time building connections to the types of reasoning and critical thinking skills that they already possess.

Legal writing programs, sensitive to the needs of novice legal writers, structure their curricula to introduce students to the conventions of the discipline. In doing so, they use some writing-to-learn strategies. For example, students generally prepare for class by writing case briefs, and most writing assignments include a specific rhetorical context and a realistic legal scenario. Moreover, writing assignments are generally problem centered, and students often use an organizational paradigm designed to help them write their analyses in a way that would be most understandable to a legal reader.

There are, nevertheless, more ways in which to incorporate WAC ideas into a legal writing curriculum. Researchers have found, for example, that writing case briefs helps students remember information about cases, but does not necessarily enhance their critical thinking abilities.

> In preparing their briefs, [some students] simply copy or paraphrase what the court said without connecting their reading of the case to their existing knowledge. In contrast, for other students, case briefing involves knowledge transformation. These students either integrate the case into their existing knowledge structures or create a new knowledge structure to accommodate the case. (Oates 2000, 21)

Busy law students sometimes save time by "book briefing," highlighting the parts of the text that seem to answer the questions likely to be posed in class. Needless to say, this strategy does not help them to integrate course material, nor does it enhance their critical thinking skills.

While organizational paradigms and role-playing may help acquaint students with the conventions of the new discipline, they may do so at the expense of helping students to build on what they already know. Most early writing assignments ask students to predict how the court will decide a given fact pattern based on legal precedents. Critical thinking is crucial to completing this task because students must question assumptions, aggressively investigate all sides of an issue, and support an unbiased conclusion. To be successful, students need to employ inductive and deductive reasoning, organize material in a coherent way, read critically, and use analogies and distinctions. Showing students the ways in which they have done these tasks in the past may help them transfer the knowledge to their new writing context. Without such explicit discussion, students may be needlessly intimidated by their task and feel ill equipped to do it.

In designing the writing workshops, I wanted to build more effectively on what students already knew by making explicit comparisons to writing and reasoning they had done before coming to law school. I also wanted to focus on their writing processes in an effort to model effective writing strategies and help them eliminate any unproductive behavior that resulted from lack of confidence. Thus, each workshop focused on one aspect of the writing process and was organized around some legal problem-solving activity. I wanted to avoid as far as possible legal jargon and use instead language and terms with which students were already familiar.

Another important feature of the design of each workshop was in-class writing. As Carol Parker (1997, 572) points out, students' writing reveals aspects of their thinking processes that may not be apparent from class discussion. The ways in which students organize discussions of legal issues reflect their understanding of the relationship of ideas; the gaps in logic may reveal gaps in understanding or unchallenged assumptions. Teachers who read students' writing gain insight into the thought processes of the individual students in their classes, their particular points of view and insights, as well as their difficulties, and the general level of understanding of the group.

While students generally do a significant amount of writing for their Legal Writing courses, little of it is done in class. In a recent survey, writing professors report that nationwide, only 7 percent of class time is spent actually writing (Association of Legal Writing Directors 2003, under "Curriculum").

Each workshop would also require students to analyze work they were doing in their legal writing classes. Workshop participants emailed me papers they had recently submitted to their writing professors, and let me know if I had permission to use their work in class. This gave me writing samples on a number of different topics that would alternately place students in the role of readers and writers.

As the time for the workshops drew closer, I became concerned about yet another potential problem. Would the students even come? Law students often feel overburdened with academic work and are sometimes quite reluctant to take on anything "extra" unless they are quite sure that it will provide an immediate, tangible benefit. This point had been brought home to me by an encounter I had early in the semester with a small group of newly arrived first-year law students. We had been discussing the importance of critical reading and its pivotal role in law school success. Realizing that the group may find some of my website materials useful, I showed them a link on one of the "Reading" pages that would allow them to hear a professor explain his reading of the first case they had been assigned in law school (Dailey, under "Reading Cases"). While several students commented favorably on the website materials, one asked a somewhat unexpected question: "How long does it take to listen to his comments?" "Twelve minutes," I replied. I saw him do a quick calculation of some complex personal time-benefit ratio. Apparently, twelve minutes was a good answer because he smiled and said, "Cool." This exchange was a bracing reminder of the realities of law school life.

Concerns about attendance appeared to be justified at first. Immediately after students received notice of the workshops, I was inundated with requests—for individual conferences. Papers were due for their classes, and panic was already rampant. Workshops that involved time spent discussing someone else's paper took time away from their own. Nevertheless, workshop participation, though initially tiny, started to grow within the first week, evidently encouraged by word-of-mouth student assessment.

Each workshop began with some problem-solving activity that involved in-class writing. The first workshop, for example, focused on the invention stage of the writing process and centered on the types of critical thinking involved in generating ideas for a legal memo. Using the metaphor of a cauldron to describe the rough draft (Bean 1996, 16), I told students that we were going to explore what types of critical thinking they needed to throw ideas into the "pot." The students then brainstormed possible answers to a simple legal question. After a discussion of the process of solving the problem, we looked at several pieces of student writing to see whether they contained all the elements we had identified as being essential.

Although each workshop contained many of the same structural features, the exercises and activities varied significantly depending on the pedagogical goal. In the reading workshop, for example, students read a fact pattern posing a hypothetical legal problem and one relevant case. Using website materials, we examined how an "expert" legal writer (in this case Mary Schairer, one of the writing professors) read the case within the context of the problem. As we listened to Prof. Schairer's analysis and looked at her marginal notes on both the assignment and the case, students took notes comparing her strategies for approaching the materials with their own. They compared her marginal notes and annotations with their own notes on a case they had read recently in class. As a closing exercise, students were given the beginning of a second case relevant to the analysis of the original problem. Using the reading and critical thinking strategies we had discussed, they wrote a prediction of the outcome of the case and the court's reasoning.

Workshops on other aspects of the writing process began with similar writing and problem-solving activities. Some required students to rewrite paragraphs or sections of papers, while others involved different types of responses to a problem. To work on organizational skills, for example, students made a diagram to use as a visual aid in a talk to a group of hypothetical high school students about a trespass statute.

Not surprisingly, uninspired writing prompts produced uninspired writing and discussion. For the revision workshop, for example, I originally asked students to list the qualities of a good legal memo. When this seemed to elicit canned responses right out of their textbook, I changed the prompt:

> You are a partner in the law firm of Samuels, Jacobs & Hill. One of your oldest clients has come to you with a complicated tax problem. You have asked one of your new associates to do the preliminary research on the problem and write a memo predicting how the court will analyze the client's facts. You've decided to give the associate some guidance by telling her the five characteristics of a memo that are most important to you as a reader. What are they?

Putting the students more concretely into the role of reader made a significant difference in the quality of the ensuing discussion.

One of the significant advantages of the in-class writing and problem solving was that conceptual problems were quite graphically represented when we examined the student writing. For example, in the critical thinking workshop on brainstorming, students generated ideas about whether a young man had acted recklessly when he threw a rock that damaged a statue. Most students used the definition of "reckless" and a case summary to generate arguments, counterarguments, and further questions. A few students, however, ignored the question and focused on whether the defendant had acted "intentionally," another element of the statute that had a different definition and would, of course, be analyzed separately. This initiated a discussion about basic assumptions of legal analysis. Addressing such fundamental problems on the spot proved to be a significantly better alternative to having the student write an entire paper, submit it to the professor, and then wait a week for written feedback. Identifying potential problems also gave me the opportunity to suggest individual conferences with students to review strategies for reading cases, taking notes, and organizing legal analysis.

One drawback of the in-class writing projects was that they left students vulnerable to embarrassment when their misconceptions were obvious to the rest of the group. To alleviate this concern, I encouraged participants to work in small groups if they felt more comfortable doing so. Surprisingly, many of them preferred taking the risk of working on their own. One student said he wanted the challenge of seeing if he could find a good solution, while another told me that though she had made a mistake in solving one of the problems, she was glad to have had the misconception pointed out to her. Despite these assurances from the students, I continue to be concerned about this issue. One part of the solution is certainly making sure that the workshop environment is comfortable enough for students to be willing to take risks and fail.

The low-risk atmosphere of the class was also important when we discussed the student's formal written work. In my own classes, we had always done peer editing, but this was more easily accomplished, I thought, where the same students had been together for several weeks and had developed a rapport. In the workshop setting, there was less control over the composition and dynamic of the group. Moreover, since the students were writing about a variety of legal issues, I wasn't sure if they would be able to critique each other's work effectively. Although this concern was generally unfounded, there were, in fact, a few times when this was a problem. As their assignments became more complex, however, I was more selective in my choice of writing samples and provided more contextual information about the legal issues.

Despite some minor drawbacks, using student writing samples was invaluable because it grounded our discussion in work in which they were highly invested. Although some students were initially reluctant to have their own papers discussed, even anonymously, they gradually began to realize that no one had submitted a perfect paper and that many of their classmates had similar difficulties in doing the assignments. This collaborative analysis of student papers gave us the time to reflect on the reasoning and rhetorical choices that went into each draft so that the writer's thinking seemed to become more transparent. As a result, the process seemed to encourage a comfortable atmosphere for asking questions and a classroom dynamic conducive to revealing areas of difficulty.

At its best, this part of the workshop provided opportunities for real insights. The most enlightening exchanges occurred when I let the student work speak for itself and encouraged classmates to think through the answers to a peer's question. In one workshop, for example, students explored various organizational paradigms before settling on one that they believed best suited legal reasoning. In this case in particular, my decision to trust the students and resist the temptation to intervene in their discussion paid off because they were able to discover for themselves a link between organization and legal reasoning.

Conclusion

Some aspects of the writing workshops are difficult to evaluate because there are so many factors that contributed to the progress of each student's writing abilities over the course of a semester. It is clear, however, that the writing-to-learn principles I had used in my own classes were also effective with first-year students in the workshop setting. The emphasis on critical thinking throughout the workshops encouraged students to reconsider their perception of legal writing as formulaic. The in-class writing and problem solving revealed strengths and weaknesses in discrete aspects of students' reasoning processes and provided opportunities for self-assessment and reflection. In addition, the peer critiques broadened students' understanding of audience and provided them with more writing strategies. They seemed to appreciate the cooperative learning environment, and as the semester progressed, they gradually gained confidence in their writing skills. I came away from the workshops convinced that given the opportunity, students will guide each other toward better, clearer writing.

The learning process was also, of course, reciprocal. The workshops gave me an opportunity to observe these bright, energetic students tackle all kinds of problems with patience and determination. The night students, in particular, showed tremendous stamina as they struggled through difficult problems after a full day of work and an evening of classes. Seeing the writing process in action provided me with insight I could apply in individual conferences and in designing materials for my website. The in-class writing and problem solving helped me to uncover student strengths and misconceptions that would otherwise be more difficult to find.

One of the more interesting developments that resulted from this project was quite unexpected. When the announcement of my workshops was circulated, the first two responses I received were from colleagues who were interested in learning more about what I was doing. We have recently begun some intriguing conversations about incorporating writing-to-learn strategies into the law classroom.

References

Association of Legal Writing Directors, "2003 ALWD/LWI Survey Report," Legal Writing Institute, *www.alwd.org/alwdResources/surveys/surveyNDX.htm#2003survey* (accessed September 14, 2004).

Bean, John C. 1996. *Engaging Ideas: The Professor's Guide to Integrating Writing, Critical Thinking, and Active Learning in the Classroom.* San Francisco: Jossey-Bass.

Dailey, Susan R., "Legal Writing Center," *www.faculty.quinnipiac.edu.law.dailey/index.htm* (accessed September 14, 2004).

Dewitz, Peter. 1996. "Reading Law: Three Suggestions for Legal Education." *Univ. of Toledo Law Review* 27: 657–73.

Oates, Laurel Currie. 2000. "Beyond Communication: Writing as a Means of Learning." *Legal Writing: The Journal of the Legal Writing Institute* 6: 1–25.

Parker, Carol McCrehan. 1997. "Writing Throughout the Curriculum: Why Law Schools Need It and How to Achieve It." *Nebraska Law Review* 76: 561–603.

Williams, Joseph. 1991. "On the Maturing of the Novice Legal Writer: Two Models of Growth and Development." *Legal Writing: The Journal of the Legal Writing Institute* 1: 1–34.

6

Blogging Across the Curriculum

Pattie Belle Hastings
Assistant Professor of Interactive Digital Design

Valerie Smith
Assistant Professor of English

This is a work in two voices. Pattie Belle Hastings (**PBH**) works in Interactive Digital Design (IDD). Although she has only fairly recently begun working with Writing-Across-the-Curriculum at Quinnipiac University, she has been incorporating Design Journals in her classes for years. Hastings believes that the process of analyzing design, articulating ideas, and expressing thoughts in writing seems to help many design students clarify thinking, understand creative processes, and take ownership of the course material. Journaling assignments, she finds, are especially useful for understanding interactive design concepts, such as usability, navigation, or "data" versus "information," from students' projects and readings. Journaling also helps students learn to articulate and communicate visual information and processes orally, which is critical in client relationships or postgraduate studies. Writing to Learn (WTL) exercises, Hastings believes, help her students attain the cognitive goals she sets for them.

Valerie M. Smith (**VMS**), who teaches both freshman and advanced writing courses and has been actively involved with Writing Across the Curriculum at Quinnipiac University for three years, is a self-described technophobe. Smith's interest in weblogs grew out of a presentation on weblogs by Hastings; her initial desire was to explore the ways in which they might be helpful to expand students' awareness of audience. She wanted to examine how such an expanded awareness of both potentially anonymous and familiar audience members might impact what and how students wrote.[1] Her work with weblogs has encouraged her to experiment even more broadly with a variety of Writing-Across-the-Curriculum concepts, such as WTL and linked assignments.

PBH and VMS: We chose to write this piece in imitation of a blog-type format for two primary reasons: (1) Because we each work within specific disciplinary conventions, we thought a blog-type format, in which we would each retain our own particular voices, might best help us to illustrate and to explore the differences between such conventions. At Quinnipiac University we recognize and value the importance of different disciplinary conventions. We encourage both faculty and students to acknowledge the significance of such differences and the difficulties such differences can often create for both students and faculty. (2) We were attempting to mirror the types of conversations between blogs that we find so interesting. We often ask our students to respond (in writing) to each other's blogs, thereby generating useful dialogues, discussions, and insights both about content and the processes of writing and revision.

What Is a Weblog?

PBH: A weblog (aka blog) is a live online journal that can be easily and instantly updated. A blog can be a frequently posted list of interesting websites, or a personal diary of events and thoughts, or a combination of the two (among many other things). The newborn publishing world of weblogs seems to be having a significant impact on digital culture, communication, education, and publication. (A recent example is the proliferation of political blogs that sprang up around presidential candidates, parties, and news agencies before the 2004 election.) Bloggers are constantly defining and debating the definition of a weblog.[2]

VMS: Weblogs are a fairly recent cultural phenomenon, too recent to be fully understood just yet, too wildly mushrooming to be ignored or casually dismissed.

A Brief History of the Weblog

PBH: The history of the weblog is constantly being revised and debated, but most basic facts are agreed upon. The original weblogs were mainly lists of links to interesting sites created by Web developers and designers in the mid to late nineties. Some included a brief introduction, description, or review of the site link, and some were simply straightforward lists of links.

As Internet time passed and the number of bloggers grew, the definition expanded to include more opinion sites and journal/diary-based sites. This growth was fueled by the creation of free and easy weblog services, such as Blogger and LiveJournal. Now the population estimates of active weblogs are in the hundreds of thousands and it has become a worldwide phenomenon that has even been spoofed on the television show, *The Simpsons*.

Weblogs in and Around the Classroom

PBH: Weblogs are increasingly being used in education by researchers, teachers, and students. Professors are keeping research blogs, requiring students to blog, or creating course weblogs. Students are keeping course blogs and/or personal blogs. Scholars are studying and writing about the weblog phenomenon, while keeping weblogs about weblogs.[3] As I write, the first Web Log Research Master's and Ph.D. are being awarded.[4]

VMS: When I first began working with weblogs, I didn't find much pedagogical advice that seemed useful to my specific needs, so I ended up "blogging by the seat of my pants," so to speak. The two things I knew for sure were that blogs could provide easy access to student work for fellow students and instructors and that they had a potentially very wide audience. I have worked with weblogs in three classes now, and I will discuss each class individually below, considering what I have learned in the course of my explorations.

PBH: In graphic design and related visual disciplines, learning journals (usually called design journals or sketchbooks) have been used to document design research, to collect design and typography notes, to collect design samples and references, and to reflect on assigned readings. I have been using these types of blog projects to introduce WTL exercises in my courses.

I first introduced weblogs in my course called Literature and Writing for Interactive Art. It seemed to make sense that for an introductory course on interactivity and content creation, the journaling process should take the form of a live online weblog. This also allowed for the addition of hyperlink references to related sites and subjects within their reflections—a critical aspect of most projects that are created in the Interactive Digital Design program.

Many design students are unaware of the kind and amount of writing that occurs in the field. Some assume that there is no writing at all and are attracted to the program based on this false belief. This mistaken belief makes a portion of the population of my classes resistant to writing of any kind. Fortunately, the majority of my students fall into the "I'll do it because it is required and easy for me" or the "I'll do it and love every minute of it" camps. In reading the weblogs of these students, it is easy for me to follow their successes and difficulties within the course material, as they Write to Learn, and to discover how each student thinks or processes the content. Throughout the journals, I am able to witness students' growth in absorption, retention, connections, and articulation. For example, the following post is from a sophomore in one of my animation courses, where the students are learning the processes and techniques of creating animated narratives:

Monday, September 06, 2004

"My Scene" Animations

I went on the Barbie site and checked out the My Scene animations there. My 5 year old sister enjoyed watching them with me while I was babysitting. Who knew homework could be so convenient?! Anyway, I was watching the short animations at My Scene and I noticed a couple of things about the animation itself. I noticed that the objects that were standing out the most were brightly colored and more often the center of the scene. For example, when one of the girls was talking, she was brightly colored and the center of the screen. In addition, the background used a dull color scheme that hardly moved at all. In the short film entitled "Does She Buy It?," the whole background is mostly black, white and grey. However, in a shot of a rack of clothes only one of the shirts is colored yellow, making it stand out. This shirt is picked up by one of the characters, which defines that the shirt was important to notice.

I also observed the minimal movement that the characters provided. When they spoke, their facial features did most of the moving. I assume that the creators wanted the viewer to focus mostly on what character was saying. Also, when movement is supposed to be portrayed, in some scenes just the background is what is really moving. For example, in part 3 of the same film "Does She Buy It?" the girls are supposed to be dancing at a club, but instead of their bodies moving, the background colors stream across along with the still figures of the girls. The idea that the girls are dancing is apparent because of the louder music and the setting that the girls are in. This shows that movement isn't the only solution to expressing an action. This not only saved time for the animators but it also made the animation more interesting.

posted by Jessica | 9/6/2004 01:58:35 PM
Jessica Sparago

Weblogs in an Advanced Writing Classroom

VMS: The first class I'll discuss was a small (fifteen-student) Advanced Creative Nonfiction class, in which the focus was on writing the autobiographical essay. Many of the students were not English majors, but they were people who envisioned themselves as serious students of writing. Weblogs worked quite well in this class, especially as students began to go back and revise their previous posts in response to peer commentary.

I visualized weblogs as "safe, experimental spaces," in which students would post weekly (five-hundred-word-minimum) experiments with the writing techniques that we were studying. They might then choose to link the work from their blogs to their longer class projects. Blog assignments were generally fairly open: the students were asked to incorporate one of the interesting writing techniques we discussed in class this week into a short piece of autobiographical writing. I reminded students to draft, revise, and edit before posting, and then to reedit following posting to ensure readability. My goal, at this point, was to raise awareness of craft, to encourage experimentation, to enhance awareness of audience through the use of a potentially very public medium, and to encourage classroom community through the sharing of work. I began using weblogs as a WTL tool, but with slightly higher stakes, because of the more public nature of the process. To begin with, everyone read everyone else's blogs, took notes on what worked or didn't work, and then participated in weekly, oral, classwide blog reports, aka peer review.

In some ways, this system of "blog-reporting" worked well immediately: it really built a strong sense of community in the classroom; students looked forward to reading each other's work, and they looked forward to hearing what others had to say about their work. In other ways, it didn't work well; there was too much back-patting and not enough critical engagement to make the responses useful for forward movement as writers. This was solved by a classwide discussion on the usefulness of comments, followed by some readjustments generated by this discussion.

At this point in the class, I assigned smaller blog groups (of five) so that students were responsible for a smaller, but more in-depth, body of commentary. All comments were still being delivered orally from notes, but within small groups that were reassigned weekly. I also suggested that they start posting weekly self-challenges by filling in the blank: "In this blog, I wanted to challenge myself to . . ." At this point, a little competition seemed to develop between students, centering on who would push themselves further as a writer each week. Even though they were assigned small groups, many students would read beyond their group so that they could see what others were working on, congratulate each other, and garner ideas for new developments from each other. At this point, many students chose to link the material in their weblogs to their more formal assignments, a suggestion I had made earlier in the semester. They could draft, receive commentary, revise, and link their short WTL works to their longer pieces. Many students chose to post their finished pieces on their weblogs as well. Several students announced that family and friends were frequent visitors to their sites and that they wanted their family and friends to see their finished versions of earlier works as well.

Things I learned: (1) Weblogs appear to work well in small, advanced classes. (2) Weblogs appear to work well when students are committed to the subject at hand. (3) Blogs can encourage a "dynamic rhetorical interchange" between students, thus helping to build classroom community.[5] (4) Because of their accessibility, weblogs are useful for WTL and linked assignments and provide easy access for peer commentary. (5) Students in this class developed a strong sense of each other as audience, but when I asked whether or not they thought the potential for a wider, more public audience had any impact on their work, several said, quite frankly, that they'd forgotten these were such public venues. Note to self: stress the potentially public nature of blogs over and over and over again throughout the semester. (6) Blog commentary, like any form of peer review, has to be handled carefully to be useful; periodic reevaluations of the usefulness of commentary are helpful.

Weblogs in Digital Design Classes

PBH: I use weblogs in most of my classes now, so I am going to describe how I use them in general terms across the courses. My courses are capped at seventeen students maximum, due in part to the nature of creative studio courses, but mainly due to the number of computer workstations in the lab. I, too, am interested in the potential weblogs offer for expanding audience awareness. Student blogs are publicly available. This means that anyone can visit and read the weblogs at any time—other students, friends, family, and anyone with Internet access. Although it is possible to create private weblogs, part of the assignment is that the students distribute their URL to the members of the class, friends, family, and that they read and comment on each other's posts. My hope is that with the public nature of the blog in mind, the students would be more concerned with creating thoughtful, cogent postings and with rewriting, editing, and proofreading before they hit the "publish" button.

"What do I write about?" is always the BIG question when we begin the blog project. The weblogs are meant to be a journal of the course, the readings, the learning, the creative processes, and if the student is inspired, life itself. I see this reflection as critical to raising the student beyond software interface and use to thoughtful participation in the creative process and the beginning of becoming a designer.

I have them start with reading the assigned texts (or sites), working through the assigned software tutorials, and design homework. They are required to write at least two to three five-sentence paragraphs per week, but many go far beyond the requirement. I instruct them to make notes as they read or analyze works and while they are in the process of researching and designing. I suggest that they go back over these notes and reflect. Was there something in particular that grabbed their interest? They can begin writing or they can continue with my prompts until they come up with a place to start.

For those who may be stuck, I have a series of questions that they can ponder:

"What inspires me and why?"

"Why do I like or dislike a particular design (color, typeface, website, etc.)?"

"What has someone else written that I like or dislike and why?"

"What am I learning about design, creative processes, and standard practices?"

"How does this new information connect with what I already know?"

"What have I learned today?"

"What problems am I having?"

"How can I improve?"

When it comes to writing the posts, I instruct students to use a word processing application and then cut and paste the final draft into the Blogger posting box. I also tell them to be sure to rewrite, edit, read it out loud, and proofread carefully before pressing the "publish" button. Do they do this? Well, to be honest, not as often as I had hoped. Many of the students log into Blogger and write stream of conscious, without ever looking back.

Although I created my weblog assignments as WAC projects, I now see these assignments as a cross between WTL and WID assignments. My main goal is for the students to delve deeper into the course content and to make it their own. At the same time, more and more software developers, interactive designers, and visual culture workers are keeping (or being required to keep) weblogs for a variety of professional purposes.

The following is an example of the intersection of WTL and WID in a student's blog:

Saturday, September 18, 2004

Narratives 101: Personal Narratives Lying Within Inanimates

As human beings we feel the need to relate to our surroundings. To touch, feel, and smell all of our experiences. The more we experience these interactions within our environment, the more we begin to create a library of stories or narratives. Narratives provide a building block for the development of our own personal character. Movies, television and books are all examples how our culture and school systems use narratives on a daily basis to entertain and inspire us. However, the vast majority of the public probably doesn't realize the smallest of narratives around us.

When first exploring the idea of narrative, I thought of the stereotypical story of one's life. This can be illustrated in a movie or a book, as mentioned above. Yet as I began to embark on this topic, narrative can boil down to an even simpler approach. An average individual may pass an everyday object that isn't seen as anything more. But if we take a closer look the object has distinctive features that can uncover the story beneath the exposing layers. A lamp, a tea cup with a chip off the top lip, a dent in our passenger side door, these are all narratives. These "battle scars" depict the story of our lives.

This type of narrative can be thought of as the art of investigating a crime scene. There are clues or silent witnesses that hold the solution to uncovering the truth. The slightest imperfection is a bookmark into the history of that object or person's life story. Other examples of narratives are songs and paintings. How many of us associate the events of our lives with songs, an old photo or a pressed flower? The relationship between the living and the inanimate world are linked together by our emotions and thus creating bits of narrative in our lives.

posted by Nessie @ 11:29 AM
Vanessa Rubano

The Blog Learning Curve

VMS: My second experiment with blogs took place during a two-week, January intercession, study-abroad course on travel narratives. This class of fifteen students consisted of mostly juniors and seniors. My goals, at this point, were to work with weblogs as WTL assignments once again. We needed to learn course content quickly, which is what the more directed assignments I developed were designed to do. I supplied the parameters for daily postings in the form of specific exercises, each one geared towards incrementally increasing their understanding of the issues involved in both the crafting and the study of travel narratives in relation to our primary and secondary texts. Each weblog allowed students to incorporate their observations as travelers, while at the same time asked them to do so in a manner that would stretch both their technical skills as writers and their ability to think critically about theoretical course material. Each assignment was closely and explicitly linked to their final, formal assignment. In this sense, the weblogs acted as a writing portfolio, since the final assignment asked students to analyze their work from the perspective of the critical framework supplied by our theoretical material.

Students set up their blogs, sent each other their weblinks, and were responsible for their first post before we ever left the United States. They were also required to share their weblinks with at least five other people (friends and family members) in order to enhance their sense of audience. I set up weblog commentary in a more directed manner as well. Because of the intensity of the workload, I immediately broke up the class into smaller blog-report groups to allow them enough time to read and comment daily on a few blogs without overburdening them. This meant I broke them into groups without having first established a classroom community. The class was divided into three groups of five; written peer comments were to consist of one item of praise and two suggestions/pieces of advice on something the writer might approach differently. I wanted to keep the idea of a safe, experimental space, but also to ensure that the commentary was as helpful as possible; we didn't have time for the type of self-adjustments that had taken place in the previous class. Peer commentary, again, counted as a percentage of the class participation grade.

Things I learned: (1) Linked, directed assignments work very well to move students efficiently through course material. (2) It is very important to have an established sense of writing community before breaking off into smaller blog groups. In this case, the community dynamic that had developed in the earlier class did not replicate itself, possibly because we never had a chance to establish a writing community. We did not have enough of a community to really make blog commentary work—although many students reported helpful comments from their friends and family members. (3) Grading peer comments through a system of checks, check-pluses, and check-minuses was really not very helpful for either myself or the students. I want to make sure students read each other's work and produce useful commentary on it, but many students seem reluctant to undertake such a project unless there's a payoff (or threat) in the form of a grade.

The Unforeseen, Unusual, and Unexpected

PBH: I require my upper-level course students to add statistics codes to their site so that they can track the number of visitors and visitor data. I had hoped that blogging would provide insight into online community and site traffic building. What I hadn't foreseen was the impact it would have on the community in the classroom. While there are glimmers of experience with online communities and networking, the real payoff has been the camaraderie and community development in the classroom. I find I have a closer bond and connection to the students, but the best result has been the connections made among the students themselves. This connection wasn't really happening much before: I had a room of people trying to hide behind their monitors. I am now witnessing friendships and the sharing of knowledge and support, as illustrated in the following student blog:

Wednesday, April 07, 2004

As far as the class projects go, wow. There were some really good projects that people in the class made, especially Rafael's and Bill's. Both of these animations were so well done, and I was amazed to see such awesome talent come from our class. However, after looking at what of the rest of the class did, I feel as though I could have done something better. I am happy with the way that mine came out, but I know I have more creative ability than just moving a mask around. If I have time this summer, I would like to tool around with Flash and maybe do another poem animation (I really liked this assignment) and see what I can come up with.

Posted by: Eddie / 12:39 PM
Eddie Pryor

There are specific requirements I outline in the project description that tie in directly to the interactive course content (WID-focused material). The first is that students must have a minimum of one link within each post. The second is that they must read each other's weblogs and make comments on at least one per week. (When I make reference from here on to "links" and "comments," I mean hyperlinks and the comment feature within the Blogger software that allows a viewer to leave a comment directly on someone's weblog site.)

The hyperlink is probably the most basic and important form of interactivity. My goal is that the frequent and eventually fluent use of the hyperlink within the student's writing will foster the kinds of mental and research hyperlinks that promote creative breakthrough. As far as the requirement for links is concerned, I suggest the more, the better. The students tend to start out by re-visiting course content links and sites they already frequent on their own. As the semester progresses, the links become more interesting, unusual, and out of their normal sphere of surfing or research, as illustrated in the following example:

Sunday, September 12, 2004

Perspective

After reading the first chapter of *Pause & Effect*, I can honestly say I'd never been fully aware of all the interwoven forms of multimedia. Sure, I'd seen the movie references in TV Guide and the extras on the DVDs, but I'd never given it much thought before.

For reasons beyond my knowledge, I kept thinking about the Disney parks. There, they use many forms of interwoven interactivity as well as forced perspective. The buildings on Main Street are not actually 3 stories, but by the angle of the windows they can appear to be. Some rides have different forms of content, for example, the Buzz Light-year ride is based on a video game. The rider scores points for all the targets that are hit with the "laser." I guess from now on I will have to pay attention more closely to the different media forms.

Forced Perspective (article link)

Delusion by Design: Architecture and Manipulation at Walt Disney World (article link)

posted by Sarah-Jane @ Sunday, September 12, 2004
Sarah-Jane Bolling

When it comes to commenting on the posts of classmates, the results have been mixed. I am trying to develop useful blog commentary and have been inspired by Val's experience and insight. One outcome I had not completely imagined is the response from the "public" that some of the students have received. Public responses have been one of the most powerful experiences for the individuals involved and have come in the form of more contact from friends and family, messages from well-known Web developers, and correspondence with other Web designers. Fortunately, this has all been positive so far. After the first two weeks of posts, I instruct the students to send the URL of their site to a minimum of five people, and I post a list of links to each student on the course weblog that I keep in order to enhance the students' sense of the public availability of their work. Here's an example of a student commenting and elaborating on another's observations:

Tuesday, September 14, 2004

Your Blog or Mine . . .

I just finished reading Ame's review of "Teddy and Anna," and I came across many similarities in our thinking when trying to understand the short pieces.

Ame explained that the first impression the title gives is a "cute and cuddly" feeling, most likely geared towards small children. After watching these short movies, the viewer will begin to notice that this story has value, and is in no way a cute cuddly movie about a young girl and the games she plays with her stuffed teddy bear. I agreed again with Ame when she says that each episode gets darker in feeling. We both noticed the early-silent movie theme, using dialogue boxes between frames, and I agreed with her when she said this addition furthers the dramatic feeling of the animation.

When I viewed the Teddy and Anna site, I was most impressed with the use of color, and maintaining a similar palate throughout the series. There are no contradictions or off-sets with color because everything pretty much encompasses characteristics of a certain palate, in this case yellow.

Ame noticed something I hadn't, and that is the characters aren't lined in black. They are more lifelike this way, but I can see that these types of movies might more often than not call for outlines to stick with a "cartoon-ish" theme. Outlines on characters normally take away from their liveliness; however put the characters in a light that can be more exaggerated, manipulated, and attractive to the eye.

After reading all of Ame's ideas on this short animation series, I started to brainstorm about how to construct an animation such as Teddy and Anna using the skills taught in the tutorial. When characters moved, I could see how adding frames with slight changes would create this illusion of movement. I also gained some knowledge of using monochromatic tone to create a different feel instead of just coloring things as they should be seen. To create such a unique animation, many factors should be thought of before starting in order to decide which things will catch a viewer's eye, and even better; please him.

posted by louiedog @ 9:03 AM
Alex Vaughn

Traveling Blogs

VMS: My third experiment with weblogs in the classroom took place this past semester. It was a 200-level Essay as a Genre class (twenty-five students), in which the focus was on contemporary American travel narratives and travel theory. Students are sophomores, juniors, and seniors, with only a sprinkling of English majors. Assignments include weekly reading response journals, weekly blog postings, two longer critical discussions of the readings and theory, and the writing of two longer travel narratives, the second of which must address some of the complex issues raised by travel theory. Each weblog had a specific link to whichever of the longer projects we were working on at that moment. I provided a variety of prompts, some of which were highly directed, some of which were quite open-ended, all of which were designed to help students with a variety of different learning styles[6] to learn course concepts, aid in the critical thinking process, and/or link to longer, more formal assignments.

Blog reports in this class were once again completed in small groups of five. New groups were assigned at three points during the semester. Readers would take notes and provide one item of praise and two suggestions or pieces of advice. They exchanged notes, discussed their blogs briefly in class, and were then given the opportunity to revise their blogs according to each other's notes before I read and graded their final blogs. This strategy appears to work well because students can choose how much or how little they will pay attention to each others' commentary. By placing the responsibility on students, this strategy has, at least temporarily, solved the problem of grading blog commentary. By the end of the semester, students know each other and they are used to blog commentary. I collect blog commentary only sporadically, and most seem to be willing to push each other forward as peer readers and as writers.

What I have learned this semester: (1) While not unproblematic, blogs can work in larger classes, even with students from a variety of majors, who may not be one hundred percent committed to the work at hand. (2) Making the links between their blogs and their larger projects as explicit as possible seems to encourage the majority students to take both their own and others' blogs more seriously. (3) Using a variety of blog-prompts works well in responding to a variety of learning styles. (4) Multiple WTL assignments on the same course concepts are very helpful, particularly when linked to revision and longer assignments. (5) Linking blog reports to the opportunity to revise blogs before being graded seems to have worked well.

Postscript

PBH: I have been amazed that some of the students continue to keep a weblog after the course is over. Most of the students have a few of my courses during the program, so they have to revisit the weblog assignment again. They often use the original site they created and pick up where they left off with more comfort, confidence, and appreciation for the process. If interactive design students successfully keep a blog for part or all of their study, they can use this site as a project in their senior design portfolio. This has become a powerful incentive for savvy design students.

I have found that my attempts at incorporating electronic versions of WAC assignments and techniques in my courses have fulfilled all the promises advertised in the literature, and then some. Oh, and did I forget to mention how much less paper I have to handle, organize, file, or return now?!

Notes

1. For more on this see Charles Lowe and Terra Williams' "Moving to the Public: Weblogs in the Writing Classroom" at *http://cyberdash.com/book*.

2. Summer of 2003, with the aid of a university technology grant, I created a website devoted to my course weblog assignments called "Blogging Across the Curriculum."

I had envisioned this site as a starting point for the work at the beginning of the semester and as a resource and touchstone throughout the semester. Any time a student becomes stuck or confused with the writing or requirements, or simply needs a bit of inspiration or clarity, it is all there. On this site you will find links to sources on all subjects discussed in this essay from academic researchers to technical how-to's: <*http://mywebspace.quinnipiac.edu/PHastings/bac.html*>.

3. Ibid. I have links to many resources on academic weblogs on the *Blogging Across the Curriculum* site.

4. Kaye Trammel received her Ph.D. on May 13, 2004. For a dissertation that examines celebrity blogs, more information can be found at *http://kaye.trammell.com/blog/*.

5. In "Welcome to the Blogosphere: Using Weblogs to Create Classroom Community," Thomas Nelson and Jan Fernheimer note that "the sheer numbers of bloggers ensures that the blogosphere is a site of dynamic rhetorical interchange" (2) (August 2003).

6. John Bean's chapter on "Engaging All Learners" provides much useful information on the construction of appropriate Writing Across the Curriculum exercises to respond to different learning styles (San Francisco: Jossey-Bass, 2001), 37–52.

Writing Assignments in Computer Programming Classes

David S. Herscovici
Associate Professor of Computer Science

As a computer science professor, my main goal in the first few programming classes is to teach students the programming skills they will need to complete the subsequent courses in the program. The question naturally arises as to what role, if any, is appropriate for formal writing in such a course. As pragmatic individuals, computer scientists would incorporate writing into a course only if we are convinced it furthers the larger overall goals of the course. In this chapter, I explain how I use writing-to-learn exercises and other formal writing assignments to foster and reinforce the thinking skills required to write good programs, thereby supporting the primary goal of the class, and I give examples of writing exercises I have used in my classes.

There are many similarities between the process of writing an essay and programming a computer. It is no coincidence that we speak of *writing* a program. A well-written program must be well structured and well designed, and it requires multiple revisions, just like a well-written essay. It is precisely *because* of these parallels that formal writing assignments can help our students be better programmers. Since they already have some idea how to organize their thoughts in a written assignment (admittedly some better than others), we can leverage this ability to help them structure their ideas for a program: we can use the more familiar skill of writing to help them acquire the new skill of programming.

One could argue that by insisting that students document their code with suitable comments, good variable names, modularized code, and other features associated with good programming style, we already require that they consider the presentation of their final product—precisely what other disciplines address through formal writing.

Unfortunately, simply requiring students to use good programming style and techniques does not teach them how to do so. Some students write the assigned programs by writing code haphazardly. When their code does not run correctly, they tinker with one part of the code and then another until it finally behaves correctly. These students do not learn to look at the overall structure of a program in ways that would ultimately save them significant amounts of time, and they do not make the necessary connections from one assignment to the next. Because their approach to the programs is haphazard, their code is similarly confused. A few students make it through the early assignments, but become lost when we discuss more complicated concepts, in part because they never really understood the ideas underlying the previous topics. We must continually ask ourselves how we can help our students succeed in these classes.

Writing assignments are a useful tool for challenging students to think rigorously and for combating their difficulties in doing so. Often, these assignments are significantly more effective than programming assignments, especially if the students are struggling with the programs. Perhaps the most successful techniques involve a combination of related writing and programming assignments in which we encourage the students to see the connections between the various modes of expression. For example, we can ask them to organize in writing their ideas about the design and structure of a program formally before they write the actual program. This can be done as an in-class exercise, with the students working individually or in groups, or it can be assigned as homework, which may then be discussed in class or simply collected. By separating the tasks of structuring the program and of writing the code, we encourage the students to see these as distinct parts of the process. By using the same program for both parts of the assignment, we show them the connections between the two parts. That organization also comes through in their programs, and we can discuss in class the extent to which creating the written document helps them produce better code and better-documented code.

Programming 1: Designing Programs

CSC 110: Programming and Problem Solving is our version of Programming 1—the standard first course in computer programming. We teach the Java programming language, and the format of the course includes three hours of lecture and one hour in the lab. While some students have some prior programming experience in another language such as C++ or Visual Basic, for most this course represents their first exposure to programming. Often the students do not understand the level of rigor and of detail required to write a program. To help them acquire this skill, and motivated by my experience as a member of the Writing Across the Curriculum Committee, I created a lab manual that includes the programming assignments as well as some writing-to-learn exercises for use over the course of the semester. Programs are assigned in lab and are due the following week. The writing-to-learn exercises are used as in-class exercises. In each case, they are designed to reinforce topics covered in class by having the students write about the topic in relation to a specific program, and in each case the student is subsequently asked to write the actual program.

The first such exercise is done in conjunction with one of their first programs. A standard assignment for a first programming course is to write a program that converts a temperature in Celsius to its equivalent in Fahrenheit.

I give an in-class exercise based on such a program (included at the end of this chapter). However, instead of writing the code, I ask them to describe in words (not code) each step the program would take as specifically as possible. They then show the output of their program when the user enters the Celsius temperature of 37 degrees, given that the result is 98.6 degrees Fahrenheit. We discuss the exercise at the board, and after that, they repeat the process (describing each step as specifically as possible and giving the output), either for a program that computes batting averages based on the number of hits and at-bats entered by the user, or for a program that computes the sum of five numbers entered by the user. I collect and comment on their work for this second program, but I do not assign a grade. To reinforce the connection between the program descriptions and the actual programs, I return their work the following day and have them write these programs as an assignment in the next lab. I have now used some version of this project three times, and my informal assessment is that it clearly helps students struggling with how to approach writing a program. This exercise is especially useful for the students when they ask for additional help, because we can then encourage them to develop a language for communicating about programming, and the exercise helps both them and us to understand the extent to which their thinking is "fuzzy." It is particularly helpful to do this early in the term. The exercise also helps students with previous experience develop more insight on the topic by giving them a different cognitive approach to programming.

Having the students describe the steps involved in computing the sum of five numbers addresses another issue as well. When confronted with this program, students frequently do not recognize that they must save a running total of the numbers already processed in a separate variable. Furthermore, even after writing this program, they forget to keep this total when asked to compute the sum (or average) of numbers input in different ways—for example, numbers that are stored in an array, passed into the program on the command line, or all entered on a single line and broken up by a StringTokenizer (a common technique in Java). They also do not recognize that they must similarly keep a running product when asked to multiply a collection of numbers. Writing assignments like the one described above help them make these fundamental connections by encouraging them to reflect and to understand the process they use to solve the problem without the help of a computer before they teach the computer to solve it by writing the program.

Writing assignments also improve students' understanding of objects and object-oriented programming. Java is an object-oriented language: relatively complex programs are generally written by creating *objects* that interact with each other to perform the desired work. Using objects, however, adds additional structure and complexity beyond the other techniques taught (selection, repetition, modular programming, etc.) as part of a programming course. Object-oriented programming requires careful design. The programmer must decide what the necessary objects are for the program, and what each of these objects can do. If we teach objects at the beginning of the course, as current trends support, we are teaching object design at the same time that we teach program design. If we teach objects later in the course, as I prefer, the students must change their approach to programming, performing essentially a paradigm shift as they move from text to object. In either case, writing exercises can show students the basic design principles required to use object-oriented techniques effectively.

For example, I include in the manual an exercise to define the characteristics (data and operations) that are relevant for a bank account, and I also have the students design characters (giants and ogres) in a role-playing game. Both of these exercises are included at the end of this chapter. I use the giant/ogre problem as an in-class group exercise. The only description I give of how the program would use giants and ogres is that giants try to kill ogres and vice versa. I want to encourage the students to use their own imaginations and to decide for themselves what criteria are relevant. My goal is to have the students consider a giant or an ogre as an entity (object) that could be used in a program, and to design the object in a general way so that it could be used in more than one program. They must decide what data describes an individual fighter, and how fighters can interact with each other and with the main program. We discuss this assignment at the end of class, and the students generally come up with appropriate ways of designing the objects. In the following lab assignment, they write a program using a simple version of the giants and ogres as a way of establishing the connection between the design of an object and how it is used in the context of a program. At this point, some students generally have trouble making this final connection and writing the code correctly. However, fewer students struggle with this program now as compared to before I included the writing-to-learn exercise. Also, by working through the exercise, the students gain a better understanding of how a giant or an ogre (or by extension, a bank account or a student) can be a separate object that interacts with the rest of the program. While I am still looking for ways to address the issues better and more completely, for most of the students there are fewer details that I have to fill in as a result of the writing exercise.

Programming 2: Designing a Large Program

The sequel to the introductory programming course at Quinnipiac is Data Structures and Abstraction. This course is designed to teach students techniques to build larger and more complex programs than the ones they write in Programming 1. Whereas in Programming 1, I generally assign roughly one program a week (perhaps a total of twelve programs), in the second semester, I assign four large programs, which together account for half the student's final grade (two in-class exams and a final account for the rest). The students have between two and four weeks for each program and are encouraged to start early.

We use the text *Data Abstraction and Problem Solving with JAVA: Walls and Mirrors*, by Frank Carrano and Janet Prichard. The text begins with a discussion of software engineering and the life cycle of software. This is a description of the stages a program goes through from its initial conception to its finished form (though arguably, a program is never completely finished). The topic generally seems rather abstract (and therefore difficult) to the students, especially in comparison to their experience from Programming 1, but it lays the groundwork for the rest of the course.

The first two phases in the life cycle of a program are the *specification* and the *design* of the program. The specification is a description of how the program interacts with and what it looks like to someone running the program, and the design describes what it looks like to the programmer; that is, it describes the internal structure of the program, including the data structures and the algorithms used. For example, if we were to think of a person eating a hot dog as a program, the specification might describe the person's hand putting the hot dog in his mouth and the action of his mouth chewing it, and the design might describe the internal process of digesting the hot dog. Perhaps not surprisingly, since both documents describe the as yet unwritten program, students are sometimes confused as to the distinction between the specification and the design of a program.

For the past four times I taught this course (including two at a prior institution, before I learned about the Writing Across the Curriculum movement), I have required students to hand in an *initial design* as part of each of their assigned programs (the assignment itself serves as an informal specification). They are required to give a narrative description of the data structures that are part of the program (how the information will be stored internally), and of the main algorithms in the program (how the information is manipulated). To help them understand what is required, I also give out a specification and design of a different program: one that plays tic-tac-toe (included at the end of this chapter). To give them the maximum benefit of this portion of the assignment, I make a point of returning the designs the next time I see them, especially for the first few programs. This allows them to use my comments in writing their programs.

In a writing class, it makes sense to require an outline as an early rough draft for an essay assignment, even if that outline might change in the course of drafting and writing. The instructor and the student could then examine the overall structure and direction of the essay and make sure these are appropriate without becoming caught up in the sentence-level detail. An initial design could be viewed as an outline for a program. It is true that this assignment is a descriptive document, so its format differs from that of a Java program—the final product they hand in—just as an outline differs from an essay. However, the format of a written program would not be a useful rough draft for several reasons. If the students write a program as a first attempt, they must either debug their program to make it work, or settle for a nonworking program. It takes a significant amount of effort to debug a program, and while doing this, they are focused on the small details of the program, such as fixing a specific compiler error. This focus keeps them from taking a good look at the overall structure of the program. Just as with an essay, it is counterproductive to spend the considerable time fixing small details of a program when the overall structure of the program may require siginificant revision. The alternative is to work on the overall structure of the program in the form of written code and to ignore the programming errors. However, the errors are generally distracting, so there is a natural tendency to fix the code as one is writing it, and it is difficult to remain focused on the overall structure. Furthermore, once a student has spent time writing code, he or she is motivated to use at least portions of that code, even if the overall structure is found to be flawed. The program then loses its coherence, as some of the code was originally created to fit a different overall structure. Finally, if we accept a nonworking program as our intermediate product, there is no real advantage to creating a *program* instead of a document written in plain English, as the latter takes much less effort to write for most students.

There are some variations of this assignment as well. On occasion, instead of collecting their designs on the day they were due, I simply lead discussion on what belongs in such a document and allow them to revise their design and hand it in at the following class. Other possibilities, which I have not used, are to have the students work in groups on a design, either of an assigned program, or on a completely separate program, or to have them comment on each other's designs.

I have several goals in mind by requiring the students to present an initial design of their programs and having them submit this design as a separate document prior to completing the actual program. I hope to help the students clarify their thinking and approach to the program, to show them how good design leads to better programs, to start them thinking about their projects early, to clarify the distinction between the specification and the design of a program, and to give myself the opportunity to comment on their initial ideas, both to direct their thinking in profitable ways and to catch students who do not understand what is required of the program (or to allow them to recognize that they do not understand what is required). While I have not tried to quantify the outcomes from this additional requirement, overall, I consider it quite successful. It has helped students understand the distinction between specification and design, and the students who complete the class have a deeper understanding of how to approach writing a program as a result of this assignment. Unfortunately, the students do not always start early (or write the required initial design). I think this is usually because they either do not understand what I am asking for, or because they simply do not understand what to do for the program (and therefore, what to include in a design). While I am disappointed when this happens, these are the students who would not be able to write the program in any case, and this assignment at least helps me find out who these students are and approach them earlier in the programming process (even before the first assignment is due). I am quite committed to this particular assignment.

In my experience, focused writing assignments are the best way to help the students focus on the structure and design of their programs before they actually sit down to write the programs. Having them write about how they expect their programs to work before the program actually exists develops their ability to understand the programming process and makes them better programmers.

Programming 1 Exercises
Designing Programs

1. Suppose you are writing a program to convert a Celsius temperature entered at the keyboard to its equivalent in Fahrenheit. List, in order, the steps your program would follow when a user sits down at the keyboard to run the program. Describe each step in words, without using code. Be as specific as possible. You may assume that your program knows the formula for converting the temperature, even if you do not.

   Give sample output for your program if the user enters the temperature 37 degrees Celsius (the result is 98.6 degrees Fahrenheit).

2. Now suppose you want to write a program that computes batting averages. The formula for a batting average requires the number of hits and at-bats (the user will enter these values). List, in order, the steps your program would follow when a user sits down at the keyboard to run the program. Describe each step in words, without using code. Be as specific as possible.

   Give sample output for your program if the user asked for the batting average of a player with 150 hits in 400 at-bats (the batting average would be 0.375).

3. Now suppose you are writing a program that prompts the user to enter five numbers and prints the sum and the average of the numbers entered by the user. List, in order, the steps your program would follow when a user sits down at the keyboard to run the program. Describe each step in words, without using code. Be as specific as possible.

   Give sample output for your program if the user enters the numbers 10, 20, 30, 60, and 80 (the sum is 200).

Designing Objects

1. Bank Account

   Suppose you want to write a program that maintains balances and other information relevant to bank accounts. To do this, you will create a BankAccount object.
   - What information might you keep about a BankAccount?
   - What would you expect to be able to do with your BankAccount objects? What information should a BankAccount be able to give to the program about itself?

- What information is needed when a new BankAccount object is created?
- What data and methods would you use to describe a BankAccount object and to give it the required capabilities?

2. Fighters in a Role-Playing Game

   Suppose you want to create a simple role-playing game. Your program will consist of giants and ogres that attack and try to kill each other (giants try to kill ogres and vice versa).
   - How would you keep track of how close a fighter (a giant or an ogre) is to death?
   - What characteristics of a fighter might be important in such a program?
   - What would you expect your fighters to be able to do? What information might your fighters need to tell your program?
   - What data and methods would you use to describe a giant or an ogre, and to give them the required capabilities?
   - Would there be any differences between your giant and your ogre class?

Programming 2 Sample Design

Specification

Write a program that plays tic-tac-toe against the user. The program first asks the user who should play X (i.e., who should go first). If the user chooses to play O, the program makes the first move. It presents the user with a board representing the current position and asks where the user wants to make a move (requiring the user to choose an empty square). The squares are represented by the numbers 1 (top left corner) through 9 (bottom right). This is repeated until there is a winner (one player gets three in a row, column, or diagonal), or no more moves are possible. At the end of the game, the program offers to play again.

Design

The Data (Current Position)

The current position is stored in a two-dimensional, 3 × 3 array of characters, declared with the line

    char[][] board = new char[3][3];

Then, board[0][0] refers to square 1 (the top left corner), board[0][2] refers to square 3, and board[2][2] refers to square 9. The characters X and O represent the players' moves, and a space represents an empty cell. In general, board[i][j] refers to square ($3i + j + 1$), and a square n is represented by board[(n − 1)/3][(n − 1) % 3].

The Algorithms

Choosing a Move

The program chooses the move that maximizes the value of the position, computed by the function described next. It temporarily tries each move, evaluates the resulting position, and removes the potential move. If the value is larger than the previously computed maximum value, the new maximum is saved, along with the square that generates the new maximum value. The computer does not play optimally using this strategy. It is possible to beat the computer.

Evaluating the Position

The value of a position is determined by computing a value for each of the eight possible winning lines (rows, columns, and diagonals), and adding those values. The value of each line is computed as follows:

- If a line contains no X's or O's, or if it contains both X's and O's, its value is 0.

- If a line contains only the comptuer's tokens (e.g., only X's if the computer is X), the value of the line is:

  100 if it contains three tokens (e.g., three X's)
  10 if it contains two tokens
  1 if it contains one token

- If a line contains only the opponent's tokens (e. g., only O's if the computer is X), the value of the line is:

  −100 if it contains three tokens (not possible, as the game would have been over before this turn)
  −50 if it contains two tokens
  −5 if it contains one token

For example, if the computer is O, the following position is worth *−8*: the value of the first two rows are *0*, the value of the third row is *1*, the value of the columns are *0*, *−5*, and *1*, respectively, and the values of the diagonals are *−5* and *1*. Adding these numbers gives a total of *−8*.

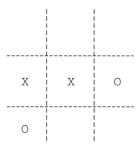

Linked Writing to Learn Assignments in a Computer Science General Education Course

Mark E. Hoffman

Associate Professor of Computer Science

Prior to my introduction to Writing Across the Curriculum (WAC), I started developing two projects in which writing was emerging as a critical component. Through my experience with these projects, I came to realize that writing was a necessary part of learning and that it was necessary for students to engage ideas and to refine their thinking. The relatively new course Introduction to Internet Studies immersed students in academic investigation of the social, cultural, and ethical implications of the Internet. During its first semester as a general education course with a mandated writing component, I started using the new projects and became aware of WAC.

As I learned more about WAC, I found that my growing intuition about writing as an important component of engaging and thinking about ideas was right. I found it reassuring to know there was evidence to support my intuition, resources for integrating writing into my course, and a community of collaborators. Over the summer, armed with my emerging understanding, I further developed the two projects.

As originally implemented, both projects followed a similar strategy: an activity to gather some basic information followed by a short writing piece to capture the experience, then an essay on a question concerning the activity. Although the strategy seemed to work, I felt that many students were only superficially engaging each project's ideas. The essays were rigid and tentative, telling me that the students did not fully understand the ideas they were writing about, and the range of ideas they considered was narrower than I had hoped. (To be honest, some of the poorer-than-hoped-for performances were due to my own inexperience with this type of project.) Having recently learned about expressive writing and linked assignments, I saw them as a way for students to more fully engage the ideas of each project, giving them more confidence and material for their essays. *And* I was more confident knowing that I was on the right track and that resources were available to support my efforts.

The revised projects consciously employed linked writing-to-learn assignments. An activity remained central to each project; however, more writing tasks were added to give students opportunities to engage ideas from more perspectives before they wrote essays. For example, after the short writing piece, each student was asked to create a "Why List" (Burniske 2000). A Why List is a discovery technique in which students ask open-ended "why" questions that they answer; each subsequent "why" question is derived from the previous answer. Why Lists give students an opportunity to generate new insights and a richer understanding of their experience. I also added a draft essay with a peer review. My comments on the draft essay focused on requesting evidence for unsupported statements, challenging assumptions, and pushing students to consider alternate points of view. My objective was to link multiple writing forms, including the Why List, forcing students to rewrite, and, therefore, to reengage the ideas in each project. The essay was now the product of many opportunities to engage ideas in many differing forms.

The first semester I used the revised projects, students complained that the course was too much like English. I had used linked writing-to-learn assignments for additional projects, but then I realized they were not an integral part of the process. Students saw the assignments as disconnected writing exercises. Armed with constructive feedback from the students, I continue to revise the original projects to strengthen their linked writing-to-learn foundations and to integrate writing assignments within each project's objectives.

Using the linked writing-to-learn assignments, I have found that students consider a wider range of ideas in their essays. Students are able to write more fluidly since they have a better understanding of what they are writing about and what they want to say. Students also express themselves with greater confidence. In the remainder of this essay, I discuss the two projects, the Great Good Place Project and the Age of Missing Information Project, in detail.

The Great Good Place Project

The Great Good Place Project is based on "third places" where people informally congregate outside of home and work, which are first and second places, respectively, described by Oldenburg in *The Great Good Place* (1989). Virtual communities are one manifestation of the integration of the Internet into society, so the opportunity to compare virtual communities to third places is an engaging way to examine how community is formed on the Internet. We consider the question: Can virtual communities be third places? Oldenburg, even in his latest edition, does not discuss the influence of the Internet on third places. Rheingold in *The Virtual Community* (2000) does, but leaves the question unanswered. Students must form their own opinion, and, in the process, consider social implications of the Internet.

Students' first task is to find a definition of "virtual community" and to post it to a class discussion board set up for the project. In class, small groups create a composite definition. The student groups then create a list of similarities and differences between third places, as described in a quote from Oldenburg, and virtual communities. Both are posted to the class discussion board. Since one characteristic of a third place is its "playful mood," some students mistakenly take this to mean a "relaxing" place that includes places where one is alone, like a beach or hiking trail. In-class discussion clarifies this and similar misconceptions. The idea of "place" is new to most students; the assignment and subsequent discussion allow them to engage the idea in two different ways.

Students are next asked to interview someone who works full-time and has experience using the Internet. For the interview, each student devises a set of questions to gather information on the interviewee's experience with the Internet, virtual communities, and third places; the questions are posted to the class discussion board. Good interview questions require a clear understanding of both forms of community, especially their similarities and differences. Students revise their tentative understanding from previous tasks and build it into a new form. The same student groups now form a single list of questions from their individual lists. The lists are discussed in class, further engaging the ideas of community, and further clarifing the interview objectives.

About one week is given to conduct interviews. A favorite interviewee is a parent or older sibling, but some students chose summer employers or faculty members, and one student interviewed the men's ice hockey coach. I take a few minutes at the beginning of class to ask how the interviews are going. We also consider how the interview medium (in person, over the telephone, through email, or in instant messaging) shapes the outcome.

Students post transcripts of their interviews to the class discussion board. In class, I select students to comment on their interview, how it was conducted, and what the person they interviewed thought about virtual communities and third places. These students expose a wide range of issues and ways to understand them. For example, many students believe that anonymity online causes people to be deceitful. One interview raised the point that anonymity may actually encourage greater openness than face-to-face conversation. Students see that anonymity can promote two very different results.

To this point each task requires students to engage the idea of community in greater depth. Each requires them to write something from scratch, not merely edit previous writing. The next task uses all that they have done to this point as raw material to create a Why List. In class, we discuss the purpose of the Why List, which is to develop new insights. Students are asked to reflect on their Why List: Was it helpful? What did they discover? What went wrong? From their Why Lists, each student selects one interesting question-answer pair as the basis for a thesis statement for an essay on the third place/virtual community question. Along with their Why List, students post their Why List reflection and thesis statement to the class discussion board.

The next task requires students to write a draft essay around their thesis statement. In class, I discuss the general form: a thesis paragraph, paragraphs supporting the thesis, and a concluding paragraph summarizing the argument. I leave the door open for other formats—in fact, I encourage them—but most essays follow this form. The objective is to engage the question, this time by taking a side and supporting it. Students are required to use quotations from their interview, and they are encouraged to use classmates' interviews. Most students effectively quote from their interview; a handful use classmates' interviews. Since the interview transcripts are posted online, students are required to cite these online sources properly.

Students publish their draft essays as Web pages to a personal Web space provided by the University. Each student reviews another's draft essay. A reviewer downloads an essay Web page to review, edits it, then publishes the edited essay Web page to her own Web space. The review requires students to make fairly straightforward annotations, such as underlining the thesis statement or highlighting misspellings, as well as more thoughtful comments, such as whether the thesis is clear or the argument presented by the author is well supported. In addition, I provide comments on the ideas included in the draft essays. Regardless of how good the essay is, I pose questions to push students to think about what they have written in a different way.

Using my comments and the peer review, students are asked to revise their essays for final submission. Clearly, students are expected to edit their work, but the greater objective is to rethink their essays. I encourage them to revise, rather than to merely edit; however, students are inclined toward directly addressing comments with a quick fix, such as inserting a new sentence in a paragraph without disturbing the rest of it. In class, we discuss the benefits of revising, the opportunity to rethink the essay, and the writing process. Grading is based on timeliness of submissions, quality of the content, structure, and mechanics.

Great Good Place Project Results

I have been pleased with the results of the project. Even students who produce poorer essays incorporate interesting ideas that emerge from the linked writing-to-learn assignments. There are fewer knee-jerk type reactions, such as "a virtual community cannot be a third place without face-to-face communication." Even if this argument is offered, it is usually better considered and better supported. I do not expect or encourage any particular response to the question, because I want each student to come to a personal conclusion.

The Why List is an interesting facet of the project. Students who take the exercise seriously gain valuable insights. One student, in looking back over her Why List, commented that she knew the conclusion she was going to reach before she began the exercise, and was not surprised to get there:

> My Why List basically went from the differences between talking online and at a third place, to respecting someone's feelings and views. I have my own opinions on the differences between a third place and a virtual community, but I tried to keep my answers as open and agreeable as possible. I tried to control the questions and answers as much as I could, and I also tried not to repeat myself. I knew ahead of time where I wanted to end up with this list, and I actually think that my list is boring and predictable.

In class, I used this student's observation to discuss the purpose of the Why List. This student's list might be considered "boring and predictable" because it was not allowed to develop new insights.

For me, an interesting and enjoyable part of the Why List is helping students recognize their own interesting ideas. As in the next example, the student begins to explore the "weaker attributes" of communication, the notion of "a perfect person," and the importance of "tone" in communication. Subsequent discussion in class include the notion of physical presence in community and the ability to "lurk" online. Any one of these ideas could have been used to build an thoughtful essay:

Q: Why is a physical 3rd place better than a virtual 3rd place?

A: Because in a physical 3rd place, people are closer and relations have a stronger bond because you can get to know a person better in the physical world. And in the virtual 3rd world, a person would willingly give their positive attributes but not so much their weaker ones.

Q: Why is it important to know a person's weaker attributes?

A: Because you can get to know a person better—a perfect person is non-existent, unless one makes themselves to appear that way on the Internet, plus, tone and body language is also not seen and they are important devices used to communicate.

Q: Why is tone so vital for communication?

A: Because if a person's voice is getting louder, for example, you know that you might have upset them.

The next student considers the question from a different perspective. Instead of comparing the strength of a relationship, she considers the amount of time spent online. In using the term "virtual third place" in this context, the student defines a qualitatively different concept. She does not realize the significance of how it differs from the third places and virtual communities discussed to this point:

Q: Why can virtual communities be considered a third place?

A: Because some people spend most of their free time on the Internet, accessing virtual communities of some sort.

Q: Why does that make a virtual community a third place though?

A: Because the virtual place is frequented more than a physical third place, it becomes a virtual third place.

Q: Why can it be considered a third place if you are not physically there?

A: Because though everyone may not be physically there, they are through the use of their computers.

In her Why List, the next student asked the typical question about why would someone lie online. In this case the medium is chat; however, she moves in the more interesting direction of multiple simultaneous chats and the meaningfulness of each conversation:

Q: Why would people use chat th[e]n if they are just going to be lied to?

A: Because it is a quick way of communicating.

Q: Why is it so quick?

A: Because you can type quick to multiple people.

Q: Why do you type to multiple people?

A: Because the reason you are chatting online is so you can talk with multiple people instead of having one conversation with a person on the phone, even though the conversation online is less meaningful.

Q: Why is your conversation online less meaningful than your conversation on the phone?

A: Because you are typing quickly to many people so it is hard to type things that really mean anything. If it was that important[,] most times you would just call the person.

Reflecting on her Why List, she concludes that "instant messaging is not really deep conversation." She also concludes, "the questions kind of swayed away from the original," which is true since her first question was, "Why do you think that virtual communities hinder adolescents from growing socially?" The idea she overlooks is the tendency to maintain multiple simultaneous chats and their impact on the ability to form a third place online.

These are wonderful opportunities to build students' confidence in their own ideas, to get them to consider their ideas in greater depth, and to explore the question proposed by the project from many different directions. Student writing produces this kind of recursive thinking and contributes greatly to the investigation.

The Age of Missing Information Project

I think writing can go beyond text as we have become accustomed to it. I have begun to explore ways that images, hyperlinks, and text formatting might be used to promote thinking. Students in the course Introduction to Internet Studies learn basic HTML so that they can explore these ideas. In the Age of Missing Information Project, I modified the process used in the Great Good Place Project to produce a multimedia, Web-based essay, rather than a text-based essay. The project is based on ideas from McKibben's *The Age of Missing Information* (1992) in which he recorded and watched all ninety-three cable programming channels in Fairfax, Virginia, over a twenty-four hour period, then spent twenty-four hours alone in the woods near his home in the Adirondacks. The book is about his observations comparing the experiences. We perform a miniversion of McKibben's experiment by taking a nature walk as a class for about one hour, then have each student spend one hour using the Internet. Over the course of the project, we explore these two experiences and work toward developing a Web-based essay built around an idea that emerges from the process of comparing them.

After the nature walk and Internet hours, students record "first impressions" that can be referenced for later tasks. There are no formal requirements other than to record enough to retain experiences that might otherwise be lost: thoughts, feelings, sensory experiences, or whatever students considered worth recording. After using the project for about a year with a text-based essay as the end product, I was struck by the fact that in one particular class, a number of the "first impressions" records were almost poetic rather than short, informal narratives. The following is an excellent example; the format is poemlike, rich in detail, and the observations unique:

Nature Walk:

- temperature [rose] as we got deeper into the woods
- specks of sunlight on the fallen trees and patches of moss
- the stream rushed out of the lake, made a loud crashing sound
- didn't see any animals, though I saw many tiny burrows
- smell of dust and pollen, which cause my throat to dry up and nose to run a bit
- tiny green buds on the tips of branches
- as we walked up higher the path seemed to become more narrow and soon enough we were almost at the edge of a cliff, looking down upon the edge of the stream that turned into a pool
- the pool/stream/lake changed colors, now it was a copper color
- the dirt was a burnt sienna, with patches of bright green moss
- really quiet, just looking around
- passed a house with a man talking outside on the phone
- stepping over fallen tree trunks

Internet Hour:

- repetitive
- the screen brings the world within my reach
- you can go anywhere and look up anything
- waiting for screen/pictures/sites to load
- the people I talk to on AIM annoy me
- talking on AIM sometimes pointless
- I want to kill the pop-up adds

- the sites I view are very random (from history sites, to celebrity fan sites)
- I am the ruler of my laptop
- my eyes hurt from staring at the screen for too long
- so comfortable where I am sitting and surfing
- multitasking—watching TV, listening to music, searching the Web, talking to people both in the room and on the Internet
- surfing the Internet gets old to me, it seems that I lose interest quickly

I pointed out these "first impressions" records to the class and proposed that we modify the project to take advantage of this and other interesting variations. The students were receptive, but were not sure exactly what *I wanted*. After a couple of days of thought and conversation with students, we decided to make the final product a Web page containing text, images, and hyperlinks that illustrated and explored their two experiences, nature and the Internet, and provided some comparison as intended by the original project.

Age of Missing Information Project Results

Some students felt more comfortable with the text-based essay as originally assigned, but added images and links to enhance the text. For example, a word like *tree* might be hyperlinked to a tree image. Others inserted thumbnail images in the text in place of words, such as a tree image in place of the word *tree*. One student formatted a poem in the shape of a Christmas tree. Other students relied more heavily on images and used short text snippets to hold the images together. One student even used pictures of himself humorously to illustrate his nature walk and Internet experiences. Some students, such as the student who wrote the "first impressions" record above, wrote poetic text interspersed with pictures. Other students wrote one section on nature and a second section on the Internet; still others interleaved the text and images of their experiences. A couple of students even went beyond the scope of material covered in the course to incorporate sounds in their Web pages.

Everyone participated; no two projects were even close to identical and all were creative. We spent the better part of a class period holding an exhibit where students displayed their work and explained how and why they constructed their projects as they did. In a survey at the end of the course, students reported that the project was fun (80 percent) and educational (47 percent), but 20 percent found it too easy. For the Great Good Place Project, 53 percent considered it fun, the same percentage found it educational, and no one found it too easy; however, 33 percent reported it was too much work. I think part of the reason students considered the Age of Missing Information Project more fun and easier is that it did not require them to write a text-based essay. From the results, clearly they thought about the questions at the heart of the project, but they were freer to explore the ideas beyond the restrictions and familiarity of text. I consider both projects to be successes in that students explored the underlying questions in some depth from a variety of perspectives. Using hypertext required students to select linking text and to think about its meaning and destination; using images required students to support their work with an appropriate image and to decide how to integrate it into the overall work. The ability to format text in various layouts, fonts, and colors required students to think about what these features provided in support of their work. All these require the same kind of thinking provided by changing text-based formats in the Great Good Place Project.

Parting Thoughts

I find grading is my greatest difficulty. Even though I understand that I am using writing to think, I still feel inadequate grading essays. Providing a grading guideline has been helpful, but I do not feel comfortable giving too much detail. Students tend to give me exactly what I ask for. If I provide too much detail, it precludes exploring different approaches, but if I do not provide enough detail, many students feel uneasy. This is something I continue to work on. Resources like *Engaging Ideas* by Bean and *New Directions for Teaching and Learning, Writing to Learn: Strategies for Assigning and Responding to Writing Across the Disciplines* by Sorcinelli and Elbow have helped a great deal.

References

Bean, J. C. 1996. *Engaging Ideas.* San Francisco: Jossey-Bass.

Burniske, R. W. 2000. *Literacy in the Cyberage.* Arlington Heights, IL: Skylight.

McKibben, B. 1992. *The Age of Missing Information.* New York: Plume.

Oldenburg, R. 1989. *The Great Good Place.* New York, NY: Paragon House.

Rheingold, H. 2000. *The Virtual Community.* Cambridge, MA: MIT Press.

Sorcinelli, M. D., and P. Elbow. 1997. *New Directions for Teaching and Learning, Writing to Learn: Strategies for Assigning and Responding to Writing Across the Disciplines.* San Francisco: Jossey-Bass.

7

Writing to Learn Across the Personal Essay

The Art of Digital Pastiche

Timothy Dansdill

Assistant Professor of English and Composition

Most of the students who take English 206: The Genre of the Essay are neither English majors, nor are they particularly interested in Composition as a subject. Most take the course to fulfill part of their general core requirement in the Humanities. I title my version of this course "Theory, History, and Practice of the Personal Essay." My goal for the course is that students will come to understand the experimental, hybrid character of the essay—that "[t]he essay," in Lopate's words, "is a notoriously flexible and adaptable form. It possesses the freedom to move anywhere, in all directions" (1995, xxxvii). Our anchor text is Phillip Lopate's inestimable *The Art of the Personal Essay: An Anthology from the Classical Era to the Present*. Students learn the epistolary and diarist traditions of writing that flow into the personal essay, and that these traditions contribute to its artfully dodgy mixture of elaboration and digression. I want them to appreciate, with Lopate, that unlike the "well-made" short story or sonnet, "there is no guarantee that the personal essay will attain a shapeliness or a sense of aesthetic inevitability" (1995, xxxviii). So despite its "being already unified by a strong 'I' perspective," the personal essay's lack of a "formal" guarantee makes it a contradictory, even mysterious, form for students.

Once we encounter Montaigne as the so-called Father of the personal essay, students are more or less ready to accept that his apparently disordered mix of personal reflection and classical citation is part of a complex rhetorical and artistic tradition I have dubbed the *pastiche effect*. The historical, theoretical, and rhetorical objectives of my course all take root and achieve different stages of fruition in this pastiche effect. Once students recognize that Montaigne's essays are a hybrid of already ancient academic and autobiographical modes that have been bred out of the academic pedigree we call the college essay, I make the case that they need to historicize and theorize the personal essay in relation to their own college writing.

A central question I have students ask themselves is: If Montaigne's new attempt at the ancient art of composition follows from a pastiche artist's way of selecting whatever he or she needs from epistolary and confessional, academic and argumentative genres, then how might we adapt and appropriate his pastiche effect to our own practices as college readers and writers of the essay? Montaigne was, most essentially, *writing to learn* when he announced his various attempts to achieve what he called "Self Portraiture." I believe that all teachers of Writing Intensive Courses (WIC) who wish to experiment with Writing to Learn (WTL) assignments using digital technology will understand that the pastiche effect of students' collaborative sampling and rearranging of personal and academic discourses will intensify an interest in writing that can travel across the curriculum.

Of course, one would expect most any English course, never mind one devoted to the essay, to be already Writing Intensive, as well as Reading Intensive. I have discovered, however, that many of my colleagues who teach Literature, rather than Rhetoric-Composition courses, are either not conversant with, or are not interested in pursuing the experimental opportunities that spring from the common developmental history of the personal essay and the reader's journal. By requiring students to keep Reader Response Journals (RRJs) that serve as a commonwealth of students' selected quotation and analysis, and that in turn inform the "pastiche" essays they will attempt, I am both extending the multimodal tradition of the personal essay, and modeling a WTL approach for instructors from all disciplines who are considering how to make their courses more writing intensive.

Toby Fulwiler, in his *College Writing: A Personal Approach to Academic Writing,* (1991) understands the interanimating tendencies of the Journal and the Personal Essay when he reminds us of the spectrum of personal to impersonal writing. "For academic purposes," he writes, "I would suggest a judicious blend of diary and class notebook, taking from the diary the crucial first-person pronoun 'I' (as in 'I think' and 'I wonder') and taking from the notebook the focus on a given subject matter" (1991, 45). I read Fulwiler's invitation to mix and match the pure diary and the pure disciplinary note-taking mode in student's journals as itself a manifestation of the intermixed histories of the personal essay and the arts of pastiche. In reading and writing across the history of the personal essay my students will need, at the very least, to develop something like this "judicious blend" of citation and response.

They will also need to develop something like Hoesterey's "selection theory" of the pastiche artist to enable a greater sense of the "formal features found in different masters." The way I have designed students' Reader Response Journals (RRJs) around Lopate's introduction to his anthology is meant to develop their theoretical and practical powers of selection. When they begin to quote from and respond to the forerunners of the personal essay, and most particularly to Montaigne's essays, in their RRJs, students come to see that the personal essay is attempting a new kind of composition. They see that Montaigne was considering any number of metaphors from the arts of putting things together that would suggest "simply a mixture of diverse elements" (Bowen 1996, 55). Upon observing students' response to Montaigne as *pasticheur*, I began to wonder whether one could propose a "selection theory" for the art of pastiche that would involve what Lopate calls "Quotation and the Uses of Learning" and serve as a WTL exercise across the college curriculum.

Remembering Montaigne as Pastiche Artist

Although Lopate does not connect Montaigne's creation of the personal essay to the larger history and practice of the art of pastiche, the analogies he uses to describe both the genre and Montaigne's own style are very much in line with what Hoesterey calls "The Semantic Field of Pastiche." He quotes from Montaigne's "Of Books," where he speaks of his "quoting habit": "For I make others say what I cannot say so well . . . . I have to hide my weaknesses under these great authorities" (in Lopate 1995, xli). In Lopate's section on "Quotation and the Uses of Learning," students recognize that whereas the impersonal essayist is more like a careful, earnest chemist, the personal essayist "is like a cook who learns through trial and error just when to add another spice or countertaste to the stew" (Lopate 1995, xxxix). I then seize upon the cooking analogy and run through Montaigne's own restless comparisons between the kind of composition he is attempting and the various arts of putting things together.

Lopate then concludes that "Montaigne made such a *mosaic* of his and others' words that quotations became a kind of baroque tilework overlaying his *Essais*, without compromising his originality" (1995, xli, emphasis added). I share with students the findings of Montaigne scholars, such as Barbara Bowen, that he has compared his essays to "only a piece of badly joined marquetry," or the art of inlaying and joining different types of wood, metal, stone; to "bigarrure," or the art of mosaic tile roofing; and to "fagotage," or the art of stacking random lengths of cut wood into a stable pile (1995, 58).

Of all his comparisons, however, it is Montaigne's description of his essays as "fricassee," or the art of making a stew, that enables me to make the case for the pastiche effect. I draw the fricassee comparison into line with Lopate's stew analogy and then conduct a brief semantic history of pastiche. Part of what makes a Montaignean "fricassee"—or better yet, since *pastiche* derives from *pasta* and *pâté*—so (un)savory is his own mix of shameless self-portraiture with classical citation. I remind students of our reading of his "On Some Verses of Virgil" and how Montaigne ended by stuffing it with classical citation, whereas he began his earliest attempts relatively free of quotations—what he calls "borrowed beauties." I say they should now reconsider closely Montaigne's original textual rearrangements and take his model from their weeks of reading into their various forms of *writing across* the history of the personal essay. Montaigne, I tell them, was, in effect, *cooking* his own RRJs when he set out to attempt this new genre, and they should attempt to do so as well. I exhort them to declare themselves *pastiche artists of the personal essay.*

Sketching—and Stretching—the Arts of Pastiche

Pastiche has the immediate virtue of capturing and connecting students' contemporary senses of how artists across the humanities, and even physical scientists, go about mixing and messing with their materials. I remind students that if pastiche is unfamiliar to them (and it is), collage, with its scissors and paste protocol, is universally memorable from childhood, and carries none of the connotations of "bad imitation" or "fraudulence" that still attach to the art of pastiche, which "retains its ties to the older hodgepodge *pâté* in signifying "a mess," "confusione mentale," "or bad work" (Hoesterey, 2). When *collage* comes into play, "paste" comes up immediately, its semantic link to *pastiche* obvious yet compelling. "Glue" and "cut" follow from paste. When I ask for the *digital* equivalent of pastiche, the entire class recognizes the use of Cut/Paste functions on their laptops. The most cursory denotation/connotation session around *pastiche* helps students see that what Hoesterey calls "pastiche structuration" covers ancient painting, traditional cooking of pasta dishes, right on down into our most basic digital options.

From this vantage, I ask for the contemporary musical manifestation of pastiche structuration. Students instantly pop in with the latest permutations of "hip-hop." They are conversant with the terms of its restless "sampling" and "mixing" across all previous musical and lyrical forms. Because hip-hop artists sample/quote, mess/mix with *whatever* they need to make a new song, perhaps it is time for teachers of writing and their classes to devise what Rice calls "the pedagogical sampler" that would enable a writer to look "at the various distinct moments she has collected and figure out how these moments together produce knowledge" (2003, 465). The question of how new knowledge is produced through pastiche even captures students majoring in science, who see clear connections to pastiche in "gene splicing."

Quotation and the Uses of Pastiche in Reader Response Journals

I require that students become familiar with the many defining qualities of the personal essayist and the personal essay that Lopate defines in his masterful introduction. Lopate identifies and exemplifies twelve major characteristics of the personal essay that include "Cheek and Irony," "Contrariety," and "The Conversational Element." Particularly relevant to the pastiche effect is his category, "Quotation and the Uses of Learning." Students' RRJs are simply modernized versions of the kinds of "commonplace books" that Montaigne decided needed to be "messed with" when he attempted his discursive sketch books of the self. They must quote three extended passages from an assigned essay and then respond to each selected passage by choosing from three required points of view. I summarize the guidelines for quotation and commentary below.

> For one of the two essays we read by a personal essayist, you need to bring to class a typed document of approximately 150 words (not counting the quotations you have chosen), containing the following range of responses:

> One entry must be "expressive" in which you try to relate the quotation to your own personal experiences and cultural orientations—or where you explore the author's profound difference from your view and identification with the subject under discussion.

> One quotation/response must be "transactional" where you communicate how and why the personal essayist is exemplifying one or more of Lopate's twelve defining characteristics of the personal essay.

> One entry must try for a mix of transactional and expressive—a "mixed mode" of writing in which you review previous journal entries and attempt to make *both* a topical *and* a personal connection between, say, Shonagon's hatreds or annoyances with those in Hazlitt; or between Cereta's cheek and irony and Edgeworth's; or between Addison's approach to death and Seneca's; or Montaigne's "quotation and use of learning" versus Bacon's.

The RRJs themselves follow a kind of *pastiche structuration* and suggest something of a "pastiche effect" as students add to them week by week. By mixing and matching the parallel histories of the commonplace book and the personal journal, students are in effect starting the art of the pastiche essay that began with Montaigne. The best RRJs virtually codify the pastiche structuration of the personal essay.

I teach three times a week, and we generally cover two essays by a given essayist in one fifty-minute meeting. I require a RRJ for particular essayists, and even determine which of the two essays we read require attention in a given RRJ. Of the thirty RRJs I require of students over the course of a semester, roughly half are determined by me so that we can accumulate a common stock of "raw material" for pursuing what I call "the art of digital pastiche." By giving students the freedom to select half of the assigned essays for their RRJs, I hope to reinforce the development of a "selection theory" that Hoesterey believes is crucial to pastiche structuration and to achieving a pastiche effect in an essay that will draw from the required RRJ entries. In all RRJs, whether predetermined by me or student-selected, the same three-part organization is required. Students find the Lopatean view the most onerous, of course, since that view requires a continuous return to his introduction and a varied application of the range of his defining categories for the personal essay. This double act of academic referencing exercises students' growing sense of a selection theory in ways that the other two "personal" and "intrapersonal" selections do

not. Though all three views in a given RRJ fall under WTL and WIC pedagogies familiar to all WAC proponents, the explicitly "academic" task of the
Lopatean view represents cross-disciplinary opportunities that I entertain in the
essay's final section. In addition to completing an average of two RRJs each
week, I ask students to:

> Select/Copy one of your three entries from the RRJ I have required for a given
> essayist and Paste/Post that section (quoted passage and specific point of view
> in response) to the corresponding Web-based "Discussion Board" that I have
> activated and titled.

For example, if I require an RRJ on Montaigne's "Of a Monstrous Child," the
corresponding "Discussion Board" will use that information in its title. Students will select and copy one section from their corresponding RRJ section
from the RRJ Word Document-Folders they save and maintain on their laptops.
The semantic fact that they digitally copy and paste this RRJ section is not lost
on them, but they are still not certain how this accumulated, but highly heterogeneous, mass of quotation and response—this Web-based "hodge-podge"—
will come into play when they attempt the art of pastiche.

Starting the Art of Digital Pastiche

Nearing midterm, after students have attempted one Personal/Expressive essay, as well as one Transactional/Academic essay that applies Lopatean categories to either a single essayist's work, or to a set of related essays by several
essayists, I remind them of the stock of RRJ excerpts they have been posting
on BlackBoard's "Discussion Forums" since the second week of the course.
Though I have made the case for pastiche structuration throughout the historical and theoretical aspects of the course, students tend to forget why they are
performing a particular task until the time comes to put that task into the immediate practical effect of a writing assignment. This weekly process of selecting from completed RRJs is yet another facet of their required freedom to
develop a selection theory and practice that would enable their own eventual
attempts at pastiche.

We pause in our reading and writing across the history of the personal essay to marvel at this immense amount of RRJ material posted out on the Web.
I bring my computer to class and hook it up to a terminal and project the Discussion Boards on a wall screen. I open each Forum, starting with Seneca. I use
the "Collect" option on the Discussion Board to simultaneously display students' collected RRJ selections for each essayist/essay set we've read. In a
class of twenty-five students, and with ten such forums, the math is easy, but
the sum of their archived writing is astounding—approximately two hundred
and fifty entries on the History of the Personal Essay from Seneca to Beer-
bohm. An average of fifty words in each student's pasting/posting on a given
Discussion Board (not counting the word count of the quotation) yields an

immense amount of writing, or "raw material" to be refined by the prospective *pasticheur*.

I give them guidelines for starting their own pastiche experiments using their word processors' cut and paste functions to sample and remix from the Discussion Boards dedicated to the history of the personal essay from Seneca to Steele. In summary, I tell my students they have to look back at the Blackboard "Discussion Boards" and practice pastiche by selecting *whatever* they need from their peers' texts, but they must break—in fact, *cut* away entirely—the Texts of the Canonical Authors whom they and their peers have quoted in the design of their various reader responses. They do this by copying an entire Discussion Board—on Montaigne's "Of a Monstrous Child," for example—to a new Word document on their laptops. When they go through and cut away all cited material, they are left with the texts of their own and their peers' "reader responses." From this more "personal" mass of heterogeneous material students must create a pastiche essay. I hand out the ground rules for practicing *digital pastiche*, but first try to give them a bit more historical precedent for what they are about to undertake.

Rules and Tools for Pasticheurs

Jay David Bolter, who reminds us that "disrupting the stability of the [printed] text . . . belongs in a "tradition" of experimental literature that has marked the twentieth century" (2001, 138), has shown us how the tradition of experiment with linear print is now undergoing a new technological shift with the advent of electronic writing and the digital arts at the close of the twentieth century. Richard Lanham also writes of the Dadaists' "prophetic mélange" that helped launch the tradition of "experimental humanism" (1993, 33). To convince and inspire my students that they are not breaking with, but remaking, this experimental tradition, I remind them of an American tradition of pastiche. Ezra Pound cut up Eliot's rather drab conventional poem to help create "The Wasteland." Gertrude Stein practiced pastiche in her poems, and John Dos Passos used it throughout his USA Trilogy novels. And William S. Burroughs, perhaps the most notorious of pastiche artists, launched "The Cut Up Machine" in 1959.

> All writing is in fact cut-ups. A collage of words read, heard, overheard. What else? Use of scissors renders the process explicit and subject to extension and variation. Clear classical prose can be composed entirely of rearranged cut-ups. Cutting and rearranging a page of written words introduces a new dimension into writing enabling the writer to turn images in cinematic variation (Skerl 1985, 102).

But most interesting to students, however, is Tzara's "How to Make a Dadaist Poem." It draws on the collagist, hands-on predilections of children who wish to cut up and repaste the world of their readerly experience. As an artifact of pastiche structuration prophetic of digital pastiche, it also confirms Lanham's observation that "the electronic screen fulfills an already existing expressive agenda rather than prophesying a new one" (1995, 36).

> Take a newspaper./Take some scissors./Choose from this paper an article the length you want to make your poem./Cut out the article./Next carefully cut out each of the words that make up this article and put them in a bag./Shake gently./Next take out each cutting one after the other./Copy conscientiously in the order in which they left the bag./The poem will resemble you./And there you are—an infinitely original author of charming sensibility, even though/unappreciated by the vulgar herd.

In my "Rules for Writing the Pastiche Essay" I model both the spirit of Tzara's Self-*Author*-izing Identity and Burroughs' Cinematic-Jump Cut extension of Tzara. Having been attuned to the ways personal essayists handle their "personae," particularly in our tracing of Montaigne's variable use of the first person—from "I" to "We"—students are more or less ready to attempt the pastiche essay as hybrid of personal and interpersonal voices and visions. Here is a condensed version of those rules.

> Select quotes and responses from one or from many Boards. Create a Desktop Document titled: *Pastiche: Raw Materials.* Start Copying and Pasting to it your selections. When you have enough raw material—your Selection Theory will let you know—*Cut away all material quoted from Authors' Texts; Save only writers' texts.* These texts are class property—raw materials in common. Cut away unnecessary text. What's left we'll call your *Pastiche: Refined Raw Materials.* Keep Cutting/Pasting according to your "selection theory." Include text from every writer: no one must be cut out. Add new text to give your Pastiche sense and shape. Paste Your Pastiche into the New Discussion Board I have titled *Class Pastiche.* And there we are—"infinitely original authors of charming sensibility!"

I give my students a week to make their Pastiche Essays. I ask that they attempt a seamlessness of structure, but a Montaignean jumpiness is just fine. They need to come up with a title that, much like Montaigne's titles, points toward an apparent center of topical gravity. We post them to the "Discussion Board" of Blackboard, but I also print them out and we read them out loud in class.

I stress that no quotation marks are needed to designate the work of another writer. I remind them that we all now know quite a bit about ourselves as reader-responders, having shared our favorite passages and best examples of commentary. I assure them that, far from encouraging the theft of another's ideas, our continuous, cumulative online exchange of canonical and collegial texts in preparation for the creative borrowing of pastiche is as far from *plagiarism* as a group of family play dates is from *kidnapping* (the literal meaning of plagiarism.) Still, legitimate concerns about what academic integrity means in college reading and writing, and how its standards must and can be managed will persist among some instructors who might wish to consider digital pastiche as a WTL exercise. Hoesterey's history of pastiche clearly suggests that the practice's reputation as the preserve of copycats and artistic frauds may play into a suspicion that encouraging the pasticheur in our students will lead to bad or empty work, mental confusion, and unleash the plagiarist.

In his essay, "Collage: Your Cheatin' Art," Peter Elbow describes a very different approach to having students engage in perusing and using the "borrowed beauties" that Montaigne calls the citation and use of the learning of others. What I find most telling is his sense that the more instructors include, rather than preclude, textual experiment, and the more local, student-produced, texts instructors weave into a course design that focuses attention on a specific genre or tradition of canonical writing, the greater the academic integrity. Why? Because students are both privileged as authors in their own right, while at the same time they are kept focused with localized reading and citing—commenting from only those texts that are integral to the course design. Our kids (in college) don't stray from their (Textual) neighborhoods if everything they need in a course is right where they work at their play and find play in their work. Or, as Rob Carrigan, writing on the problem of journalistic plagiarism has noted, "It is harder to plagiarize when your news is local, local, local." Without very localized, very focused reader-response journal–type WTLs and a pedagogical ambiance of shared, collaborative integrations of course content, most instructors should not be surprised by violations of academic integrity. Generalized content courses that assign a slew of readings, and then ask for a generalized "research paper" are generally most vulnerable to a digital cut and paste, patch-writing job full of cribbing from the Web.

My experience with hearing about instructors' problems with student plagiarism tells me that they do not make the texts—Canonical or Collegial—a part of a larger course design consciousness about academic integrity as the continuous redescription and reintegration of authorial and student writing. Some instructors might be understandably apprehensive that digital pastiche might model more permissive, even subversive, attitudes about academic integrity, and a course like the one I have described does make the difference between creative reinvention (pastiche) and outright academic theft and dishonesty. The students very quickly grasp the clear difference between the two.

The pastiche effect promotes creative boldness and emotional openness about the big personal and public issues of human existence that have been covered academically in their readings from the canonical personal essayists whose citations now operate in absentia, veritable "ghosttexts" adumbrating each pastiche of peer reader response. From Seneca and Shonagon to Steele and Stevenson, revelations of death, love, sex, loneliness, hatred, desire have made their extrapersonal appearances to students as readers across the personal essay.

Mixed with this astonishment is a sense of collaborative achievement. Students as readers across the personal essay now can begin to see themselves as *writers* across this most hybrid of genres. What Montaigne calls his "vagabond nature" in how he uses quotation from his authorial forebears is suddenly showcased and shared between students whom I cajole into playing the role of a textual vagabond—a *pasticheur*. I briefly consider two variations below.

Implications for "Modeling" Digital Pastiche as Writing to Learn

In deliberately mixing academic purpose with artistic play, I recognize that not all instructors across the college curriculum will wish, with Craig Stroupe, to experiment with "hybrid composing environments such as those of electronic communication [that] are characterized not by their purity, but by their dynamic, social hybridity" (2000, 619). Most instructors will understand that even if the arts of pastiche depend for their effects on "Classical rhetoric, which was built on a single dominant exercise: modeling" (Lanham 1993, 47), they might wish to experiment with writing to learn using more conventional, or "pure," forms of "modeling."

Yet whatever our experimental attitudes about mixing or messing around with students' personal and academic discourses in the production of knowledge, all of us have to face with Lanham that "[t]he world of electronic text has reinstated this centrality of modeled reality" (1993, 47). And, as we see through Hoesterey, the history of pastiche prior to the advent of the electronic text is all about imitating and modeling dominant realities. In my two suggested variations for using pastiche, I have reversed my own play/purpose model that has students cut away authorial text and paste/post students' texts. I do so to appeal to instructors who tend to privilege purpose over play, and who wish to model transactional over expressive or poetic tactics. Both suggestions presume the maintenance of an RRJ for the course.

> Students compare/contrast peers' online postings of a given author's three clearest or three muddiest points and learn how peers read for meaning. Brief commentaries that remix, and perhaps refute, peers' "selection theories" are then posted on a new discussion board to teach collaborative and critical sensitivity. As a WTL and Self/Peer-challenging "exercise preliminary to an essay," students discover uncanny centers of shared citational gravity.

> Students write a pastiche essay that incorporates one different quotation on a given author posted by each student in the course and attempts to "patch write" the gathered quotations into a coherent explanation of the author's general drift. Students write a pastiche essay that incorporates quotations from several authors posted by peers across several discussion boards and the pastiche writer connects the significance of his selections of from his peers' citations.

Variations abound, but the central pedagogical point to keep in mind when considering how electronic writing and digital pastiche might advance the centrality of writing-to-learn exercises across all WAC programs is that we must be willing to open our courses to the screens and the locational matrices of online learning and start posting materials according to the rhetorical models and needs of our disciplines to see what it is we want students to learn through digital pastiche.

Final Thoughts on the Place of Pastiche in the Age of Digital Composition

Even after their exposure to its presence in the origins of the personal essay, and some reminder of its modern manifestations across all the arts, the role of pasticheur remains alien to students and probably suspect for most instructors, and not only because of the conflation of the pasticheur with the plagiarist. The alien nature of pastiche stems, I believe, from the split between "creative writing," or the expressivist-poetic side of composition, and "critical writing," or the analytical-transactional side of college composition. Patricia A. Sullivan's characterization of writing about significant experiences, that it "both embodies and disrupts one of the principal binaries structuring the current field of composition: our bifurcation of personal writing and academic discourse" (2003, 43), goes to the heart of why pastiche writing might not be considered a legitimate practice, even in the rather open heuristic territories of WTL.

Richard Lanham traces the enduring high-tension bifurcation of creative/critical writing modes to "the bistable oscillation between use and ornament, between purpose and play" that began with Rhetoric itself (1993, 47). This bistability of purpose and play has evolved in the contemporary terms and outcomes of Rhetoric-Composition into a serious bifurcation in not only how English Studies is to approach the teaching of college writing, but how WAC programs are to negotiate the essential creative play of WTL techniques into the more serious purpose of Writing to Communicate (the discourse of a given academic discipline).

According to Lanham, the word processor, with its powers of selection and rearrangement has pointed the way, "above all, [to] a pervasive reversal of use and ornament, a turning of purpose to play and game, a continual effort not, as with the Arnoldian canon, to purify our motives, but to keep them in a roiling, rich mixture of play, game and purpose (1993, 50). Dedicated to (re)turn us to this "roiling, rich mixture," Digital Pastiche is a "Creative Writing to Learn" exercise has deep roots in the modernist hybrid, and indeed, ancient matrices of the reader's journal, the personal essay. Those roots, as we have seen, now promise new routes of writing to learn by virtue of the Web-ready word processor. Virtually any writing-intensive course that commits to collaborative, Web-accessible RRJs can now play seriously with digital pastiche to help students read and write across the academic curriculum in both creative and critical ways.

References

Bolter, Jay David. 2001. *Writing Space: Computers, Hypertext, and the Remediation of Print*. Garden City, NJ: Lawrence Erlbaum Associates.

Bowen, Barbara C. 1996. "What Does Montaigne Mean by "Marqueterie"? In *Language and Meaning: Word Study in Montaigne's* Essais, edited by D. Berven, 54–60. New York: Garland.

Brush, Craig. 1994. *From the Perspective of the Self: Montaigne's Self-Portrait*. New York: Fordham University Press.

Carrigan, Rob. 2004. "Your Cheatin' Art." *Newspapers and Technology, http:// www.newsandtech.com/issues/2004/07-04/nt/07-04_carrigan.htm.*

Elbow, Peter. 1998. "Collage: Your Cheatin' Art." *Writing on the Edge*. 9: 1.

Fulwiler, Toby. 1991. *College Writing: A Personal Approach to Academic Writing*. Portsmouth, NH: Boynton/Cook.

Harvey, Gordon. 1994. "Presence in the Essay." *College Composition* 56: 642–54.

Hoesterey, Ingeborg. 2001. *Pastiche: Cultural Memory in Art, Film, Literature*. Bloomington, IN: Indiana University Press.

Lanham, Richard. 1993. *The Electronic Word*. Chicago: University of Chicago Press.

Lopate, Phillip, ed. 1995. *The Art of the Personal Essay: An Anthology from the Classical Era to the Present*. New York: Anchor/Doubleday.

Montaigne, Michel de. 1976. *Complete Essays of Montaigne*. Donald M. Frame, trans. Stanford, CA: Stanford University Press.

Rice, Jeff. 2003. "The 1963 Hip-Hop Machine: Hip Hop Pedagogy as Composition." *College Composition and Communication* 54: 472–85.

Skerl, Jenny. 1985. *William S. Burroughs*. Boston, MA: G.K. Hall.

Stroupe, Craig. 2000. "Visualizing English: Recognizing the Hybrid Literacy of Visual and Verbal Authorship on the Web." *College English* 62: 607–632.

Sullivan, Patricia A. 2003. "Composing Culture: A Place for the Personal." *College English* 66: 41–54.

Tzara, Tristan. 1995. "How to Make a Dadaist Poem." In *Poems for the Millennium,* ed. Jerome Rothenberg, et al. Los Angeles, CA: University of California Press.

Young, Art. 2003. "Writing Across and Against the Curriculum." *College Composition* 54: 472–85.

8

Writing in Political Science

Sean P. Duffy
Associate Professor of Political Science

When I began teaching five years ago, I drew on the teaching skills I had learned or observed as a graduate student—skills limited to leading discussion in a seminar environment, or presenting material in a large lecture format. I had never questioned where or how my students would gain the skills necessary to reading complex material in my discipline, political science, and I had assumed that students' writing skills would be perfectly aligned with their comprehension of the material. In short, I didn't consider reading and writing to be skills that I was responsible for developing as an instructor in my discipline. Needless to say, like so many teachers before me, I was disappointed in the results I got and had a hard time assessing what my students were learning, or if they were learning at all. When I joined the Writing Across the Curriculum (WAC) committee at Quinnipiac, I began to discover tools I could use to become a more effective teacher. My participation in a Bard College "Writing to Learn" workshop the summer after my first involvement, and my work on the committee since, have given me real tools to incorporate into effective teaching in political science. I did not join Quinnipiac's WAC committee as an advocate of writing across the curriculum (and in the disciplines); I became an advocate because of what I have learned from my involvement. In this piece I hope to demonstrate some of the success I have had in using writing to foster students' critical thinking skills, their understanding of discipline-specific material, and their ability to write using social science conventions.

Linked Assignments and Writing Instruction in Introduction to Political Science

One of the first courses I was asked to teach was the generalist's introduction to political science, our PO101. Over the years, this is the course I have taught most often, as I teach several sections a year. When I first designed the course, my goals for the class were both to convey a general understanding of the topics and approaches used in political science and to promote an understanding of complex ideas, the ability to think critically, and the ability to construct a logical argument in writing. All these are skills that I think are central to my discipline; I believe they are also values central to our idea of a liberal education in general.

Initially, I assigned a fairly heavy writing load on the assumption that such practice would help students build the kinds of skills they had begun to learn before they reached my class. I assigned three critical reflection papers—scattered throughout the semester—that asked students to focus on issues in the news, one "theory paper" that asked them to make a persuasive argument based on philosophical or theoretical material, and one descriptive paper, a country study. I was under the assumption that simply requiring this kind of writing would accomplish my objectives, and I was repeatedly disappointed with the work that was turned in. It didn't occur to me that there was a role I could play in developing good writing beyond simply providing opportunities for this kind of transactional writing. After learning something about WAC, however, I revised my course to incorporate three new approaches: linked assignments, explicit attention to writing instruction, and the integration of writing-to-learn exercises in class. I was willing to modify my expectations as to what subject-specific content we could cover in favor of the possibility that my objectives for the course could more adequately be met.

Linked Assignments

Originally, I had required students to write their three short reflection papers on issues in the news. My objective had been to use these papers as a vehicle for focusing my students' attention on current events and how they are connected to material we were covering in class. I wanted to get them in the habit not just of reading a good newspaper regularly, but of critically reflecting on the issues they confronted. As initially constructed, I had no expectations that the three papers would differ from one another in any way other than the subject issue selected by the student. The work I received was disappointing. Students seemed genuinely confused as to what I was asking them to do. Most turned in summaries of an article in the newspaper. The best were able to identify the major issues; many couldn't. Very few even *began* the task of critically evaluating what they were reading.

In restructuring this assignment, I made explicit (and different) goals for each of the three reflection papers so that each paper builds on the skills developed in the previous one. The papers are portrayed as part of a single assignment (in three parts), where the installments are due in quick succession— three weeks in a row. This collection of writing is then linked to the following assignment, the "theory paper," by linking the goals and lessons of the first assignment to the second. The first of the reflection papers requires the student to describe the treatment of an issue in the news; I ask students to isolate and summarize the essential message of the article. I also ask them to begin integrating critical evaluation by articulating the conclusions they draw from the article and the question the article raises for them; these I ask them to link to some assessment of how the author may have *intended* the reader to react. The second paper follows by asking the student to identify the way another writer makes an argument, specifically in an opinion piece from the op-ed page. This assignment asks the student to build their analytical skills by deconstructing the way a writer creates an argument. The final of the three short assignments requires the student to make her own argument, very much modeled on the opinion piece evaluated the week before. These skills—essential to persuasive writing—are then carried over to the "theory paper" assignment a few weeks later. Throughout the whole process, time is spent in class practicing the skills required.

Before the first paper is written, we look at a news article as a group and select the major points reported, those that seem objectively verifiable, and those that appear to have some subjective component. Before the second paper, I pass out an opinion piece from the op-ed pages, and we isolate the author's thesis and the points she uses to support her thesis. Here, I ask students to consider the different ways the author seeks to persuade and how the thesis may not actually be stated. Before the final paper, I take some class time to give students practice writing thesis statements related to issues that concern them, then discuss how they would support such a claim.

I have recently found support for using such a linked approach in political science classes in several articles published in my discipline's practice-oriented periodical publication.[1] Clifford Bob, in a September 2001 article, discusses his experience with breaking a research paper into several "guided assignments," proceeding from question identification through outline and draft, and on to final product, with feedback and peer review at every stage. He finds that such an approach has several advantages: it communicates high expectations, it averts last-minute writing (and makes plagiarism more difficult), and it familiarizes students with the way scholarship is produced in political science—exposing them to how we think about politics, conduct research, make arguments, draw conclusions, and communicate our ideas.[2]

In an earlier article, Pamela Zeiser relates her experience with shorter, related assignments. Her experience also supports my approach: "Short, frequent writing assignments are particularly effective when they are different but related," she writes. For her, a series of linked assignments serves two purposes: they "make the thinking and writing process visible to students," and they "teach . . . students the benefits of revision and seeking and responding to feedback." For Zeiser, such an assignment structure helps to break down and demonstrate the different steps necessary for critically evaluating a topic and writing effectively in our discipline. Zeiser also emphasizes the importance of clear guidelines and the careful articulation of explicit goals for each assignment in order to get the best results.[3]

In-Class Writing Instruction

In a much earlier piece in *PS: Political Science and Politics,* David Londow introduces a bibliography of writing resources for teachers of political science by making the separate, but related points that "Time spent on class or group discussion of student papers in progress is time well spent," and "If we want our students to write well *in political science,* we may have to teach them to do so ourselves."[4] While I don't spend time reading and workshopping student writing in *this* class, I do take specific time from class to break down the skills necessary to read, evaluate, and write about the issues in the context of such an assignment. In addition to the exercises mentioned above, I also spend time in class discussing what I believe to be some central precepts to writing in political science. First, I discuss with students the difference between persuasive, descriptive, and expressive writing. While expressive writing can be a useful approach in some aspects of political science writing (I encourage students to do it to help them focus on the aspects of a research topic in upper-level classes, for example), I emphasize to students that persuasive and descriptive writing are far more commonly done in political science. Consequently, the focus of writing in political science is either on the *reader*—changing the way he or she thinks about an issue—or on a subject being described. In particular, I link the writing assignments described above to the goals of *persuasive* writing: namely, clearly articulating a thesis and logically developing an argument to support it, with the objective of convincing a reader of the validity of the thesis.

When the class is preparing for the longer "theory paper" assignment, I also spend some time in class discussing principles of analytic writing and scientific logic. In particular, we review the concepts of falsifiability (to be interesting, one must be able to imagine the *alternative* to the position the student is taking), begging the question (ensuring that students, in making their point, aren't simply deferring the issue), circular argument (assuming the conclusion in order to make the argument), and post-hoc explanation. Finally, in discussing thesis statements, I emphasize that the most interesting theses take the form of statements of fact,[5] statements of value, or statements of explanation.

Writing-to-Learn Exercises

Finally, I have experimented with short, in-class writing exercises as a way of encouraging writing practice and (more importantly) as a way of reinforcing the content and ideas at the heart of the class. In order to facilitate such response-oriented writing, I have organized the course around three essential questions that I make explicit to students as organizing devices for course structure and objectives guiding the choice of content: "Why do we need government?"; "What's the best form of government?"; and "How does government structure affect outcome?" In particular, I have found two approaches to be particularly valuable. To help students to situate the course content in terms of these three questions, I continually raise them as I introduce new material. In particular, close reading and freewriting exercises can help students consider new material in the context of these larger themes. Often, I select a passage from the assigned reading and have a member of the class read it out loud. I follow this with short writing exercises that may ask students in their own words to identify the thesis and supporting points, to respond to the claims made, or to restate the main focus of the material. These short writing assignments can then be used as material for discussion of the readings and, by extension, the subject content of the reading.

Similarly, I have had success with integrating writing into classes that have taken on a more lecturelike approach. In particular, I like to use two- to three-minute freewriting exercises, asking students to take the last few minutes of class to write whatever comes to their mind in response to that day's class: ideas they had that they didn't get to express or discuss, questions they have, or what they believe the main "take-away point" of that class is. Occasionally, I collect these as a way of seeing what my students are thinking; more often, I hope that these comments, written into the students' notes, help them to digest the material for that day in a way they can access at a later time.

Writing and the Question-Driven Research Project in Upper-Level Classes

Another place I have had success with the integration of Writing Across the Curriculum–inspired technique has been in my upper-level seminars in Political Science. I use the upper-level seminar as a vehicle for teaching students the major research conventions in our discipline. Assigning a research paper can be a particularly frustrating experience for many teachers. As Bob states, "For both students and faculty it is frequently unsatisfying . . . [resulting in] papers that deal with a broad topic rather than presenting a sharp thesis."[6] Often the work turned in is poorly focused, poorly integrated, and poorly written. Some work, including Bean, suggests substituting shorter writing assignments or linked assignments.[7] Nevertheless, the research paper is an important vehicle for building and communicating knowledge in my discipline. Not only do I feel it is important to teach the conventions of a research project (and the kind of thinking that it requires), but I have also found that students gain a great deal of satisfaction from successfully completing such a project. However, to be successful, it is important to coach the students through the process. As Bob has found, breaking the process down and working through each stage in class can be a productive way of handling the research assignment.

In my upper-level classes, I introduce research in Political Science as being essentially question-driven, so the first stage of the process is oriented toward exploration.[8] This involves the use of more expressive kinds of writing both in class and on the student's own time. In a class on nationalism and identity conflict I taught a few years ago, I had my students each write a research question on a piece of paper, then pass it to another class member. It was expected that class members would contribute whatever ideas they had to the question at large, then pass it along. Periodically, each question sheet would come back to its originator, who would read the ideas contained and update his question to reflect his current thoughts. While I used a low-tech approach for this exercise—paper—it is the sort of thing that easily could be incorporated into a series of online linked discussions. During the fall of 2003, I experimented with a combination of interactive writing, freewriting, and guided journals in my advanced seminar on terrorism. One venue for this exploratory writing was done in a public forum, using an electronic discussion board. While the forum was guided in that I asked students to use it to exchange ideas about the readings for the week, I also found that students engaged ideas much more broadly in ways that, as Bean would say, avoid early closure. A private journal was also kept by each student (I checked them for depth of thought three times during the semester) where I asked them simply to engage in fifteen minutes of freewriting on their paper topics—either process or content—once each week.[9] I was very pleased with the results. I found that the discussion board prepared the group to *continue* discussion of the week's work in the class (rather than trying to initiate discussion), and my students themselves referenced it as one of the highlights of the course that allowed them to get far more out of the material than they otherwise would have.

Building Writing to Think and Learn into a Political Science Curriculum

Because I work in a fairly small department, I have the opportunity to teach courses at all levels and to work with students several times during their careers at Quinnipiac. This makes it easy for me to establish my own curricular goals and to implement them without yet convincing the rest of my department to follow suit.[10] Recently I took the opportunity to map my goals for each level of course I teach to writing (Writing to Learn/WTL) exercises I use to promote those goals, and formal (transactional) writing assignments I assign in courses. The map at this stage is based on courses I teach at the 100-level (Introduction to Political Science, described above), the 200-level (including a writing and methodology/writing in the discipline [WID] class I have developed for political science majors), and 300-level special topics seminars.

My goals for 100-level classes (my Introduction class being a case in point) are to develop students' critical thinking skills, introduce some political science content, and expose students to the way a political scientist looks at the world. Accordingly, I find writing-to-learn assignments that facilitate reading comprehension, content assimilation, and critical evaluation and analysis to be the most helpful in achieving these goals. Formal writing assignments that build on these skills, such as the ones I discuss above, help to complete the writing and learning process at that level.

At the 200-level, where I tend to have a higher proportion of students who have an interest in pursuing studies in political science beyond the introductory level, my goals build on those for the 100-level by emphasizing more critical *analysis,* and introducing both methodology used in political analysis and a more concentrated approach to specific subject matter. Thus, I hope that students will begin to build their skills and knowledge in my discipline. I have structured my 200-level Foreign Policy class around a linked series of short assignments that ask students to grapple with the subject matter in a way that also progressively requires a higher order of thinking. The first of the three papers asks students to look at a particular issue and *identify* the major foreign policy challenge. In this paper, I am looking for accurate summary of material relevant to their finding and the ability to paraphrase it, or explain it to the reader. The second paper asks them to identify the aspect of the foreign policy process they believe is most important. Here I am asking them for more application and analysis of the material introduced in class, and to begin to structure a critical analysis of the material we have discussed. The final paper asks them to make full use of their critical and analytical abilities by responding to a proposition about current U.S. policy. Specifically, I ask them to clearly state their position, develop it with rational, logical argument, and defend it against the strongest aspects of the opposing view. To lay the groundwork for these assignments, I make use of writing-to-learn exercises in small- and medium-sized group work once each week in class.

The focus on writing and analysis skills particular to political science is the purpose of the methodology course I offer, where the specific goals include socializing majors into the way we ask and pursue questions in political science. Introducing students more formally to hypothesis formation, causal reasoning, and research skills can be accomplished in activities such as drafting, redrafting, and peer review of particular *types* of writing in the discipline. At this stage, I use some reflective expressive writing exercises to help students begin to explore where their interest comes from and how they can shape their interests into a research project or more effective persuasive writing in the discipline. At the 300-level, where I have mostly political science majors and require a great deal of subject-specific reading, I build on the skills introduced in the methodology course and emphasize activities oriented toward reading comprehension and assimilation, and writing to facilitate a research project, as I have already discussed.

Assessment

The lessons I have learned from incorporating Writing Across the Curriculum goals and techniques into my political science courses are still largely confined to impressions.[11] Nevertheless, I can state with confidence that I do notice a difference. With respect to my introductory class, three general lessons have become apparent. First, I had initially expected that a refocus of the class on writing-based learning would necessitate cutting the content I covered in the class. I was willing to make this sacrifice in the hope that the material I did cover would be more effectively learned and that my goals for teaching critical thinking and logical argument would be more closely realized. Therefore, I initially cut about 15 to 20 percent of the content for the course (it had already been too much to cover in a fourteen-week semester anyway). About midsemester, I was pleasantly surprised to note that I could start adding content back. My students were learning the material more effectively, and it wasn't taking that much more time. By the end of the semester, I had added most of the material back to the course, where it has remained ever since.

A second pleasant effect of this approach was a greater level of involvement in the class. Students participate more when they understand more clearly the goals of the class and are given an opportunity to think, reflect, and organize their thoughts before they're asked to share them. Even if I give them an opportunity to write their ideas down only occasionally, their increased level of confidence and engagement carries over into classes and discussions more generally.

I have also gotten better writing out of my students. By restructuring what is essentially the same set of writing assignments, I have realized a way to teach the conventions of writing that I expect my students to use. Consequently, papers have been easier to read, and therefore to grade—cutting down on the time I was spending on grading written assignments. Students are also taking more interest in their papers. I have more students seeking me out after class or in office hours to discuss their papers and how they can make them better, and I have had a marked increase in the number of my students who seek assistance with their writing in our learning center.

Finally, my students themselves have expressed higher levels of satisfaction with the course. Our department asks students in all our classes to fill out a departmental evaluation form at the end of the semester. Questions range from those asking students to rate the course on different elements to those asking more open-ended questions. In comparing the evaluations I had received for different sections of this course the year before I implemented the changes to those of the sections that had incorporated the changes, I was surprised to see a genuine qualitative difference. In particular, student comments on content coverage and comprehension, course organization, writing instruction, and skill enhancement were very encouraging. Not only did students have more to say (and of a positive nature) in these areas, but they also indicated by their comments that they understood my objectives for the course and had adopted them as their own.

Conclusions

My involvement with Quinnipiac's Writing Across the Curriculum project has been very rewarding for me as a teacher. Not only has it given me real tools for more effective teaching, but it has also given me the framework for envisioning what I do in any particular class in a context that includes what I am doing in other classes, what my colleagues are doing in political science and elsewhere, and what my students are doing across the curriculum. Every time I plan a new course, and with each reiteration of an existing course, I attempt to incorporate more writing of an informal nature to help my students with reading comprehension and learning. Similarly, I have learned more about setting specific goals for my formal writing assignments in a way that can be linked to the cognitive development I encourage in the *way* I present material and facilitate its understanding in my classes. Admittedly, many of my ambitions in incorporating WAC principles into classes are larger at the beginning of the semester than I am often able to realize in practice. However, even *some* use of these principles has had very positive effects on my teaching and on student performance in my classes.

Notes

1. *PS: Political Science and Politics,* American Political Science Association, Washington, DC.

2. Bob, Clifford. 2001. "A question and an argument: Enhancing student writing through guided research assignments." *PS: Political Science and Politics* 34 (3): 653–55.

3. Zeiser, Pamela A. 1999. "Teaching process and product: Crafting and responding to student writing assignments." *PS: Political Science and Politics* 32 (3): 593–95.

4. Londow, David Z. 1993. "Writing in Political Science: A Brief Guide to Resources." *PS: Political Science and Politics* 26 (3): 529–33. Emphasis in original.

5. By this, I mean statements where the author is asserting something *as fact.* I instruct students that, in political science, what in other contexts may look like opinion is usually stated as fact, supported by appropriate empirical evidence or logical reasoning. Statements of value, similarly, are often asserted in much the same way, but usually involve a *normative* commitment.

6. Bob, op. cit.

7. Bean, John C. 1996. *Engaging Ideas: The Professor's Guide to Integrating Writing, Critical Thinking, and Active Learning in the Classroom.* San Francisco: Jossey-Bass. Bean advises that we need to change the way we teach a research paper if we are to avoid the kind of writing where students "patch together" material taken from other sources, often falling into poor habits verging on plagiarism. Among other approaches similar to those discussed above, Bean also suggests "consider several short research assignments or a structured assignment that breaks projects into stages." See Ch. 12, pp. 197–214.

8. Bean introduces several ideas for exploratory writing in Ch. 6 (pp. 97–118). My uses have come close to what he suggests as "focused freewriting," "e-mail networks," and "open-ended" and "semi-structured journals."

9. I have found the following source particularly good with reference to how a journal assignment can be used and evaluated in a social science course. Of course,

Bean also gives good guidance in these areas: Varner, Donna and Sharon R. Peck. 2003. "Learning from Learning Journals: The Benefits and Challenges of Using Learning Journal Assignments." *Journal of Management Education* 27 (1): 52–77.

10. Ultimately, I hope my colleagues will be persuaded to incorporate much of what I have learned into their own teaching. At that time, we might talk about generalizing our expectations throughout our Political Science program. We are still in the early stages of implementing a WAC approach at Quinnipiac, however—there is plenty of room for growth!

11. See the chapter in this volume on assessment for more on how we are beginning to plan more systematic, objective assessment.

9

Evaluating Writing Across the Curriculum Programs

Suzanne S. Hudd
Assistant Professor of Sociology

The evaluation of writing has more or less naturally evolved on our campus during the past couple of years. Several of the faculty members involved with our Writing Across the Curriculum (WAC) program independently decided to examine whether the strategies we had used in our classes were effective in helping students to reach their writing goals. In conversation with colleagues across the country, our WAC program director learned that such spontaneous and unsolicited effort on the part of faculty to evaluate WAC activities is somewhat unusual. Why did a group of us see the need to assess our writing experiences? What were our goals? How have we begun to translate our individual efforts at assessing WAC into a campuswide effort? What have we learned from the evaluation process so far?

This chapter elaborates the answers to each of these questions. First, I describe why evaluation is an essential component in WAC program development. I then outline a list of general factors that must be considered before designing a campuswide methodology for WAC evaluation. Next, I present our institutional WAC evaluation form, along with a discussion of the goals inherent in our approach and a description of our plans for beginning the systematic assessment of WAC. Finally, I report on my own experience implementing the WAC evaluation form and the ways in which I have used the form to modify the writing component in my classes.

Any discussion of WAC evaluation must consider the evaluation process on several different levels. As a first step, the success of individual WAC exercises within specific classrooms can be assessed; for example, does peer review alter the quality of student writing? At the next level, the instructor may wish to evaluate the overall writing experience within a specific class; for instance, did the WAC exercises in this course help to improve student writing and thinking?

Finally, the assessment of the overall campuswide WAC program requires both data from individual classroom experiences and information that addresses the faculty and administrative perspectives on the role of writing in student learning. Such "higher-level" evaluation data are gathered to document the potentially different effects of writing across disciplines in relation to the institution's overall mission. At each level, the collection of evaluation data is important to ensuring that the practice of the writing program continues to fulfill its goals, both within individual classrooms and across the entire college campus.

In this chapter, I will emphasize classroom-level evaluation, but I will also briefly identify a set of administrative considerations related to writing evaluation. As our WAC program has evolved, I have shifted roles from an administrator in support of WAC to a faculty member who incorporates WAC exercises in my classes. Each of these roles has informed my approach to WAC assessment, and as such, I feel it is impossible to discuss the evaluation of WAC in the classroom without giving equal consideration to the institutional infrastructure through which the WAC program is implemented and its critical role in facilitating the success of WAC in the classroom.

Reasons to Evaluate WAC

The most obvious reason for evaluating WAC is to ensure that the teaching methods and exercises we employ in our classes are achieving their intended goals. We implement a writing exercise with some sort of outcome, or series of outcomes, in mind. The process of evaluation, if it is undertaken appropriately, enables us to discern whether, and to what extent, students experience these outcomes. In this regard, WAC evaluation serves the more subtle purpose of helping us to clarify our writing goals for a particular exercise, or moreover, for the course in general. So, for example, if I choose to include a peer-review exercise in my class, what kind of feedback do I want the student writers to receive from their peers? Do I expect the reviewer to learn anything from the process? On more than one occasion, I have been forced to clarify the goals and expectations for a particular writing assignment as I begin to consider how to evaluate the student writing experience. Thus, the first reason to conduct WAC evaluation is actually two reasons: to verify that our goals for each assignment are achieved, and by default, to improve the quality of our assignments.

The need for student feedback is a second important reason to undertake formal assessment of WAC. As faculty members committed to WAC, we may read about WAC techniques that seem applicable to our classes or learn about them from our colleagues. Even when a WAC method has been tested and evaluated with students in other subject areas, ongoing assessment of its applicability to one's own students is important. Our students may not experience the positive results we expect them to achieve from a particular assignment for any number of reasons, including their major, their level of academic development, or the "fit" of the assignment with the conventions of our academic discipline.

One might imagine, for example, that a peer review session in an English writing class with only sixteen students might yield very different results than a peer review session in a Sociology class with thirty students. In order to apply the same peer review process in each of these two classrooms, an instructor would need to be attentive to both class size and subject matter. Because WAC techniques are implemented by instructors with varied teaching styles in a wide variety of instructional settings, evaluation is crucial to ensure that WAC exercises are adjusted to account for situational factors that may affect students' writing experience.

Proponents of WAC are generally committed to excellence in teaching. We spend a great deal of time discussing writing and incorporating writing into our syllabi to improve educational outcomes. As such, a third reason for evaluating WAC exercises is to document whether our efforts have made a difference. Where they have, we can also use student feedback as the basis for ongoing improvement of the exercises we employ. Many of us use examinations to discern whether our students have mastered essential course concepts. Likewise, we must "test" ourselves to learn whether the goals we intend for the writing in our classes are being achieved. In this regard, WAC assessment serves as a vehicle for demonstrating excellent teaching: I establish a goal for an assignment, I assess student performance of the goal, and I review the evaluation data to verify that the students' experience with the assignment is consistent with what I expect. If I observe a discrepancy between my expectations and the students' experience, the evaluation feedback can be used to correct the assignment to facilitate the achievement of course objectives.

Those of us who are committed to the importance of WAC as an educational tool are sometimes charged with advocating for WAC programs and funding. WAC evaluation provides concrete data that lend support to our personal assessment of the important relationship between writing, thinking, and student learning. A statistic, such as "85 percent of my students claim that their writing was improved as a result of taking this class," can be much more compelling than ad hoc impressions that my students are working hard to improve their writing. Comparative data can offer particularly strong evidence to document WAC success. Natural opportunities for comparison present themselves by virtue of the fact that some faculty use WAC routinely while others do not. Aggregate data that contrast class performance or qualitative differences in the way students approach the writing process in WAC and non-WAC classes can be used to foster an increased awareness among faculty and staff of the effects of emphasizing writing in the syllabus.

WAC evaluation is important for one final reason: It encourages faculty collaboration and facilitates a shared understanding among the faculty and students of WAC program goals and the role of writing in the institutional mission. On our campus, efforts to assess the writing experience in isolated classrooms led to the creation of a subcommittee that was charged with preparing a common evaluation form that could be voluntarily used by any faculty member on campus to assess WAC techniques. It became evident as our meetings evolved that while, on the surface, our goal was to document the effectiveness of WAC, a more important common denominator had emerged: our commitment to improving student learning, writing, and thinking. In this regard, WAC evaluation assumes a broader role. It enables faculty to observe the commonality of our goals and experiences. It creates community.

Factors That Affect the Evaluation Process

WAC evaluation is not a "one size fits all" process. Rather, the evaluation of WAC programs must incorporate an understanding of a wide array of factors. A number of factors may affect the structure of the WAC evaluation process on a particular campus, including the type of data the program wishes to review, the commitment of campus resources for the purpose of WAC evaluation, the goals of the WAC program, and the stage of WAC program development. I elaborate briefly on the possible effects of each of these factors next.

1. The Type of Data Required

Any instructor who assigns a paper will also grade the paper. Grading is the most basic level of writing evaluation. In grading papers, we assess the written *product*. To what extent can our students convey their thoughts effectively in the written word? The effect of WAC on the written product can be readily assessed through an evaluation of the final grades for a particular written assignment in a particular class. Within a single classroom, we expect that there is a consistent framework across which the papers have been assessed. Even where there are teaching assistants (that is, multiple graders), a grading grid can be used such that common products receive a common grade. As an evaluation tool then, grades provide us with the ability to calculate the percentage of students who have met or exceeded the basic requirements for the assignment in terms of the quality of their written work. In the majority of classrooms, analysis of the written product is typically quantitative: How many students succeed? To what degree they are successful? How many students fail?

The evaluation of the writing *process* constitutes a second level of WAC evaluation. Do our students approach their assignments differently as a result of the WAC program? Do they think about their writing, or approach the writing process differently as a result of the WAC exercises we have used? These data may also be quantitative, obtained through an instrument similar to our campuswide WAC evaluation form presented at the end of this chapter, or they can be qualitative, obtained via discussion or in written, open-ended feedback from students. Data that document changes in students' perceptions of the writing process constitute an important intended effect of WAC. As WAC instructors, we seek to change the way our students approach the writing process, the manner in which they think about their writing, and moreover, their view of themselves as writers. While writing assessment can begin with data on performance (for instance, do students in the WAC class perform better on a departmental exam?), a comprehensive assessment must necessarily incorporate information on the effects of WAC on our students' approach and attitudes toward writing as well.

2. Commitment of Resources for WAC Evaluation

Our early efforts at WAC evaluation required the time and energy of dedicated faculty who recognized the importance of documenting the effects of WAC in the classroom. The development of a campuswide evaluation process, however, must consider the availability of resources that provide dedicated funding and staffing for WAC assessment. Dedicated resources are necessary to ensure that the evaluation process is comprehensive, ongoing, and efficient. Likewise, an administrative commitment is essential if the evaluation process will be designed to assess the writing progress of the entire student body in a standardized way over time and across disciplines.

As WAC instructors, many of us have informally observed a difference in the ways our students approach their subject matter and in the process by which they prepare their papers. While data from our classrooms provides an important first step in documenting this transition, we must also be concerned with understanding the effects of WAC at the institutional level. While I have advocated strongly for gathering these data, and have collected separate information on the writing process in my own classes, this left me with ninety separate writing evaluation forms to tabulate and analyze. Are there simple ways to assess the effect of WAC on the writing process in the absence of institutional resources committed to gathering these data? One possibility is to incorporate documentation of the writing process as part of the assignment. My students are typically required to submit their topic, a thesis statement, an outline and a rough draft—each comprising a section of the grade—prior to submitting their final paper. Thus, my grade book automatically documents the degree to which students have participated in the process, as well as their success at these various stages.

While there are simple steps that individual faculty can take to document the effect of WAC on both process and product, a comprehensive effort to assess students' writing experience across the disciplines requires a commitment of institutional resources. On our campus, the evaluation of writing will ultimately be coordinated through the Assessment Office. However, as the commitment of faculty to writing assessment grows, as we hope it will, the staffing needs there will likely expand. Thus, while WAC assessment can begin at the individual faculty level, if it is to be sustained over time and achieve a quality that facilitates a broad discussion of writing goals in relation to the institutional mission, then an institutional commitment, both in terms of staff and funding, is necessary.

3. Goals of the WAC Program

An appropriate plan for writing assessment is founded on the goals and objectives of the writing program. This is true both within individual courses, as well as for the evaluation of a campuswide WAC program. In the previous section, I highlighted the important interrelationship between the evaluation of written assignment and classroom goals. Here, I would like to elaborate briefly on the importance of examining the interrelationship between writing assignment goals and campus goals for the writing program.

The evaluation of WAC begins within the individual classroom. So, for example, as a teacher of Sociology 101, one of my goals is to encourage my students to draft and revise their papers, as I have observed that students in introductory classes often fail to incorporate revision as a natural part of their writing process. Thus, in order to assess whether I have effected a change in the writing process, my evaluation data must elaborate the extent to which students have outlined and prepared early drafts of their papers. In addition, I must also assess the degree to which the students perceive a relationship between the steps they completed (i.e., multiple drafts) and the quality of their final written product.

If WAC evaluation is to achieve its ultimate goal, however, it is important to consider not only the immediate goals within a particular class—in this case outlining, drafting, and revision—but also higher-order goals for the writing program in implementation of WAC evaluation. For example, one of our campuswide goals for WAC is to enhance students' critical thinking skills. If, through the in-class grading and evaluation process of the assignment I describe above, I also observe the evolution of the student thought process across their multiple drafts, these data can be used to in support of the campuswide evaluation agenda. Thus, if classroom goals are assessed with an eye to the institutional goals for writing, then both interests can be served. In this way, the evaluation program offers ongoing opportunities to assess the congruence between classroom and institutional goals.

4. Stage of WAC Program Development

Both the programmatic structure of WAC and the stage of WAC program development must be considered if WAC evaluation is to be fully effective. Our campus WAC program recently completed its fourth year. It was not until the middle of the third year that we put serious energy into the evaluation of WAC. In hindsight, our discussions of evaluation, and preliminary efforts to examine the possibilities for evaluation, might have begun sooner. My previous administrative experience suggests that the design of any new program should necessarily incorporate a consideration of the means by which the program will be evaluated in the long term. It may be beneficial, for example, to have some baseline data pertaining to classroom writing experiences of students before the implementation of WAC is widespread.

Programs mature, and as they do, so do the goals and objectives for the program. We have already experienced several iterations of our WAC evaluation form in just two years, and we expect further innovation to occur. Still, it is important to begin with a framework for evaluation in mind. If the goal is to learn about the "successes and failures" that can be attributed to WAC, however, we must recognize that if it is being implemented fully, WAC will continue to evolve. Thus, the institution must make an ongoing commitment to evaluating WAC program goals as well as the teaching and learning experiences associated with WAC across the campus. If the evaluation of WAC is to remain pertinent, it must be sensitive to the evolution of the program as new faculty and curricular innovations are incorporated at both the classroom and institutional levels.

Using the Evaluation Form to Inform Writing Instruction

Early on in the development of WAC, a group of faculty outlined a series of statements that served to guide the development of WAC on campus:

1. Writing is integrally related to reading and speaking.
2. WAC will incorporate both writing to learn and transactional writing.
3. WAC will be applied throughout the curriculum rather than in specific courses.
4. WAC will be used to enhance the teaching and learning that take place without substantially altering what we do in the classroom.

There were also a series of goals related more generally to the ongoing development of the program—for example, the revision of the required freshman English courses. As the program has continued to take form, it has been in concert with these assertions. Our evaluation form (Figure 9–1) was designed to simultaneously complement these broad goals and to give WAC instructors a sense of the effect of WAC on student writing. The form was developed by a subcommittee of our WAC committee, and it was constructed using pieces of the various evaluation instruments that had been developed by several WAC instructors on campus who had previously assessed the WAC experience in their individual classes. An important underlying goal of our efforts was to develop a "generic" evaluation survey that could be utilized by instructors across disciplines and who had employed a variety of WAC techniques. The WAC evaluation form is made available to instructors during WAC workshops throughout the year, and it is used on a voluntary basis.

The questions on the evaluation form have been designed first to distinguish the writing experience in WAC courses (Question 2). In my own experience using this form, I found that while the vast majority of students indicated that they worked harder on their writing (80 percent) and learned more about how to write (75.6 percent), only about half of the students (53.7 percent) felt

WRITING EVALUATION FORM

Evaluation of the Writing Component of _____

(please indicate subject area, course, and section)

1. In relation to the writing I do for my other classes, I would say that in this class:

(Please circle one number for each statement.)

	Strongly Agree	Agree	Disagree	Strongly Disagree	Unsure
I worked harder on my writing.	1	2	3	4	5
There was much more writing.	1	2	3	4	5
I learned more about how to write.	1	2	3	4	5
I could see improvement in my writing.	1	2	3	4	5
I had more discussions with the professor about writing.	1	2	3	4	5
I have been prepared for the type of writing required in my major.	1	2	3	4	5
I am better prepared to do writing in my other classes.	1	2	3	4	5

2. As a result of this course, my ability to prepare papers has been affected in the following ways:

(Please circle one number for each aspect.)

	Definitely Improved	Improved Somewhat	Has not Changed	Has Worsened
Outlining/organizing before I write	1	2	3	4
Writing more than one draft	1	2	3	4
Organization/flow of thoughts	1	2	3	4
Grammar and sentence structure	1	2	3	4
Citation format	1	2	3	4
Other (please indicate):	1	2	3	4

Figure 9–1

3. What kinds of writing helped you increase or develop your understanding of course concepts or content?

(Please circle one number for each kind of writing.)

	Definitely Helped	Helped Somewhat	Didn't help	I didn't do this kind of writing
In-class writing on a topic of my choice (3-5 minutes)	1	2	3	4
In class writing in response to a question posed by the teacher (3-5 minutes)	1	2	3	4
Journals	1	2	3	4
Short reaction papers (1-5 pages of analysis, response, reaction)	1	2	3	4
Library Research Paper with an original thesis and use of other articles as evidence to create new knowledge (5 or more pages).	1	2	3	4
Research Paper based on surveys, interviews or other self-designed methods showing the creation of new knowledge (5+ pages)	1	2	3	4
Multiple-draft writing and revision	1	2	3	4
Other. Please describe:	1	2	3	4

4. From the list above, what was the most important writing technique that helped you with your performance in this class? (Please describe how it helped you.)

continued

Figure 9–1 *continued*

5. We are interested in whether you feel the writing assignments in this class improved your ability to understand the course content. Please indicate whether you agree with any of the following statements.

Item	Strongly Agree	Agree	Disagree	Strongly Disagree	Uncertain
I understand course topics better because of the writing.	1	2	3	4	5
The writing helped me to relate concepts in this course to concepts in other courses.	1	2	3	4	5
The writing assignments helped me to better understand the way I learn.	1	2	3	4	5
The writing assignments improved my thought process in a general way.	1	2	3	4	5
I have an enhanced understanding of "real world" issues and their relationship because of the writing in this course.	1	2	3	4	5
I used the writing assignments to help organize my thinking.	1	2	3	4	5
It seemed like the writing and thinking in this class were not related.	1	2	3	4	5
I got more out of this class because of the writing.	1	2	3	4	5

6. Is the *process* of writing that you go through for your papers different as a result of this course? If so, how?

WRITING EVALUATION FORM
PEER-REVIEW EXPERIENCE

Evaluation of the Writing Component of _____

(please indicate subject area, course, and section)

Optional Evaluation of Peer-Reviewing Process

1. Please rate the value of the following elements of our peer-reviewing process in terms of their value to *you* and your ability to improve *your paper*.

(Please circle one number for each element.)

	Extremely Valuable	Moderately Valuable	Of some Value	Not at all Valuable
The suggestions made by my peer reviewer	1	2	3	4
Reading another student's paper and comparing it to my own	1	2	3	4
Using the reviewer's comments to improve my own paper	1	2	3	4
The effect of the peer reviewing process on my grade for the *papers*	1	2	3	4
The effect of the peer reviewing process on my grade for the *class*	1	2	3	4

2. Has the peer-review process affected the way you will write your papers in the future? If yes, please explain what you think the long-term effect of the peer-review process will be.

that there was more writing in the class. While the students are somewhat mixed on the amount of writing they experienced, these findings are encouraging in that one of my goals was to make the writing "invisible" to a certain extent—that is, to have the students perceive the writing as a tool for learning. The relationship between these data and our institutional goal to not "substantially alter what we do in the classroom" is clear.

The connection students make between their writing and thought processes is also evident in the evaluation data. The vast majority of my students over the past year (81.7 percent) state that they used the writing assignments to help organize their thinking in relation to course concepts. In the words of one student, "I definitely take more time to *think* about what I'm going to write now. I do realize that thinking and planning before you write makes the writing process so much easier and better." Likewise, my students indicate that writing has helped them to understand course concepts and to relate what they learn in my course to information they acquire in other classes.

Consistent with our program goal to utilize multiple WAC approaches—for instance, transactional and writing-to-learn exercises—our form is designed to examine which WAC techniques our students find most useful for improving their writing. Data gathered in relation to this question will also give the WAC committee a sense of the frequency with which faculty members are incorporating specific WAC techniques on a campuswide basis. In my classes, I found multiple draft writing to be the most helpful technique for improving writing quality. Two-thirds of the students (61.7 percent) indicated that preparing drafts was "definitely helpful," and an additional 31.7 percent stated that it "helped somewhat." All the assignments in my classes are embedded with a grading process that requires students to turn in their preliminary work, including thesis statement, outline, and first draft. These results enabled me to observe that, by and large, my students link multiple drafts with improved performance.

The final question on our evaluation form asks students about their experiences with writing before and after the WAC class. This question provides students with the opportunity to elaborate directly on how they may have begun to approach their writing assignments differently. Here, our agenda is to discern what changes in the writing process seem to be most notable to our students, and whether there may be unintended consequences associated with WAC exercises. For example, do students in WAC classes approach their reading assignments differently?

Many of my students speak about realizing the importance of taking time with their thoughts and the importance of going through multiple revisions and organizing their ideas. While students occasionally note that they will "only use multiple drafts if the instructor requires it," they more commonly describe the effects of the process as positive.

> The most important writing technique to me was outlining and also having a peer review after writing the first draft of my papers. Outlining really helped organize my ideas and thoughts. It made the writing process much easier. I'm

> glad we were required to have an outline because it generally improved my
> papers, and I don't think I would have written one if it were not required. Now
> I realize it is beneficial to *always* have an outline. The peer review helped me
> to notice errors in my papers and to write more coherently.

What has been most fulfilling to me in reading the evaluation data is that my
students speak comfortably about themselves as writers. This is quite contrary
to the reactions I often observe on the first day of class when I present writing
as a focal point of my course and a vehicle for learning. A common response
on my preliminary evaluations reads something like: "I am afraid of the writing requirements in this class." In comparing their pre- and post-class observations about writing, I am able to see that many of my students have become
more comfortable with writing. Some will go even farther, noting that this class
has changed their overall attitude toward writing. In the words of one student,
"I just want you to know that you made me feel good about my writing." Finally, I have been able to observe my students rising to the challenge they often perceive in written work: "I never had to write a paper similar to a literature review. It was very difficult for me to learn the process . . . . It was
rewarding to see the final product."

While we have initiated data-gathering on the writing experiences of our
students across campus, we are simultaneously working with several other
methods for collecting evaluation data in a more preliminary way. A separate
campuswide committee has been formed to discuss the feasibility of creating
electronic student portfolios that may be used for a variety of purposes. Our
WAC director is collaborating in this effort with the goal of using the portfolio
as a means to collect, store, and analyze writing samples. This technology, in
combination with a set of performance standards, will provide us with the ca-
pability to assess the effect of WAC on the written products of individual students over the course of their college experience. We have also experimented
with a writing focus group as a means of obtaining qualitative information that
will inform and advance our understanding of students' writing experience as
they transition through their four years at Quinnipiac.

The ongoing assessment of student writing, using multiple methods, is an essential component of any WAC program. WAC is not designed solely to affect
our students' writing ability. If this were our only goal, the evaluation process
would be relatively straightforward. Rather, we are seeking to change our students' attitudes about writing, the ways in which they think about their writing,
and their approaches to the writing process. Perhaps most importantly, we are using writing to affect critical thinking skills. In essence, we are seeking to assess
multiple outcomes: writing quality, writing process, critical thinking, student
learning, and attitudes toward writing. Thus, our assessment effort and the methods we use must be adequately comprehensive to address each of these goals.

10

A Cognitive Psychologist's Rationale for Experimenting with WAC

Shar Walbaum
Professor of Cognitive Psychology

Motivation

I can't recall a time when writing wasn't important to me. This goes back to a two-sentence essay entitled "My Address," painstakingly written on one of those buff-colored sheets of paper. In high school, I spent three years as a reporter and editor for the *Jeffersonian* and learned the value of being clear and concise. I began to learn how to think on paper. Although I started at the university as a journalism major, my attention was soon captured by the kind of psychology that addresses thinking, problem solving, and the relationship between thought and language. Now, I am a professor of cognitive psychology.

As I learned about scientific writing during undergraduate and graduate school, my earlier training in journalism stood me in good stead. I already knew that one must be alert when writing expository text, because feelings and beliefs can creep in disguised as fact. More importantly, I had a sort of budding editor's consciousness, something cognitive psychologists call metalinguistic awareness. I was able to step back and analyze my writing as if it were not mine. However, I was disappointed to find that there was very little formal training during my "higher" education in how to write in a scientist's voice. Students were left to "muscle through" when faced with the problem of research writing. One naive (and common) solution to this problem was to write research reports as if there was no researcher (i.e., using the passive voice).

Both my training in cognition and my experience as a writer told me that this was not the best way. Lack of relevant training is the main reason we have a body of research literature abounding in prose that is dense, obtuse, and just plain inaccessible. Young scientists need support and feedback as they are learning to write—just as they are learning to think—like scientists. This realization

motivated me to teach psychology students to write more effectively and to
help them see writing as an avenue for learning.

WAC 101

Fortunately, my first faculty appointment came at a time when Writing Across
the Curriculum was gaining momentum across the Mount Holyoke College
campus through the efforts of a small group of dedicated faculty (similar to the
one that spearheaded this volume). I attended workshops and heard speakers
that helped me provide better support for student writing. For the first time, I
became sensitized to the way English professors are often held responsible for
the quality of student writing, as if freshman composition could train all students to write in all disciplines. It gave me the opportunity to find others in
biology, math, and political science who not only saw writing as a behavior to
be shaped, but also as a tool for the development of thinking.

The main (idiosyncratic) rule I carried away from my WAC training experience at Mount Holyoke was to "Stop marking up every page." (I also toyed
with "Never use a red pen," but eventually decided that problems with written
feedback rarely have to do with the color of the ink.) I learned that less is more;
my old editing habits were very likely overloading students with too many details. As a consequence, my feedback was probably being ignored. This is just
what Jean Piaget, the eminent theorist of cognitive development, would have
predicted (Piaget 1972). If we have no way of making sense of new stimuli, we
resolve the resulting cognitive disequilibrium by just filtering them out. For example, if I overheard a conversation between a Peruvian couple, I would be in
a similar position. Although I know a little Spanish, when it is spoken collo-
quially, I experience information overload and simply stop listening. This is an
adaptive response. If someone wants me to understand something that is being
said in Spanish, he or she must speak clearly and simply (presenting me with a
moderate amount of cognitive challenge). Similarly, if I want a student to understand what I am saying about his or her writing, I must express it clearly and
simply. In other words, cognitive development is possible only when new information is moderately disequilibrating. (Of course, as a cognitivist, I was kicking
myself for not figuring out this rule sooner.) During my three years at Mount
Holyoke, I learned to "zoom out" as I was reading student work and to look for
patterns, whether in terms of micro or macro structure or content.

My WAC Experiments

In 1991, I became a permanent member of the psychology faculty at Quinnipiac University and, in the mid-nineties, I had the great good fortune to move
into an office next door to Mary Segall, then Director of Freshman English.
Mary and I shared many wonderful conversations about cognition and writing
. . . she became my on-campus WAC guru. Partly through her influence, I took

on the goal of trying to integrate writing development into all my courses. What follows is a description of a few different ways I tried to do this.

One course that presented a special challenge was Introduction to Statistics in Psychology. In faculty discussions about WAC, I had heard many statements like "Sure, WAC is a great idea, but how could one reasonably be expected to apply it to math?" I suspected writing, like reading and talking, belonged throughout the college curriculum. So, to begin with, I asked students to write essays on their best and worst experiences in math classes. These essays gave me a way to identify, and later to address, student concerns. During the course, I regularly asked them to write more than one way of defining a term like "standard deviation" or "statistical significance." Similarly, on every quiz and test, I stressed the relationship between words and numbers by asking them for clear and concise descriptions and explanations. I had students put statistical concepts into their own words because I knew it would strengthen their understanding. In addition, once they articulated what they understood, I had a better shot at shaping that understanding. I found that, for many students, a verbal emphasis in statistics made the material much more accessible. Writing helped them think.

In one early experiment with writing, students brought in four-page drafts of a term paper for a "round robin" session about halfway through the semester. The students sat in a circle. I collected and then randomly redistributed the papers. Their instructions were to review the paper and offer the author feedback about clarity, organization, missing information, or anything else that struck them. Comments like "Great work!" were not allowed, because I wanted them to get past the "criticism = bad person" equation. After about five "rounds," I reallocated the papers and they began again. Halfway through the hour, my directions changed to include, "Begin with the last two pages." I no longer do this activity, but it was zany and fun while it lasted. Students got feedback from many different points of view, they had a shot at seeing how their peers were writing, and they spent one hour thinking about effective writing.

In another experiment, I tried "process writing." I wanted to work with a form of writing that would help students become more aware of the role metacognition plays in writing. Generally speaking, metacognition is thinking about one's own thinking. (A few paragraphs back (back) I used the more specific term of metalinguistic awareness, or being aware of how one is using language.) My inspiration for promoting metacognitive awareness was early research by Ann Brown, an innovative researcher in the area of metacognition. For example, Brown and Campione (1977) found that educable retarded children could be brought up to age-norms in reading if they were trained to use self-monitoring strategies. The children were taught to do the following: When you get to the end of a paragraph, ask yourself, "Do I understand?" If the answer is yes, keeping reading. If it is no, reread the paragraph. The children learned to use the instructions, transferred them to new reading tasks, and greatly improved their reading comprehension. Brown concluded that one component of retardation, at least at this level, was a reduced tendency to spontaneously self-monitor. Other research tells us, in contrast, that one distinguishing characteristic of "experts" (in domains such as physics or chess) is their strong tendency to check their own understanding as they are problem-solving (Chi, Feltovich, and Glaser 1981). It appears that self-monitoring plays a key role in intellectual progress. Many subsequent studies have shown the value of explicitly helping students (of any age) to self-monitor and self-test as they are learning (Schneider and Bjorklund 1998).

I began my "process writing" activity by asking students to draw lines down the middle of several pages. Then, I asked them to write a brief essay on a topic. The left side of the page was to be used for free or "stream of consciousness" writing relevant to both the topic and the process of writing. (In cognitive research, this activity results in "verbal protocols.") The right side was for additions to the essay proper. The spacing of the different entries paralleled their relationship in time. For example, the essay sentence written on the right:

"All children experience trauma at some point."

might be followed by a thought written below and to the left like:

"Why did i say ALL? It should be SOME."

A revised sentence would follow on the right, and so forth.

Process writing can reveal to both the reader and the writer how thoughts are linked to the written word. This activity was valuable to me, as a reader, because I could glimpse the writing process in action. I could see which questions and concerns were coming up and which weren't. It was valuable to writers because it underscored the importance of planning and revision in good writing, and it provided an avenue for effective self-monitoring.

I have also experimented with Writing Enhanced courses. Student comments like "Why should you care about my writing—this is a psychology course!" led me to try using a "WR" designation (to represent a writing course). I thought the designation might help everyone start on the same page (so to speak). After a few tries, I decided to simply infuse all my courses with writing tasks. If I think that there is a reciprocal relationship between good thinking and clear written expression, then a substantial writing component belongs in each of my courses. My response to that comment is now, "I emphasize writing because it is a powerful tool for learning about any topic, psychology included."

The Paper Project

Through experimentation, I eventually developed an integrated set of writing activities that I can apply to any course in psychology. This "Paper Project" (shown at the end of the chapter) creates many opportunities for the exercise of expository writing skills and the development of content knowledge. I refined it while teaching Child and Adolescent Development. The developmental course often attracts younger, less experienced college students who typically need academic support in many areas, writing certainly being one of them. I decided that it was a perfect candidate for an in-depth paper assignment, because it surveys many different theories and a large body of research. From the outset, I had no interest in being handed a traditional term paper assignment during the last week of class. I wanted to be part of the process and to use the term paper as an opportunity to teach about how to write and think like a psychologist.

The template for the Paper Project consists of eight sequenced tasks, starting with a thesis paragraph and ending with a final draft. Some tasks are aimed at helping students conduct library research and summarize sources (without plagiarizing). Others are designed to help them to write clear and well-organized expository text. As each task is completed, I have a chance to offer personalized and relevant feedback; the project is designed to provide many such "teachable moments." At the semester's end, the term paper is handed in as part of a portfolio of previously completed and reviewed work. This portfolio offers me the opportunity to retrace the steps the student took during the development of the project. It partly serves a mnemonic function for me; although by that point I am familiar with each project, I need to be reminded about details. Most importantly, the portfolio gives me a way to examine each individual's progress, taking into account all the work that has gone into the project.

During the semester, students face three deadlines for handing in sources and summarizing them. For each deadline, two sources are summarized, so students have reviewed six sources by the time the rough draft is due. At least another six sources must be summarized and handed in by the final draft deadline. Looking at their sources gives me a chance to tell whether students are searching the literature effectively and, if needed, redirect them. In some cases, I need to reteach the contrast between a popular and a professional source.

As far as the notes are concerned, I stress that I expect them to be real working notes—not typed, not neat—summaries of only that information they plan to use. Looking at notes lets me easily conduct preemptive strikes on plagiarism and, in a related vein, enables me to effectively redirect a student who uses highlighting as a substitute for note-taking. Notes tell me what the student thinks is a main idea versus a minor detail or whether he or she is even aware of the need to notice these qualities. In general, summarizing is an advanced literacy skill, often not mastered until graduate school (Brown and Day 1983). By working with notes, I can help students to more effectively summarize scientific literature.

The development of the paper takes place in stages: thesis paragraph; one-page outline; extended outline; rough draft; and final draft. The least familiar of these is the bridging stage between the simple outline and the rough draft—the extended outline. It is a mix of structure, prose, cited sources, and source notes with all parts not necessarily equally developed. It is used to emphasize the importance of organization in effective writing. The extended outline is also a wonderful tool for directing the student's attention toward sections of the paper that need to be developed either conceptually or in terms of background research.

The structure of the Paper Project gives students the time and support they need to do some in-depth research on a special topic and to show me their best writing. While skilled student writers sometimes balk at the need to go through the stages, and bristle at the feedback, they are invariably proud of the final result. (I think we don't do enough to help our good writers. Too often, perhaps out of a professor's sense of relief, their papers simply receive an A and a comment like "Great work!") For those students who are less skilled writers, the project gives them needed practice and many opportunities for success.

Talking WAC with Psychologists

In 1997, at the annual meeting of the Eastern Psychological Association, I found myself making the following argument to a roomful of cognitive psychologists: not only were they capable of integrating writing development into their courses, but they were also just the folks who should do it. To make my argument, I relied on research in expertise. First, I described what we know about the cognitive consequences of expertise (Glaser and Chi 1988). I related those consequences to their development as psychology scholars and professors. I wanted to help them to recognize their own expertise as readers and writers of expository text. (I anticipated that they would lack self-confidence in this area, a common source of WAC reluctance for non-English professors.) As psychology experts, I pressed them to understand that they already have the pattern recognition capabilities to automatically perceive both micro- and macroglitches in student writing. While allowing that they probably need practice to provide the most effective feedback, I emphasized that the goal was well within their grasp.

Second, I used expertise research to remind them that we (as cognitivists) know how novices become expert: novices need domain-specific practice coupled with effective feedback (see, for instance, Ericsson 1996). All theories of expertise agree on this point, regardless of whether they emphasize the role of talent and motivation. For psychology majors, domain-specific feedback is feedback about effective expository writing using APA (American Psychological Association) style. Who better to supply this feedback than professors with expertise in APA style? In conclusion, I argued that we could hold our students to high standards of expository writing only if we provide them with relevant learning experiences.

Conclusion: It's About Scaffolding

Lev Vygotsky, who focused on sociocultural influences on cognitive development, coined the term "scaffolding" to describe what adults contribute to children's development (Vygotsky 1962). Adults don't make development happen, he argued, but they are still crucial to the process. They provide carefully chosen opportunities for learning, opportunities that are tuned to fall within the child's "zone of proximal development." In other words, adults use environments, objects, and even other people to surround the child with challenges that are just beyond his or her current intellectual reach, but are close enough to carry the possibility of being met. (Notice the parallel to Piaget's idea of moderate disequilibrium here.) Grown-ups provide nudges when a child is stuck and a shoulder when he or she is discouraged. An adult who is "tuned in" notices and praises new achievements and, then, turns right around and presents the child with a new puzzle. As the child meets the challenges and solves the puzzles, he or she develops new cognitive skills and attains greater knowledge. This is Vygotsky's explanation for intellectual progress.

Piaget recognized that many adults may not learn how to use abstract or logical reasoning or may exhibit it only in a single domain of their lives (Piaget 1972). However, young adults have considerable potential in this area, having reached Piaget's pentultimate stage of cognitive development, Formal Operations. When we integrate writing into college courses, we provide scaffolding for young adults' intellectual development. We create opportunities for domain-specific application of scientific reasoning.

Through various writing assignments, such as those that comprise the Paper Project, I have tried to promote students' cognitive development. The assignments themselves challenge the students intellectually and push them to refine their writing skills. The structure of the tasks, the way they are sequenced, and my feedback all provide scaffolding for the development of students' writing and their understanding of psychology. I enjoy being a witness as students develop into better writers, more knowledgeable scholars, and clearer thinkers.

References

Brown, A. L., and J. C. Campione. 1977. "Training Strategic Study Time Apportionment in Educable Retarded Children." *Intelligence* 1: 94–107.

Brown, A. L., and J. D. Day. 1983. "Macrorules for Summarizing Texts: The Development of Expertise." *Journal of Verbal Learning and Verbal Behavior* 22: 1–14.

Chi, M. T. H., P. J. Feltovich, and R. Glaser. 1981. "Categorization and Representation of Physics Problems by Experts and Novices." *Cognitive Science* 5: 121–52.

Ericsson, K. A. 1996. "The Acquisition of Expert Performance." In K. A. Ericsson (ed.), *The Road to Excellence* (pp. 1–50). Mahwah, NJ: Erlbaum.

Glaser, R., and M. T. H. Chi. 1988. Overview. In M. T. H. Chi, R. Glaser, and M. Farr (eds.), *The Nature of Expertise* (pp. xv–xxxvi). Hillsdale, NJ: Erlbaum.

Piaget, J. 1972. *The Psychology of Iintelligence*. Totowa, NJ; Littlefield, Adams.

Schneider, W., and D. F. Bjorklund. 1998. "Memory." In W. Damon (ed.-in-chief) and D. Kuhn and R. S. Siegler (vol. eds.), *Handbook of Child Psychology* (Vol. 2, pp. 467–521). New York: John Wiley.

Vygotsky, L. S. 1962. *Thought and Language*. Cambridge, MA: MIT Press.

The Paper Project

Syllabus excerpt:

The completed paper will be a literature review of some area within developmental psychology. It will be completed in a series of steps. At the Final Draft deadline, you will hand in a portfolio of all your work on this project along with my earlier feedback and your polished draft.

1. Topic paragraph

   Give a brief description of your topic and a couple of questions you will try to answer.

2. Two sources and working notes

   Select professional, academic sources. Notes should be in your own words, detailed enough for you to use when you write. Ultimately, you will hand in 12 sources with their corresponding notes, 8 of which should be primary and from recent, refereed journal sources. I expect you to develop working notes on every source you use.

3. One-page outline

   Identify four or five major areas of inquiry and points to consider within each.

4. Two sources and working notes

   See item 2.

5. Extended (5–6) page outline

   Use this outline to integrate your sources. It can be a mix of briefly noted and more developed material. At this point, you should be working from a word-processing file.

6. Two sources and working notes

   See item 2.

7. Rough draft (8–10 pages)

   Hand in all previous work and any new sources and working notes along with this draft. Every part of the outline should be developed to some degree and sources should be cited. If you are missing information for an area, that, too, should be noted.

8. Final draft (12–15 pages)

   The completed paper should be written in APA style, 12–15 pages of expository text, typed and double-spaced. Hand in all previously completed work on the Paper Project. Any sources and working notes that I have not previously seen should also be included.

11

WAC and Mathematics

Cornelius Nelan
Associate Professor of Mathematics

The discipline of mathematics and the principles of WAC do not form the easiest of marriages. Mathematics is itself more a process than a set of facts and formulas. When mathematicians "write up" their research, they do not document their personal motivations or the hard work that went into the creation of their results; they simply present a valid logical argument proving that what they have presented is correct (based upon universally accepted assumptions and definitions). The writing style is very straightforward and usually linear. In mathematics, the process of creating new mathematics usually precedes the process of writing.

When mathematicians are writing for other mathematicians, they know that the text will be closely scrutinized for correctness and completeness; there is no room for personal opinion or salesmanship in a technical mathematical paper. Thus, they tend to get right to point. Each sentence is meant only to provide information; there are almost no "throwaway" sentences used to stir interest in the subject or to simply entertain. The first sentence in a mathematics paper might be, "Let G be a nonabelian group and N a normal subgroup of G." Right to the point and already filled with jargon that will make it difficult for the nonmathematician to follow. There are also a minimal number of adjectives and adverbs in mathematics papers; even when there is an adjective, it is only used to provide more information rather than to alter or clarify the noun it is modifying. In the sentence, "Let f be a differentiable function," the definition of "function" is already set in stone, and the adjective "differentiable" tells us a little more about this particular function f and does not at all change the meaning of the word *function*. It is practically impossible to reason out the definition of a word from the context of a sentence (as many of us were taught to do in elementary school); we really have to know what the words mean beforehand or look them up as we read the text.

When mathematicians are writing for nonmathematicians, they still tend to use many of the same conventions they use when writing for an audience of mathematicians. Written mathematics tends to be very (sometimes painfully) terse. This is partially due to the nonliterary style that most mathematicians adopt, but also due to the more universally accepted and more precise definitions in mathematics than in other disciplines. Words in mathematics tend to be "potent"; a great deal of information can be communicated in a small amount of space. The role of *definition* in mathematics is often not fully understood by nonmathematicians. Definitions, along with axioms, are the fundamental building blocks upon which the entire discipline is built. Definitions often evolve over time to be not only precise, but also very functional; they are used to prove theorems and, therefore, need to be laid out in a way that cannot be misinterpreted and cannot change substantially when put into a different context. Often clarity (in the sense of being easily understood by people who are not experts in the field) is sacrificed to obtain these goals of precision and functionality.

The process of teaching mathematics presents a much different set of challenges than does performing mathematics. Mathematicians must completely rethink the way they communicate mathematics when talking to nonmathematicians. There is a need for "triggering mechanisms" to help identify and address misunderstandings and to promote a mutual understanding between student and instructor. The traditional lecture method, which produces class notes that often look and read like journal papers, does not accomplish this, but reflective writing assignments can. Writing assignments show that the instructor is interested in the opinions of the students (something mathematics instructors are not known for) and acknowledge the possibility that the instructor can learn from his or her students, something the students find very encouraging and which is entirely missing from the standard lecture format of teaching. In 1989, the National Council of Teachers of Mathematics (NCTM), concerned that traditional methods of delivering mathematical content were becoming increasing ineffective, produced a document entitled *Curriculum and Evaluation Standards for School Mathematics.* "Mathematics as Communication" is the second standard listed. The NCTM suggests that "the study of mathematics should include numerous opportunities for communication so that students can realize that representing, discussing, reading, writing, and listening to mathematics are vital parts of learning and using mathematics" (NCTM 1989, 26). These standards were intended for use by K–12 mathematics instructors, but the point is equally valid for college-level instruction.

At Quinnipiac University, the mathematics faculty teach two types of courses that serve vastly different purposes and audiences: those specifically geared towards math and science majors (Calculus, Linear Algebra, Abstract Algebra and Analysis, etc.), which give the student an idea of what it is to be a professional mathematician, and service courses (College Algebra, Business Calculus, Statistics, etc.), which are specifically designed for people who may have little or no interest in the subject matter of mathematics, but who may indeed find a use for mathematics in their other courses and in their careers. Not all disciplines make this distinction; in most cases, an introductory psychology course (for example) serves both the major and the nonmajor. Mathematics faculty at many higher education institutions started drawing the distinction between service courses and courses for majors in the fifties and sixties when it became apparent that American higher education institutions were in competition with each other to attract and retain students, many of whom have a low opinion or even an aversion to mathematics. The goals of a service course are usually perceived by instructors in terms of the acquisition of certain skills, such as taking derivatives or simplifying radicals; the overall philosophy of the course in the context of the entire liberal arts curriculum is not usually well defined. Mathematics instructors need to consider the impression that students are forming of the discipline of mathematics as a result of taking this course. Mathematics instructors should ask themselves the following questions: "Will my students take away from this class a positive impression of mathematicians and their contributions to modern society? In their future careers, will my students be able to tackle mathematical problems or actively avoid them? Will my students be able to communicate their understanding of mathematics concepts to others? Will the student be able to read and understanding mathematical or statistical arguments? Will the students be able to use mathematics to their advantage in their future careers?"

Many service mathematics courses are taught with tests and homework assignments as the only evaluation instruments, and the students work out problems using a shorthand notation that does not normally require the student to form complete sentences or use correct punctuation. We typically allow the students to abuse terminology and to incompletely explain their reasoning, as long as their techniques and solutions are essentially "correct." The quality of the student's writing is not always evaluated, not because the instructors are lazy or because the students are incapable of producing quality written work, but because we do not expect the students to be acquainted with the conventions of mathematical writing and do not think we can teach them how to "write mathematics" within the context of the service course. In a course designed for majors, the quality of their written work is much more important, and we expect to see growth in their ability to write mathematics as we see a more mature understanding of the course material.

Mathematicians do not in general attempt to teach their students how to "write mathematics," even though the thought processes used in the discipline of mathematics have a profound effect on the structure and conventions of written mathematics, as discussed above. Many mathematics instructors do not believe they are competent to teach writing or believe it is not their responsibility to teach writing. Thus, in service courses, we see reluctance on the part of many instructors to assign papers or even to assign specific reading assignments. However, as one can see from the other chapters in this book, the principles of WAC do not necessarily require us to teach our students how to write but rather how to "use" writing to help teach the mathematics. It is indeed a worthwhile endeavor to use writing assignments in service classes to help students arrive at their own understanding and appreciation of the course material. About fifteen years ago, it was common for students in all my undergraduate courses to produce two to four papers (usually short: three to five pages) over the course of the semester, most of which were a response to a reading assignment. About twelve years ago, this practice was discontinued for various reasons, mostly lack of support by colleagues. It was about five years ago that this practice of assigning papers in many of my courses was reestablished; the impetus to do this was not a discovery of WAC techniques but came about as a result of teaching a number of courses for an audience of preservice secondary mathematics teachers. It was necessary to have this group do a lot of writing in order to immerse them in the language of mathematics. WAC principles have, however, shown me how to make these papers more instructive.

If we are going to assign papers, especially in a service course, we need to have a clear idea of what we expect these papers to accomplish, and we need to have a realistic set of expectations to evaluate the papers we receive. If, for instance, we assign a paper in a business calculus course, the students' work will look nothing like a typical mathematics journal article. The proofs, if any, will be incomplete. The arguments will not flow linearly. The conclusions will not be well supported in the same sense that a mathematician would consider a conclusion well reasoned. If we want to accomplish anything at all, we have to link the assignment to clarifying an important topic addressed by the course. For example, if a goal of the course is that the students acquire a good understanding of what a derivative is, the paper could ask them to explain (to a layperson) their particular understanding of the concept of "derivative" and why we study derivatives. What we have accomplished by doing this is to make students think about a basic concept in a very different way than they would normally and to increase their understanding of the concept by having them communicate that understanding. This should affect the way we grade these papers: emphasize the expressive nature of the writing over the transactional, or in other words, be very lenient.

One of my primary goals in service classes is to promote the student's ability to read and understand mathematics texts and to use what they know to explain what they don't know. It is not my intent to have students reading journal articles, but to be able to pick up a textbook at some later date and teach themselves (or more likely reteach themselves) about some mathematical technique or concept. It is difficult to imagine that many of my students will use the quadratic formula to solve an equation in their future lives. A more likely scenario is that they would hear a term, such as p-value, in a presentation, and they should be able to go to a statistics book and read about p-values. Thus, almost all the papers assigned in my undergraduate classes require the student to read a section of the textbook and write a paper summarizing its content as if speaking to a third party or to simply write a critique of that section of the book.

As stated above, it was teaching graduate courses to prospective second-ary education mathematics teachers that reintroduced me to the idea of using writing (papers) as an instrument to help teach the course. The audience of a preservice mathematics teacher is a hybrid of the two audiences mentioned above. These students will go on to teach mathematics, but it is unlikely that they will ever create original mathematics themselves. They are generally older than the students in my undergraduate classes and generally have had extensive experience outside the college classroom that has matured them significantly. However, their interest in the discipline of mathematics runs the full gamut from not very interested to highly interested. Thus, the assigned papers do not require the students to create mathematics, but do require them to understand and comment upon written mathematics text.

During the past six summers, I have taught a course entitled MA 590: Top-ics in Pre-College Mathematics Education for graduate students preparing to be secondary education mathematics teachers.[1] It is listed as a mathematics course, rather than an education course, although its audience is entirely prospective mathematics teachers. The topics covered in the course are chosen by the instructor, but when I teach the course, the topic is the "language of mathematics" and the role that definitions play in mathematics. In this course there were two major papers assigned. The first paper was a review of a math-ematics textbook.[2] The second paper was a report on a tutoring experience the students performed over the course of the semester.

As noted above, the first paper assignment was to review a mathematics textbook used by a high school or college (in rare cases middle school) mathe-matics class.[3] The questions that the students needed to address included "How well written is the textbook?" and "How clearly is each point made?" This same assignment was given each time the course was taught, but it wasn't un-til the summers of 2003 and 2004 that the expectations and the criteria for eval-uation were clearly outlined in the class syllabus. Until that time, the syllabus just stated that the first paper, the textbook review, was due on a certain date. The original assumption of the class was that too much specification would limit creativity on the part of the students. The opposite turned out to be the case. It is only after the students know that they have accomplished what the professor is looking for that they can then become creative and look for things that go beyond the assignment. As of 2003, the syllabus contains about four paragraphs defining the goals of the assignment and explains how to get a good grade. A premium is placed on clear analysis and coherent argument.

In the summer of 2004, we tried something new. We actually practiced writing the paper during class time. We photocopied a section of a textbook, read it during class, and wrote a short (two-paragraph) critique of that passage. We then discussed what people had written and tried to form some kind of con-sensus as to which points were superficial or a matter of taste and which points actually had an influence on their understanding of the effect of using a partic-ular textbook as a teaching tool. By doing this, we were sacrificing one half hour of a two-hour class,[4] but it was definitely a worthwhile endeavor. Practicing critiquing a textbook made the students more aware of what to look for when judging mathematics textbooks and more cognizant of exactly what a mathematics textbook needs to accomplish. Thus, for the first time the students were able to identify real flaws in the particular book they had chosen to review. I received papers with very interesting and useful observations on the nature of mathematics textbooks.

Four students in my class noticed that many mathematics textbooks, influenced by the Internet, are actually trying to make individual pages look like websites. There are little snippets of information assigned to different sections of the page, not all of them related. The thinking may be that a student should be able to find something of interest on this page, even if they find the subject matter inherently uninteresting. The consensus of the class is that this doesn't quite work, first because the student did not come to this page voluntarily and could easily dismiss everything on the page, but more importantly because all these extras distract from the presentation of the core material. Books are meant to be read, and the format of the book should facilitate this rather than make it harder to follow the flow of the material.

From the student evaluations of the course, it is apparent that the students enjoyed this assignment. As prospective teachers, they appreciated the need to be able to read mathematical texts not only critically for the sake of their students, but also for their own sakes. At this stage of their careers, they are very soon going to become adept at absorbing written text if they are going to continue their intellectual development within the discipline. Reading mathematical texts for information is a skill that they are not nearly as good at as they should be. The act of writing about the textbook also enhanced the reading experience. Since they were to produce a paper, they read the book more purposefully than they otherwise would have.

The second writing assignment was a case study of a tutoring experience. Over the period of three weeks, each student in this class was assigned the task of finding a child whose class level was somewhere between sixth and tenth grade, and they were to hold three "tutoring" sessions with the student. For the purposes of this assignment, I hoped that the prospective tutee might struggle a bit with mathematics, making the exercise a little bit more interesting, but my students had to find the student through their own connections. In the first session, the tutor and tutee were to identify a topic in mathematics with which the child struggled; during the second section they were to work exclusively on that topic. Finally, during the third session, they were to do some sort of enrichment activity, something outside of the normal mathematics curriculum. While they were doing this, my students were instructed to try to convince their tutee of the value of understanding basic mathematics vocabulary.

My students then submitted a paper detailing the entire experience, but concentrating on the child's opinion of the relationship between language skills and mathematical ability. Through the six summers the course has been held, the students have in general found this assignment a bit easier than the first paper, but they seem to put less effort and thought into the second set of papers than into the first set of textbook review papers. For some, this paper seemed to be a step backwards; they were able to fall into old habits, claiming that mathematics was an inherently difficult discipline and that we really can't expect students to understand written mathematics. Most of the classes have felt that while their tutees humored them when they talked about the importance of "definition" in mathematics, few of them really saw a relationship between understanding the language of mathematics and a fuller understanding of the discipline. My students and their charges both asserted that mathematics can only be learned if the teacher is very good. Children like mathematics if they like their teacher, and if they do not like mathematics, it is usually the teacher's fault. This is a trap that mathematics teachers both set and fall into themselves. We don't want our students to become completely dependent on us. This also works against the point that I was making in the course. We were attempting to take a constructivist point of view: if students understand the language, they can create their own understanding of the subject.

In practice this second paper didn't accomplish nearly as much as it should have. So in the summer of 2004, we tried a different approach. In addition to writing the paper, the MA 590 students kept a double-entry journal describing the tutoring experience. They were to record their initial impressions following each tutoring session and then, at a later date (before writing the paper) they were to revisit their journal entries and identify how their impression of the experience had changed after completing the entire tutoring project. This has the effect of making the paper a bit more cathartic, but also a more effective maturation experience for my students.

This second paper was a revelation for a few of my students because it made them consider and express (in writing) their thoughts about their effectiveness as teachers. I have to admire people who at this stage of their career (the very beginning) can openly address their need to grow as professionals. Here is what one student had to say about the experience: "This left a significant impression on me. I think teachers must be careful with directions. The language we use in the process of teaching is just as important as the language we expect the students to develop in order to comprehend math."

The most pleasing part of this assignment was my student's willingness to be open about their thoughts and to write passionately about the subject of mathematics, a subject that they had recently decided to devote their lives to. None of the twenty papers (ten students, two papers each) I received will be publishable, even with revisions, but this is most decidedly not the point. But with luck, my students learned the value of writing as a mechanism of clarifying their own thoughts, and that it is just as effective in mathematics as in any other discipline.

Notes

1. Quinnipiac University's teacher education degree is at the graduate level, an MAT.

2. Each student picks a different high school– or college-level textbook to review.

3. This paper assignment required the students to read a mathematics book in its entirety, probably for the first time in their lives.

4. There were only sixteen classes held during the entire summer semester.

Reference

National Council of Teachers of Mathematics Working Group. 1989. *Curriculum and Evaluation Standards for School Mathematics*. Reston, VA: National Council of Mathematics.

12

Building the WAC Culture at Quinnipiac

Kathleen M. McCourt
Vice President for Academic Affairs

When I arrived at Quinnipiac in the summer of 2001, the Writing Across the Curriculum (WAC) initiative was underway, but in its early stages and with goals that were still in the process of being developed. A director had been hired the year before to oversee the effort, and he made it clear to me, as he had to the university president and my predecessor, that there could be no overnight miracles. He spoke of the need to transform the university culture, to create new values, new pedagogical practices, and new expectations. We agreed such cultural transformations take time. He was confident that he had, and insistent that he must continue to have, institutional support. While encouraged by his enthusiasm and confidence, at that point I was not certain where this program would fall among other priorities.

My previous position had been as dean of a liberal arts college where there was no doubt that writing should be paramount. Indeed, when I was a junior faculty member at that same institution, I had been involved in the launching of an ambitious Writing Across the Curriculum program that was closely woven into the general education requirements. At Quinnipiac, I had to address the question why an emphasis on writing should be a priority in a school whose primary mission has historically been preprofessional preparation in health sciences, business, and communications. While the liberal arts have long been a significant component of every undergraduate student's education at Quinnipiac, it is not the heart of the university's heritage.

My own liberal arts background continued to argue that it was one of the best things we could do for all our students. As it turned out, the accrediting associations for our professional programs were great allies in making this case. The AACSB-International, which accredits our School of Business, looks for a strong general education curriculum for business majors as well as the demonstration of writing proficiency specifically, along with other basic skills.

Our School of Communications is considering pursuing accreditation from the Accrediting Council on Education in Journalism and Mass Communications (ACEJMC); in discussions, ACEJMC representatives have been clear that the skills of the liberal arts, including writing, should be nurtured in the programs they accredit. In the School of Health Sciences, the associations accrediting our programs in such areas as nursing and physical therapy place a strong emphasis on demonstrable foundational skills, including writing. The Law School, in keeping with American Bar Association standards, has placed a strong emphasis on helping students develop written communication skills and requires that incoming students demonstrate their ability to write clearly. So Quinnipiac, with its mix of professional and liberal arts programs, became in my mind a natural for a writing program that really was designed to meet the curricular needs of the various schools.

Still, we were talking about cultural change. And it seemed clear that any significant cultural change would require that a critical number of senior faculty members buy into a new message about writing and intentionally restructure the ways in which they teach their classes. At the same time, the veteran faculty would need to communicate to new colleagues joining their departments that they really expected the pedagogical lessons of WAC to be adopted in their classrooms. This would mean getting deans and department chairs on board as well. It would mean that department committees take a focus on writing into account when reviewing course syllabi in the process of weighing progress toward promotion and tenure.

The WAC director was convinced that a balance between administrative support from the top and construction and dissemination of the program from the ranks of the faculty was the essential combination for success. Clearly the university's president and I both needed to speak publicly about our support of the program in order to convince the community that this was indeed an institutional goal. We did. In addition, the director was provided with a modest budget to invite speakers to campus and to purchase materials and lunches for faculty attending workshops.

Although the goal—to develop a first-rate writing program—was clearly articulated by the administration, the process—the way to get there—was not. The director and his committees were free to proceed in the way they believed would be most effective in winning the support of the faculty. While the director has conscientiously made progress reports and sought input from the administration, he has been pretty much left free to build the program according to his own best insights. The success of the program to date has been primarily due to the vision and the strategic thinking he brought to the process, along with the cooperation of a core group of faculty at every step. Building that committed cadre of faculty was an essential component for progress.

Early on a decision was made to link the faculty's local efforts as much as possible to national programs. The idea was to impress on this core group of professors that they were part of a national movement and to reduce any sense of isolation they might feel as they wrestled with seemingly intractable issues. Bringing recognized experts to campus to meet with faculty helped to locate Quinnipiac's program in a larger arena. The opportunity for six of the faculty to present their work as a team at the 2003 Conference on College Composition and Communication (CCCC) reinforced their sense of being at the heart of important pedagogical work. The overwhelmingly positive response of colleagues from other schools to their CCCC presentation helped these faculty members realize that their local efforts had already surpassed what was happening at many peer institutions. This was a great source of positive reinforcement. I realized quickly that the modest support provided to this group for attendance at the conference had been a worthwhile investment. Over time, some of the most committed participants have begun to feel that their efforts and the program they are building can be a force in shaping the national WAC movement.

Classes at Quinnipiac are kept fairly small with an average class size of twenty-two. Yet faculty have heavy teaching loads and the "draft, redraft" mission of WAC requires added instructor attention to each student's work. What would make a faculty member willing to invest the extra time required to respond to several versions of a student's paper? The chapters in this book, written by faculty who did invest that time, tell the story from their perspectives. As more faculty attended workshops and shared their enthusiasm for what they had learned, peer awareness began to build, and those who were unfamiliar with the program gradually began to learn more about it. Quinnipiac has approximately 275 full-time faculty members. Not all bought into the program, to be sure, but a core in each school underwent initial training and became proselytizers. The director then brought this core group of faculty members on board as fellow trainers; now they, in turn, are training colleagues in their own schools and departments, further expanding the circle of awareness and participation.

During the same time these developments were going on with writing, several other faculty committees were addressing issues central to our undergraduate programs. A key Faculty Senate committee was undertaking the work of reforming the core curriculum. At the heart of the newly approved core curriculum are three interdisciplinary university seminars, each of which will include a significant writing component. Another group was considering how best to assess student learning outcomes in both writing courses and the new core curriculum. Two years after the writing director began at Quinnipiac, the university hired a coordinator of assessment and academic research; the following year a new director of freshman composition was hired. With significant faculty input and some administrative support, these three, working as a team, put together a plan to undertake a serious assessment of how well the various writing initiatives are working—that is, the extent to which there will be measurable improvement in writing across the four years of our students' undergraduate education.

In addition to the core curriculum committee and the assessment committee, another group of faculty, the academic integrity committee, oversaw the implementation of a new policy by launching a universitywide educational focus on integrity in academic work. For obvious reasons, a significant focus of this committee's work has been on written assignments. Overlapping committee memberships and frequent conversations across groups have been necessary to coordinate efforts, maximize the impact of curricular change, and allow for systematic assessment. Writing has been a theme running through the combined efforts of these several faculty groups that are collectively contributing to the prospect of real and substantial institutional change.

Like other universities, Quinnipiac depends on its part-time faculty to supplement the staffing of courses in many of its programs, not only in business, communications, and health sciences where clinical or practical experience is invaluable to preprofessional students, but also in liberal arts courses. For writing to be truly integrated into the curriculum, we knew that part-time instructors would need to understand the pedagogy and commit to its values as much as full-time instructors. From the perspective of the student in the classroom and how she or he experiences learning, it may make little difference if the instructor is teaching a full load of courses or only that one particular course. Yet, adjunct faculty members, even when they might have the time, seldom have the encouragement or the support to engage in professional development activities.

The English department took the lead in recognizing both the importance of the role that part-time faculty play and the challenge of how to engage them as participants in the development of the writing program. When the department initiated a plan to assist faculty with the incorporation of computer technology into their writing classes, they immediately sought to include their adjunct colleagues. With significant cooperation from the university's office of academic technology, adjunct faculty members were provided with laptop computers and had access to programs for using technology in the classroom. The English department went further and proposed that those adjuncts who make a multiyear commitment to teach in the freshman writing program participate fully in faculty development activities and be provided with additional compensation for doing so. The dean and I agreed to this proposal and were able to successfully incorporate it into our budget planning. In other departments the integration of writing into courses taught by adjunct faculty remains uneven and more problematic, although a universitywide push to increase the participation of adjuncts in faculty development programs is underway.

In the fall of 2003, Quinnipiac was awarded a grant from the Davis Educational Foundation to support faculty development in the area of learning the skills for integrating writing into the various curricula. The grant award provided important affirmation to those members of the faculty who had committed time and energy to the program (as well as to the writing of the grant proposal) and provided the university with funds to launch an ambitious faculty development program that would continue through three summers and help the QUWAC team reach its goal of training seventy percent of the faculty. It also gave us further occasion to publicly proclaim the centrality of the writing program. In the first summer, within two weeks of announcement, we had signed on the target number of one hundred faculty, about equally divided between part-time and full-time.

While it is too early to declare transformation and victory, there are signs of some change in the culture. We were encouraged, for example, to see the results of the 2003 National Survey of Student Engagement, which indicated our first-year students were writing more papers, both short and long, than were their peers at comparable institutions. Assuming this early indicator really is a harbinger of change, what helped move us to this stage?

A key element was the right director, one with expertise, a clear charge, a focused agenda, and a knack for working effectively with both his administrative and faculty colleagues. The director's style is one of gentle but firm guidance and lots of positive feedback. He also believes in feeding the faculty, with both new ideas and lots of food. Importantly, deans were not left in the dark; as regular updates were provided to them, the deans could knowledgeably reinforce the goals of the program. Secondly, the director articulated a clear goal that was ambitious but attainable: a seventy percent rate of faculty participation in WAC workshops over the course of four years. The plan and its timeline were realistic; there were no illusions that this could be other than a multiyear plan. Third, the director was supported by two strong faculty committees. The EDWAC (English Department Writing Committee) assumed a leadership role in defining the writing mission of the college and laying the foundation with the English composition courses taken by all students; then the QUWAC (Quinnipiac University Writing Across the Curriculum) Committee, made up of faculty from all the undergraduate schools, was charged with moving the program beyond the English department in an incremental way, bringing in supportive faculty one by one. The resultant core group of committed faculty was essential; they signed on to be active participants over the multiple years of the plan, and their camaraderie was contagious. Finally, the faculty has been fortunate to have a very strong partner in the university's Learning Center, whose staff members have reinforced the principles of Writing to Learn and Writing in the Disciplines in their workshops and in their training of peer tutors.

The academic deans and I continue to support the efforts of the WAC team and their multiyear rollout plan because we are in agreement that the program is essential for the academic excellence we want to attain. Writing skills of entering freshmen, and too often those of graduating seniors, are not at the levels we want. An institutional focus on writing is right for our students and is consistent with the mission of the university. We are training future business managers, nurses, physical therapists, elementary school teachers, and broadcast journalists, all of whom will be more successful in their careers if they are proficient writers. Finally and pragmatically, our emphasis on writing says something extremely positive to the public about where our priorities are and how much we value our students' personal and professional success.

Supporting the WAC Initiative

A Learning Center's Perspective

Andrew Delohery

Director of the Learning Center

As we began this process, I thought that supporting a WAC (Writing Across the Curriculum) initiative would be fairly easy: bring on more writing tutors to support more students because more faculty were going to use writing as a means to evoke critical responses from their students; be more aggressive in soliciting syllabi of faculty participating in WAC; be present at more department meetings where faculty may express need in supporting the writing of their students; in short, be prepared to support more students being asked to do more writing. This initiative should represent a good opportunity—very good—considering we have a long history of supporting writing at Quinnipiac University. Consequently, it's tempting to buy into the default ethos, "We've been doing *this* anyway." Yet, as we continue forward with our WAC initiative, I'm finding that the word *this* carries significant baggage. While looking for opportunity to provide support to new programs or initiatives has been productive in the past, we are finding that we need to be a bit more introspective.

While an increase in writing seems to be happening to a degree, we find ourselves negotiating the needs and expectations of at least three audiences: students, faculty, and the institution. Each audience comes to us with specific needs. Students are focused on meeting faculty expectations. Faculty are interested in supporting their students. The institution is interested in supporting both student and faculty in an efficient, effective manner. And, within these three audiences, differences remain. Traditionally, many consider *writing* to be a product. Students write a paper, an essay, a report, and that product earns a grade. In WAC terms, the product earning a grade represents a transaction between the writer and the audience, in most cases the student and the professor. Indeed, in his text *Language and Learning* (1970), James Britton names this type of writing "transactional writing." At the other end of the gradient is the idea of process—the paper, essay, or report as a record of a thinking process. Hence, increasing emphasis is placed on what Britton has called "expressive writing," to explore ideas or opinions in the early stages of composition. In her text *Grammar for Teachers,* Constance Weaver notes that "we write in order to represent, clarify and express our ideas and feelings to ourselves and others" (1979, 56).

We are all aware of writing as product. Students are not surprised to see a research paper assignment as they peruse the syllabus. Faculty have been known to shudder as they remember their theses and dissertations. Yet we tend to identify these experiences by pointing to a pile of papers, to a product rather than to the experience through which we went to construct the thinking that pile of papers represents. Writing Across the Curriculum attempts to remind us that the expressive writing is necessary if we want to make the transactional writing better. If we want to effect significant change in the product, we need to begin with change in the process. This very premise segments our three audiences still further because each individual is at a difference place in validating process or product. We're hoping we can develop and support a community that will validate both.

With one more solid week of tutoring to go in the spring semester of 2004, the staff of the Learning Center knew that of the 2,571 tutorials we've provided, 504 of them have been in the service of writing. The demand for writing tutorials tends to claim about 20 percent of the tutorials taken each spring semester. Last fall semester, we logged 720 writing tutorials of the 4,285 taken, closer to 17 percent, reflecting a consistent demand for writing tutorials.

In addition to the peer tutoring, students have attended the weekly drop-in Learning Skills Seminars, developed and delivered by our assistant director, Judy Villa. At these seminars, offered twice each week, we can expect between fifteen and forty-five students to attend, being drawn by titles like "Tame Your Text; Read and Remember," "Run, Don't Walk from Plagiarism," and "Write the Right Essay." These seminars have proven so popular that faculty attend, looking for other methods to help their students reach their learning objectives. In fact, for the past few semesters, we have been facing a growing demand— invitations to develop course-specific seminars and deliver them during the class meeting time for best effect.

So, we have been busy and successful. Student feedback is mostly positive. Faculty are pleased with our support of their students' writing. Our numbers look good (over 40 percent of our undergraduate students used our services in the fall semester of 2003). So where's the challenge?

In "Writing Centers and WAC," Joan Mullen claims, "the connection between instructor, student, and WAC and writing centers provides generative feedback through continual reflective assessment about the learning process; in every case, language is being renegotiated, and faculty, students, and center are responding to immediate contextual needs" (2001). Our *contextual needs* are changing. Increasingly, students and faculty are changing the manner in which they find value in writing and where they find that writing. More and more emphasis is being placed on process as a means to product, partially contradicting traditionally accepted values of the product as the goal. Consequently, part of our challenge will be to continue this level of service to an academic community that is involved in renegotiations—*renegotiation* indicating that our audience will be both those with new support expectations, and those still expecting support similar to their past experience. In addition, part of our challenge will be to assist with the renegotiations themselves.

Earlier I mentioned the various elements that contribute to our success—the tutoring, the seminars, the big numbers, the community value. Taken for granted, these otherwise successful aspects of the Learning Center could be construed to work against the tenets of WAC. Perhaps I'm pushing the Damocles analogy a bit too far, but it's worth consideration if we hope to support a WAC initiative to the expectations of our three audiences.

Many students faced with a writing assignment want to know "the right way" to do the assignment. For them, the emphasis is on correctness, which means myopic attention to grammar, mechanics, and proofreading. They are too often concerned with comma splices and other aspects of proofreading than they are with any deep revision. Clearly, they often privilege form over content.

Indeed, many students coming for tutoring are most interested in the "right" answer. Given their experiences, their harried schedules, and their expectations, they have not the time, the patience, nor the desire to renegotiate themselves within the evolving discussion of new material. They want the right answer. Consequently, our response to demand for this type of support is one challenge that we face in supporting a WAC initiative. If we meet this demand by providing support that privileges writing as a product, we may send the wrong message about WAC, about what we do, and about how useful we may be. However, if we try to change the students' focus to look at aspects of their expressive writing in an attempt to help their transactional writing, they may become frustrated, thinking that this strategy can't or won't help, at least not with the initial problem that was defined.

In his text *Engaging Ideas*, John Bean discusses what developmental psychologists have called "cognitive egocentrism." According to Bean's summary, when people first encounter difficult material—students new to university or students in a course where they didn't expect to find writing—they tend to restructure the material in a way that is less threatening to them. Nothing new here, and, really, nothing wrong. However, he goes on to claim that despite the intentions of the person offering the information, "students translate those meanings into ideas that they are really comfortable with" (Bean 1996, 135). So it seems that a student looking for help with proofreading might not hear the tutor's suggestions about coherence. The student, like other students who value the service of the Learning Center, wants the right answer, rather than the observation that might challenge his or her assumptions and prompt a fruitful deep revision.

Similarly, we support many students who have been referred by faculty. In the case of writing, many professors, upon attempting to grade an essay too replete with grammatical errors, will recommend that the student "go to the Learning Center." Now, the phrase "go to the Learning Center" can serve as a euphemism for many things, including "this paper needs corrections I don't want to offer" or "this paper needs corrections I can't offer." So the student, hoping to transact the best grade for the paper, comes to the Learning Center—at the professor's behest—to get the paper fixed.

Our own diction—the language with which we present ourselves to our audiences—also runs the risk of serving this perception of correctness. Students and faculty alike look for the right answer, the rule to follow to make the presentation better, the paper well documented, the assignment clearly understood. While these expectations are valid, they can also reinforce the wrong message, potentially conflicting with the dynamic that WAC seeks to promote. Ironically, we have, to a certain degree, been reinforcing the perception of correctness through some of our own language. One of our most successful Learning Skills Seminars is titled "Write the Right Essay"; we have students signing up for repeat performances and faculty asking us to present this workshop in their classes. Yet, here is an example of the power of language and its ability to inform the support of a campuswide initiative. Using language like this, we may be perceived to be supporting emphasis on transactional writing, often to the exclusion of expressive writing. Students and faculty alike seek the format, the rules, the information that will speak to the right, the correct, the best way to present their material. Too much emphasis on transactional writing as the most important part of the writing process, implied though it may be, can reinforces the tradition we are seeking to change with a WAC initiative. Our own language can work against us.

So we need to carefully cultivate the perception of our clients, faculty as well as students. Being regarded as the ultimate editorial service will not serve a WAC initiative, nor will it serve the development of the Learning Center or the academic community it, in turn, serves. We will continue to provide very good service, following the demand of our community. Now, that demand may be changing. The degree to which it changes will be informed by the role we play in supporting WAC.

As we meet this challenge, we've begun to notice that not everyone is in the same place. Not each first-year student is totally focused on form. Members of our community—our clients—have varying degrees of need. Consequently, if we are going to continue to meet demand, we must account for the varying needs of our audiences. As we think of ways to help students and faculty renegotiate their learning, we must also continue to help those who want us to help them fix their comma splices. So, as we continue to provide peer tutoring, offer seminars, and collaborate with faculty, we will also begin to renegotiate some of our own language.

One place we'll begin to look is our contact with clients. Far and away, the greatest point of contact with clients is through our Peer Tutoring Program. Our program, certified by the College Reading and Learning Association (CRLA) to the Master Level, requires significant training of our peer tutors. While they come to us with a cumulative GPA of 3.0 or better, an A or A− in the courses they support, and three faculty references, they also undergo at least one semester of our training. This training, ten hours for each level (one through three), deals with the affective components of tutoring.

As I mentioned earlier, historical demand for writing support is around 20 percent of our total demand, with about one-third of our undergraduates using our tutoring service. Given that we support over two hundred individual courses, 20 percent for one topic is considerable. Consequently, we require a few more hours of content training for our writing tutors. Typically, we require another seven to eight hours of writing-specific training, delivered for the most part by our assistant director, who has led classes in both the English and the Education departments.

The tutor training, both the specialized writing training and the regimented affective training, is integral to how we can support a WAC initiative. The affective training develops an environment informed by the old proverb "give a man a fish, feed him for a day . . . ." Our tutors, even as they provide support, do so in a way that moves toward making them obsolete. Besides offering initial scaffolding that helps clients solve problems, they model and coach attack strategies that clients begin to internalize and practice across discipline boundaries. As our clients progress in their academic development, two things can happen. They develop adequate skills so that they no longer need us, as is indicated by our demographic history. Roughly 70 percent of our clients are first- or second-year students. The remaining 30 percent or so is roughly split between third- and fourth-year students. The other thing that happens is a change in relationship; clients continue to work with our tutors, but more on the level of peer to peer, rather than tutor to client.

So a basic premise of our WAC initiative—writing promotes critical thinking—is incorporated into our writing training. Among the various topics, our tutors are trained to focus first on "HOTs" and then, after working on HOTs, they move to "LOTs." HOTs—higher-order things—correspond to the elements one might recognize as deep revision. Here, tutors attempt to focus their clients on issues of idea development, coherence, cohesion, organization—many of the tasks that require more metacognition, which is definitely not the expectation of clients who use tutoring "to have their papers proofread." Initially, the clients, and often, their faculty, default to our tutors to provide the LOTs—lower-order things—such as punctuation, grammar, and the like before their ideas have come to fruition or have been adequately developed. In his text *Writing Without Teachers*, Peter Elbow notes that "Writing is not a transmission of a message but is a way to grow and cook a message"(1998). Elbow's claim speaks to the dynamic inherent in WAC; writing helps us think about what we want to say. Investing time in HOTs will yield a better thought as well as a better articulation of that thought. Selling clients on the inherent value of a HOTs-first approach—when they work with a tutor during an initial meeting or as they work independent of class or Learning Center—continues to be very important to our WAC initiative.

Our tutor training is informed by another perspective, as well. Our relationship with the Freshman Writing Program bears directly on our ability to support a WAC initiative. On the one hand, we need to know the objectives of our two-course first-year writing sequence. To provide a consistent level of support and a consistent message to clients, our tutors must be aware of writing faculty expectations. On the other hand, in order to continue supporting the clients—students and faculty alike—who are coming to us for LOTs-level support, our tutors' evident knowledge of specific course learning objectives gains us significant validity. The line of logic is disarmingly simple: if our tutors know what our clients will be expected to do, we should be able to provide better service. Even though we may not validate premature focus on LOTs (basic editing, proofreading, and the like), we must be in a position to support these demands. As early as the second training session, our writing tutors are oriented to supporting LOTs-focused clients, discussing topics such as "the basis for college writing success" and "constructivism and trusting the student writer."

As a regular part of writing tutor training, our director of Freshman Writing works with our tutors, training them in the very same aspects of pedagogy that are employed in faculty development. Since nearly all our first-year students follow our two-semester composition sequence (English 101 and English 102), we can expect our historic demand for writing to be at least consistent, but with more emphasis on WAC, the demand for writing support may increase. We want this support to be useful and consistent. We, therefore, make sure that our tutors know what is happening with all first-year classes in the core curriculum and with freshman English. Discussion in the tutor meetings ranges from "helping students to situate themselves in the text" to various methods for engendering deeper reading and more critical response. Included also is training in methodology to focus clients more on deep revision rather than on premature light editing. This specialized training helps our tutors support students newly come to Quinnipiac's writing expectations, ensuring that the tutors are included in the discussion of departmental expectations. It also helps our more seasoned tutors to stay current with the aims and objectives of the writing program. In addition, it allows the director of the writing program another source of information to help her evaluate various objectives. Information gathered by peer tutors and archived at the Learning Center can offer insight into the efficacy of a program and its methods.

It's interesting to note that our inclusion of department-focused training (in this case, the English department) has not given rise to any concerns about tutors being too focused on disciplinary conventions, or, conversely, tutors supporting writing in a discipline whose conventions are unfamiliar to them. Many writers have weighed in on what Kristin Walker calls "the debate over generalist and specialist tutors." Some question the efficacy of tutors who have little or no content-specific knowledge offering support to a student whose writing assignment calls for the use of discipline-specific conventions. This is a worthy concern, and one that bears directly on the success of supporting a WAC initiative, reinforcing writing as transaction and not as process. Handled poorly, this interaction could reinforce the wrong perception of the role of the Learning Center, and, in the long run, the foundation of WAC.

Implicit in the generalist/specialist discussion is an important assumption, one that bears directly on training. The assumption is that a writing tutor who doesn't share the discipline-specific content with a client will default to identifying issues of correctness, issues that we associate with our LOTs training. Indeed, this default to a comfort zone, in this case grammar and mechanics, is a common response when our authority is challenged. We tend to look for things we know, and not to think in a more global, reflective manner. (Bean's idea of cognitive egocentrism, mentioned earlier, can apply to tutors and the manner by which they field a client's questions as well.) A writing tutor asked to support writing in a convention he or she doesn't tutor for content might feel more comfortable identifying comma splices, subject/verb agreement issues, and other lower-order, editorial issues. Again, while this type of support is absolutely necessary, it must be offered at the right time of a client's writing process. If the client has had an opportunity to think about deep revision, it may be time to focus on LOTs. Offered at the wrong time, however, this type of support misconstrues the usefulness of the Learning Center and, ultimately, can hurt the premise of WAC. Consequently, tutor training takes on even more importance.

Something that helps our writing tutors offer timely support is a previous draft of the student's writing with professor remarks. Certainly, reading over the professor's comments helps the tutor focus on issues regarded as pertinent by the professor leading the class. The tutor is better able to understand the professor's requirements and better able to show more immediate return to the student seeking to improve the paper. But perhaps as important, these comments also provide a window into the orientation of the faculty member's perspective as regards writing. A faculty member more focused on editing and proofreading will provide comments substantially different from the professor interested in revision. Combinations of revision-oriented annotation and editing-oriented annotation often occur, as well. A professor may attend to both editing (LOTs) and in the same paper mention revision (HOTs). Regardless of the type of comment, this annotation can help the writing tutor evaluate to what degree the student is meeting the professor's expectations.

With the right attention to training, writing tutors can feel comfortable supporting their clients in a manner consistent with many current pedagogies, as well as with our WAC initiative. An underlying premise of our tutor training sequence is one of collaboration. Currently, many campuses are abuzz with words like "constructivism," "problem-based inquiry," and other theories that acknowledge the usefulness of collaboration. In our tutor training, we have for some time privileged collaboration as an important means not only to support our clients, but also to move them farther down the road of self-sufficiency. The dynamics of a tutorial that expects collaboration also creates an environment that supports the WAC initiative. When a tutor treats a client as a colleague, as a partner in the assignment, the client is more likely to embrace the ownership and responsibility that come with writing. In doing so, the client moves away from more simple, LOTs-type issues and engages in more sophisticated thinking about the writing. Our training helps the writing tutor supporting a client in a discipline outside the tutor's areas to focus the line of question on higher-order issues. For example, the tutor can ask many questions to direct attention to more sophisticated issues and engender collaboration. They can be discipline-specific, but from a perspective that demands the client's responsible contribution. Asking the client "Should a person writing for biology begin with a hypothesis?" requires that the client bring his or her knowledge to the table, engaging the student in thinking that collaborates toward a goal that the student ultimately defines. Here, the student brings his or her own "expertise" to the tutorial, establishing a working relationship with the writing tutor.

The questions can also engage the client from a nondiscipline perspective. Simply asking the client "What is this essay about?" begins the process of ownership, the dialectic that requires the client's reflection and expression of his or her idea. Phrased correctly, the question can ask for analysis, synthesis, and eventually evaluation from the client regarding the assignment. "Now that we've discussed your purpose, which topic do you think best supports your claim?" "Which topic is most problematic?" "Who is your audience?" "Now that we know your audience, what will be the most important part of this paper to have them understand?" "What, specifically, have you done to deliver your message to the audience you've identified?" Questions like these require more engagement on the part of the client. Consequently, these kinds of questions allow the writing tutor to create an atmosphere of collaboration more easily. The client, perhaps for the first time coming to terms with the assignment, can begin to rise above the "correctness" of the assignment and begin to think on a more sophisticated level.

There may be times when the client cannot provide the discipline-specific information. If this occurs, the tutor can make an opportunity from this deficit by recommending that the client meet with the faculty member who assigned the writing. Creating this kind of triad—professor, student, tutor—and seeking every opportunity to build from it is a tremendous benefit to all parties concerned. Students realize that this kind of behavior is appropriate at a university. Faculty are generally pleased that their students are taking time to thoughtfully address their assignments. Tutors have provided support and scaffolding in a manner that builds validity and support for the Learning Center and have done so in a way that precludes any stress of not knowing the "right" answer. All these benefits taken together create a wonderfully supportive environment for the WAC initiative.

Additionally, a discussion regarding the issues presented by the specialist/generalist discussion is helpful in another issue. It can also speak to the recalcitrant faculty member who might claim exception from helping students take ownership and responsibility for their writing. I've had many faculty tell me that "writing is not my area" or "I'm a specialist; I don't support writing."

These faculty, of course, regard writing as the product of the student's experience, as opposed to writing as a vehicle for the student's process. These are the same faculty who tend to send their students to the Learning Center for "writing" when they really mean "correctness." Helping faculty realign their ideas about writing's usefulness to their students—and ultimately, to themselves—remains a challenge. Often, we need to recognize that faculty, much like our tutors, much like our clients, are loath to leave their disciplines for a different view. Changing the dynamic of the experience, creating opportunities for collaboration, offers significant progress.

Now, changing the dynamic can be touchy. It is, however, well worth the effort. The assumption that provides the challenge is that writing is best used to produce a product. The members of our community who hold this assumption tend to be the clients and the faculty looking for our tutors to proofread the writing assignment, to help make it correct. This emphasis on product over process is the very challenge we face. Faculty making this assumption are likely to resist including writing in their classes, often citing the need to cover content, and not having the time to include writing. Note here the focus on foundational information, information like vocabulary terms and basic formulae. Like the student coming to the writing tutor for proofreading, faculty can focus on the LOTs-level of information. In this case, just as the student is interested in measuring the grammar, spelling, and punctuation, the faculty member is interested in measuring content. In the earlier strategy employed by the writing tutor working outside his or her discipline, changing the scope of the question can work here as well. In addition, not only can it help move the student toward better learning, but it can also help faculty feel more comfortable in responding to their students' writing. One of the tools we've found useful to help with this change comes from John Bean's text. Bean offers some suggestions to begin the discussion about editing-oriented comments and revision-oriented comments (67–70), including making sure not to overload papers with comments about surface-level errors and, thus, creating the impression that more serious concerns are no more serious than a dropped comma or a misplaced modifier.

In each case mentioned above, a consistent dynamic emerges. Acknowledging the different intentions of the questions and comments raised by tutors or by faculty identifies a fairly consistent parallel to the cognitive domain of Bloom's Taxonomy of Educational Objectives (Bloom et al. 1984). Posed correctly, questions that solicit a student's reflection on her motives for a particular act or decision can be very powerful. Asking the student to identify and explain what she feels is the strongest point of her writing requires other aspects of more sophisticated cognition, such as analysis and synthesis. Asking a student to explain his choice of diction given the intended audience asks for evaluation. Asking the student to identify and explain what he feels is the strongest point of his writing requires other aspects of more sophisticated cognition, such as analysis and synthesis. The student is required to contextualize the effectiveness of his discourse. The question may be in the context of a discipline, but it doesn't have to be. As mentioned earlier, the adroit writing tutor uses questions that plumb the knowledge base of the client. This type of questioning is not just a tutor survival skill, allowing the tutor to snatch a tutorial from the jaws of mediocrity. This type of questioning engages the client on a level that requires acknowledgement of his or her own contribution, which can be a powerful heuristic lesson.

I would also think that questions like these, validated by their use by "experts" (the perception of the faculty and sometimes of the tutor by the student) and the result derived from them can inform affective development as well as cognitive. A client hearing a tutor ask about audience might be influenced to think of this question on his own. A student responding to a professor's question regarding her motivation for a particular organization of topics might be better prepared next time to accept this higher-order thinking as what's expected at a university. These kinds of questions—questions that foster thinking about HOTs—disabuse students of the notion of right and wrong while moving them toward a discussion between better and best. Rather than measuring the experience by absolutes, they begin to think in terms of degrees, degrees affected by the choices made by the student as writer. Done well, this can also bring the student to a new level of awareness about his or her writing.

When identifying the challenges of supporting a WAC initiative, another issue presents itself. We need to be concerned about the way we present our services, the way we communicate with our community. We offer various methods of outreach (advertising, referral service) and feedback (professor reports, semester standings). In each case, we must evaluate our language to make sure our message is consistent and that it supports the WAC dynamic. For example, we offer faculty an electronic writing referral form. With this form, faculty can refer students to the Learning Center for specific attention. This form, located on our website, allows faculty to refer students to us for specific writing support. This form, part of which is reproduced in Figure 12-1, has been constructed to ask for specific types of information. Faculty can identify as many boxes as they like, but they must select at least one box for the page to work.

When we developed this form, we attempted to use language that would serve a community with various needs and values. We attempted to develop language that would serve the professor suggesting support for LOTs and also the professor interested in the student dealing with HOTs. We do not wish to marginalize either need. Consequently, the option to refer a student to work on proofreading speaks to the end of the process, the LOTs phase of support. There are, however, other options that speak to organization and development, which speak more to deep revision, or the HOTs phase of support. This public face of our service needs to respond to that audience I mentioned earlier, the audience involved with renegotiating its perspective regarding writing. In the same way the type of question asked of students may impact cognition and affect, the manner in which we solicit information, privileging certain infor-

Learning Center Web Referral Form

☐ Assignment Directions   ☐ Stronger Summary or Conclusion
☐ Paper Organization   ☐ Stronger Lead in the Introduction
☐ Clear Thesis   ☐ Stronger Development in Body Paragraph(s)
☐ Transitional Elements   ☐ Stronger Word Choice (Diction), Vocabulary
☐ More Sentence Variety   ☐ More Attention to Proofreading

... In respect to the reference paper:

☐ General MLA or APA Typing Format Instructions
☐ Forming the Argumentative Thesis
☐ Integration of Quoted/Paraphrased Material into Text
☐ Proper Use of Citations Indicating Sources
☐ Paraphrasing that is "Too Close" to the Original Quote

When this form is submitted to the Learning Center by clicking on the **'Submit Request'** button, a confirming email will also be sent to you for your records at the email address entered, above.

Students needing special accommodations should be referred to Mr. John Jarvis, Learning Center, 582-5390.

[Submit Request]

Figure 12–1

mation over other information, can help or hinder our ability to support the WAC initiative.

Communication with faculty has been a long-standing priority for us. Indeed, if we are to be useful, we need to support what happens in the classroom. Consequently, we maintain very good lines of communication with faculty, both giving and receiving information that will help support the student. One of the ways we maintain contact with faculty is our optional professor report. At the student's request, we send professor reports to faculty on behalf of their students using our tutoring. (Approximately 97 percent of our clients ask that a report be sent.) These reports offer specific information to the professor regarding topics covered, time spent, and possible further needs of the student. Students like to have their professors know they've come for support. Faculty enjoy the feedback this report provides, and they like the idea that their students consider their assignments to merit attention. These reports also allow our staff to identify trends that are helpful with our own development and staffing. In fact, these reports have often led to collaboration among student, faculty, and staff. These professor reports are integral in maintaining communication among the players. Given this utility, these professor reports represent another facet of our growing introspection. They represent another means by which we can serve the WAC initiative. The language we employ should inherently describe writing to clarify and to express ideas. It should assume that our audiences will be interested in writing as expression and as transaction. If we make this assumption, the language will speak to people at all places of the writing process.

Another means of communication with faculty is our Semester Standings Report. We contact faculty at the end of the semester, offering them information regarding their students' use of our tutoring. We supply various bits of information—how many students, how many times, for which topics—in the hope that it will be useful for their review. Our goal is simple—to make faculty aware of our level of support, organizing their students' declared needs by topic. (See Figure 12-2.) Through this simple email message, faculty can see another facet of their students' educational process. The information represents a self-reporting of sorts, from the student's perspective. In most cases, students come to use tutoring of their own volition, identifying topics of concern on

THE LEARNING CENTER
Quinnipiac University

Hello Professor Delohery:

I'd like to share with you some data about your students collected through the Learning Center. The information below was gathered over the course of 03FA. Over the course of last semester, 27 of your EN 101 students came in 47 times for tutoring. Below is a list of the top five topics they discussed, listed by frequency. Please contact me if you have any questions.

Topic	Frequency
Revising	33
Citations	17
Punctuation/Grammar	17
Body Paragraphs	16
Thesis Statement	16

Figure 12-2

their own and as indicated by the professor's notes on a given writing assign-ment. Of course, as the tutorial progresses, our writing tutors may steer a client toward a particular need they have identified, but the resulting topical informa-tion can provide some insight to faculty that is not available in the classroom. The topical information in this report is organized by frequency, indicating the most occurring topic of discussion first.

This report offers us a challenge as well as a window on our tutoring pro-gram. The challenge is the tone we set forth as we present this information. This tone is indicated by diction, specifically the jargon we may inadvertently employ. For example, the word "revise" takes on specific meaning in the con-text of WAC. We look for evidence of deep revision as an aspect of a healthy WAC initiative. But given our audience, "revise" may mean different things to different people. Faculty understanding this word as being substantially differ-ent from "edit" will understand the level of support we provided differently than will a faculty member who has not entered the WAC discussion. So, as mentioned earlier, we face the challenge of communication with an audience at different stages of renegotiation with writing in their curriculum.

Both of these last two aspects of communication help us meet another challenge—that of validity. We already enjoy the respect and confidence of many professors and students as regards our ability to support their writing. Again, when we qualify the term "writing" to mean product, different disci-plines have different conventions. Journalism professors require clear, concise writing. Composition faculty often expect a student to experiment with style, searching for the best way to express his or her "voice." What a composition professor may see as a positive experiment in style, a journalism professor may see as a negative exercise in florid prose. If we are going to support their stu-dents to the degree that they will send us business, we need to show that we un-derstand and value the discourse pertinent to the assignment and its audience. The Professor Report affords us the opportunity to indicate to faculty that our tutors understand and discuss discipline-specific conventions. The tutor's prose narrative can indicate the degree to which he or she understands the con-ventions and how he or she helped the client to embrace them. The Semester Standing Report acts in a similar manner. The topics listed in the report can speak to our awareness of discipline conventions. Using the terms and phrases that are discipline specific conveys our awareness of them and our commitment to support students in a manner that befits their discipline's expectations. Both of these reports provide the necessary means for continued communication and collaboration.

Increasingly, it's becoming apparent that our message about process is consistent. Keeping engaged in the discussions—whether institutional or indi-vidual—as our audience renegotiates their needs seems to be the best way to move forward. As we continue fostering and supporting the collaboration, we try to maintain discussion among the players. In fact, CRLA's notion of the triad—student, professor, tutor—as significant tool for meaningful learning places us in a good position to support a WAC initiative. Peshe Kuriloff, former director of Writing Across the University at Penn State, observed the following: "To the extent that we identify ourselves as serving the needs of students and student learning, we have an obligation to use feedback to improve learning." Here at the Learning Center, we are in a good position to help with this obligation. The challenge will be keeping abreast of the various discussions and providing useful information (support, data, and the like) to our changing audiences. We must continue to engage faculty in discussions about their disciplines' convention, collaborating on the means to better support their students. We hope to exploit these relationships primarily to move the client's perspective closer to deep revision as a normal part of the thinking and writing sequence. We also hope we can, by affecting some change to the student's attitude about thinking and writing during the tutorial, begin to inform what happens in the classroom as well.

References

Bean, John C. 1996. *Engaging Ideas*. San Francisco: Jossey-Bass.

Bloom, Benjamin, et al., eds. 1984. *Taxonomy of Educational Objectives: Cognitive Domain*. New York: Longman.

Britton, James, et al. 1975. *The Development of Writing Abilities*. London: Macmillan Education.

Britton, James, 1970. *Language and Learning*. Hamondsworth, England: Penguin Books.

Elbow, Peter. 1998. *Writing Without Teachers*. 3rd ed. Oxford: Oxford University Press.

Kuriloff, Peshe. 1999. "Writing Centers as WAC Centers: An Evolving Model." *Writing Centers and Writing Across the Curriculum*. Westport, CT: Greenwood Press.

Mullen, Joan. 2001. "Writing Centers and WAC." In *WAC for the New Millennium*. Susan McLeod, et al. Urbana, IL: NCTE.

Walker, Kristin. 1998. "The Debate Over Generalist and Specialist Tutors: Genre Theory's Contribution." *The Writing Center Journal* 18 (2): 27–46.

Weaver, Constance. 1979. *Grammar for Teachers: Perspectives and Definitions*. Urbana, IL: NCTE.

13

Decolonizing the Academy

WAC and Institutional Recognition and Reward Systems

Robert A. Smart
Professor of English

Mary T. Segall
Assistant Professor of English

In the preceding chapters, faculty members from across the disciplines have demonstrated WAC (Writing Across the Curriculum) strategies in their teaching, all of them in support of their desire to help students learn more efficiently and to report the results of that learning more effectively in formal writing assignments. Their investment in WAC was born not of institutional mandate, but of a genuine desire to improve student learning. At the time of this writing, nineteen different departments from all five schools on our campus are represented by the faculty involved in WAC training workshops.[1] Their voluntary participation is the kind of involvement that Miraglia and McLeod refer to as one crucial factor in sustaining a WAC program (1997, 48). While our contributors have embraced WAC, they have naturally selected various principles and applications of WAC as they pertain to their disciplines and as they provide pedagogical advantage in large section classes. Nonetheless, they have all approached the challenge of implementing WAC strategies with intellectual rigor. Many have found their classes enriched, as has Peter Elbow, who explains: "I can now teach a 'product' of literature by using active, experiential workshop activities I learned as a teacher of writing—and thereby increase the chances of students actually *experiencing* the literary work and the critical concepts they are studying" (2002, 535). Noteworthy in Elbow's remarks is his sense that using an essentially WAC strategy resolves the common and traditional opposition between the "product" of literature and the "activities" of the writing classroom. This theoretical "nesting," we argue, is key to the value and success of WAC programs nationally. In fact, we argue that WAC has been and continues to be revolutionary, in the sense that these programs offer the most integrated and inclusive institutional means for bringing change to all the levels of the academic hierarchy: "To effect real change in abilities as basic as writing and learning, these [WAC] programs have asked, tacitly in most cases, that instructors alter as well their perceptions of other dimensions of the academic community: for example, (1) the role of language in learning, (2) their relationship to students in the classroom, (3) their interactions with colleagues in other disciplines, and (4) the nature of the academic institution itself" (Fulwiler 1991, 179).

One of the more "revolutionary" aspects of WAC is that it provokes the question of how the university situates and values faculty work in writing (WAC). Regardless of the particular focus or application within their disciplines, our contributors demonstrate a serious scholarship attendant to WAC programs, an intellectual aspect that often goes unrecognized or is mistakenly viewed simply as "service" to the community. In the Writing Program Administration (WPA) document, "Evaluating the Intellectual Work of Writing Administration," editors Charles Schuster, Robert Schwegler, and Judy Pearce note the prevailing attitude that writing administration (as virtually any writing work in the academy), "does not produce new knowledge and . . . neither requires nor demonstrates scholarly expertise and disciplinary knowledge" (1998, 85). We would argue that the research represented by our contributors does meet the criteria for scholarly knowledge because the application of WAC principles to one's discipline requires not only special expertise in the particular discipline, but also in WAC principles and strategies. The intellectual challenge of how the integration of the two will produce better teaching (a criterion valued for promotion) and learning is, in itself, a way of producing new knowledge.

In addition to the WPA document already cited, the Academic Association of Higher Education also "advocates the viewing of multiple kinds of scholarship, including the scholarship of discovery, the scholarship of teaching, the scholarship of integration, and the scholarship of engagement," a position developed from the pioneering study of institutional rewards and promotion systems by Ernest Boyer in 1990 (Boyer 1990). Individuals such as Carrie Leverenz in her article "Tenure and Promotion in Rhetoric and Composition" (2000), poignantly reveal the personal cost to faculty who pursue academic work in writing only to find that when their work is offered as evidence for promotion, it is devalued by review committees. The broadening of the traditional definition of scholarly work is further addressed by Robert Diamond and Bronwyn E. Adam, editors of *The Disciplines Speak: Rewarding the Scholarly, Professional, and Creative Work of Faculty* (1995). The fact that professional organizations are grappling with the issue of institutional reward underscores the point that in order for faculty outside English to embrace WAC and to be rewarded for doing so, the definitions of knowledge and *scholarship* need to include the intellectual work of those faculty who analyze and quantify the application of WAC principles in their disciplines. The WPA document ("Evaluating the Intellectual Work of Writing Administration") specifically recommends the following for evaluating writing program administrators: "We urge that material and policies for evaluation of writing administration focus on these areas:

- Program Creation
- Curricular Design
- Faculty Development
- Program Assessment and Evaluation (WPA, "Evaluating the Intellectual Work of Writing Administration" 99).

While the WPA document is specific to writing program administrators, the basic tenets remain consistent with our view that faculty involved in WAC programs can and do construct knowledge that deserves scholarly recognition and reward, not least because in the most successful WAC programs that we know, faculty play a larger administrative role than most other faculty and curricular reform movements require. The WPA guidelines for evaluation (listed above) could well serve as a template, or at least a starting point, for an examination of how faculty are recognized and rewarded for their work within the institution. One promising example is evident in *English Department Guidelines for Promotion and Tenure,* from Loyola University. The revised 1998 document specifies three areas of assessment: teaching, scholarship, and service. In the first two of the five items under the scholarship category, recognition of scholarship in composition is made explicit: "(1) published or publishable work in composition, language, and literature in such generally recognized modes as historical, biographical, social, bibliographic and textual scholarship; (2) published or publishable work in criticism and theory of composition." Significantly, the language that describes rewardable scholarly and pedagogical activity specifically identifies the most contested areas within English Studies as valuable within the promotion and rewards equation of the department and the institution. If this age-old opposition within the English department can be so productively resolved at institutions like Loyola, could a resolution of the same issue with regards to WAC be so unthinkable? Both Toby Fulwiler (1991, 186) and Charles I. Schuster (1991) have suggested such a change in institutional reward systems, the latter calling for a shift in metaphors in the description of disciplines (including the study of literature) and writing in general from complementarity to something closer to Bakhtin's notion of dialogism, which "maintains the power of both" (Schuster 1991, 94).

All these issues and contradictions, played out both on our campus and nationally, have a powerful historical and political origin, one which is important to consider briefly as we explore the power of WAC to resolve these historical and political paradoxes. Anybody seeking to understand the current institutional rewards situation for faculty who devote a significant amount of their professional time to writing-across-the-curriculum would do well to begin with Stephen Arata's monumental study of the waning of the British Empire, *Fictions of Loss in the Victorian Fin de Siècle:*

> With the professionalizing of English . . . came the adoption of those "masculine" values traditionally associated with the professional: rationality, rigor, objectivity, a commitment to explicit standards governing the production of knowledge, and the embrace of that "clean cold detachment" counseled, in a different context, by Eliot. With the triumph of the professional came the promise, too, that the institutionally guided study of literature would somehow be therapeutic, that it could soothe our ills and recoup our losses. In that sense, English Studies is the unrecognized heir of those earlier professional discourses that similarly had promised the rejuvenating value of "being all attention." Indeed, since its beginnings, English Studies has been, at heart, a prospectus for cultural renewal (1996, 183–84).

With the failure of the empire, its imperial psychology shifted into the profession, and the qualities that distinguish the imperial enterprise moved along with it—an unequal economy of power and entitlement, the insistence on a "master narrative" that relegates difference to the margins of discourse,[2] the creation of a hierarchy of work in which certain tasks are "worth more" than others, and the elevation of enumeration above reflection as the central measure of accomplishment.[3] As Arata's summary suggests, understanding the history of the professionalization of English Studies also provides clear insight into some of its most protracted conflicts, most notably the ways in which institutions of higher education have valued—or not—the writing and composition work of its faculty. Yet, as Jessica Yood has recently noted, "we have yet to understand how writing by academics about their work is intimately connected to the kind of work we have done in the past and continue to do now" (2003, 526). This lack of understanding is precisely the gap in understanding that our essay tries to address, in the hope that a new understanding of old conflicts might yield new solutions.

To begin with, it's important to recognize that the success and spread of WAC programs nationally has also moved the traditional conflicts about the place of writing in systems of institutional valuation out of the English department and into the rest of the academy. As non-English faculty play larger and more important roles in an institution's commitment to improving writing across the curriculum, traditional discussions about the place of writing scholarship and service to the institution have shifted into many discipline departments, some of which have likely never had to consider writing as service and publication as part of a faculty member's retention and promotion portfolio. In her recent article, "The WAC Matrix: Institutional Requirements for Nurturing a Team-Based WAC Program," Lisa Emerson observes that "some faculty felt that time spent on long-term teaching innovation was a luxury they could not professionally afford" (2004, 56) because they would either be spending more time on pedagogy at the expense of their discipline research or "would be publishing in areas outside their primary research field, which may not be evaluated as highly as work in their primary field" (2004, 57). This expansion of a formerly narrow departmental discussion actually bodes well in the long run for creative resolutions and solutions, since much of the acrimony and entrenchment in that debate over the place of writing in our professional lives was exacerbated precisely by the same disciplinary history that gave rise to it. This is especially true in departments where the most senior (and tenured) faculty started their careers in the 1970s, when the lesser, "oral"[4] conversations about the place of writing in the academy still occupied the second tier at our professional meetings and in our professional publications, notably the MLA, PMLA, NCTE, and College English. As Jessica Yood's history of the legitimization of this conversation shows, these conversations and questions about how writing instruction and scholarship are valued in the academy and in the profession "would become knowledge in the field when pedagogy, writing research, and professional critique were published together as scholarship" (2003, 532), something that would not happen until the last decade and a half. And even now, very little has been written that addresses the implications of work in writing-across-the-curriculum programs for non-English faculty facing promotion and retention committees, even though these venues are the most important contested areas for determining institutional valuation.

One of the clearest descriptions of this conflict between writing and valuation within the discipline of English Studies is nearly twenty years old:

> As long as English professors were engaged primarily in a "pure" discipline, "applications" were devalued. Hence, rhetoric, the study of reading and writing, and all teaching were banished from the sacred laboratory—except, of course, freshman composition, which proceeded on the basis of a "purified" rhetoric that dislodged composition from its historical intellectual base. Literary studies were purified *to* theory, and rhetoric was purified *of* theory— with lugubrious consequences for the humanities. (Winterowd 1987, 257)

The tautology is clear here, as well as the distancing of writing instruction from both theory (the reasons *why*) and pedagogy (the question of *how*), which writing-across-the-curriculum programs have sought to redress across the country. If we stretch this colonization of writing instruction to the larger stage of the entire academy, then the questions we have to ask also have to be reframed. For example, when a social science faculty member addresses the writing of her students as part of an upper-level course in her discipline, is she advancing the content agenda of the course or is she "taking time out" from content instruction to address something that should have been addressed in the required composition courses that all freshman have to take? To what extent is the commonest objection of non-English colleagues to WAC development—"isn't that the job of the English department?"—the result of the schism that Winterowd described as the "purification" of literature into theory and rhetoric into "application," a practice that is by definition devoid of any real theoretical meaning? And not least important, to what extent does the WAC involvement of a non-English faculty member constitute the pursuit of academic interests that, no matter how admirable they might be, are really not the faculty member's "business," especially come promotion and review time?

This is a conundrum of our own making, created in the political trenches of writing instruction as compositionists fought for first class citizenship within English departments that were caught in a struggle for "relevancy" in an academy that saw a shift in student interest away from the liberal arts as a whole towards more "professional" disciplines that held out the promise of jobs and careers.[5] And without repeating either the theoretical ground for WAC, which is covered in the introduction to this volume of essays, or the several recent studies of WAC effectiveness, we need to mention that the development of a writing-across-the-curriculum pedagogy and theory, since the first such programs in the late 1970s, also constructed a potential opposition between the historical place of freshman composition in undergraduate education and the new mandates for WAC program development across the entire four years of that education, in all disciplines that students might major in. This potential opposition is, we argue, unnecessary. The most successful national models have, in fact, coordinated powerfully with freshmen composition programs to produce consistent and effective writing programs that stretch beyond the freshman year, without implying that what a student learns in the freshman year about writing is really unconnected to the demands of learning to write within the disciplines.[6] The most unfortunate outcome of this unnecessary pedagogical opposition is that a WAC program—which is predicated on using writing as a cognitive tool within the content classroom to advance both the course agenda and the promotion of formal or transactional writing which is enriched and enhanced by those informal reflective and recursive writing assignments—can often appear to be a separate program of writing instruction, one that on occasion can proceed along a different or, worse case, form a contradictory vector to the typical freshman writing program. A student studying in the "purified" composition program described by W. Ross Winterowd—and it is not inconceivable that this is the case, especially if one reviews the many composition textbooks that publishers circulate ahead of every book-ordering season—might in fact learn that the main concern of any writing course is negotiating stylistic skill and adhering to handbook prescriptions for "correctness." Meanwhile, our non-English colleagues who have worked with WAC principles in this same student's major classes would model a more constructivist view of writing, of writing as thinking in a systematic and productive manner about the ideas and facts available to the student in these content classes. These particular tenets have been at the heart of every WAC workshop and presentation since the program was started on campus.[7]

Part of the "problem," as Bruce Horner notes, is the predication of value on product, on "exchange value" (2000, 372), which is more difficult for

writing courses—especially Freshman Composition—than it is for more traditional disciplinary courses. We have to agree with Horner that this "discourse
of professionalism limits how we think of the work of Composition, defining
legitimate work as the acquisition, production, and distribution of print codi-
fied knowledge about writing: the production and reception of (scholarly)
texts" (2000, 375). Since teaching writing within the academy has already been
problematized by those usually charged with doing it (the English department),
the willingness of other departments and disciplines to accept WAC work as
valuable, usually at the administrative level where faculty valuation takes place
(the chairs), is low. Traditionally, "the greater the amount of knowledge produced, and the further removed this knowledge appears to be from lay knowledge [often the perception of what happens in freshman composition], the
greater is the stature of the individual professional or discipline" (Horner 2000,
375). And therein lies the issue, or rather, it is from this long-standing princi-
ple of institutional valuation that the particular problem addressed in this essay
grows. Recent efforts to change the ground for assessing the value of writing
classes within the academy, whether on constructivist epistemological claims[8]
or on claims that the activities in a writing classroom are in fact "post-discipli-
nary"[9] have provided little in the way of real change in the way that we reward
and promote those faculty—in any department—who devote a significant portion of their professional time and work to improving student writing, especially within their disciplines. As Horner correctly concludes, attempts "to define Composition in terms of its disciplinarity are either doomed to failure,
given Composition's identity with teaching, or they will transform Composition into something unrecognizable, a discipline in which teaching is periph-
eral, not central" (2000, 380).

It is precisely this "identity with teaching" that frames an argument for
valuing the work of faculty who devote their energies to advancing a WAC institutional agenda. What all the essays in this volume speak to is the fact that
by advancing a WAC program through sustained and broad faculty development, students become better students, in that they come to understand how
knowledge is constructed and mastered, and they learn to frame what they have
learned more competently within the writing expectations of their discipline
majors. Teachers also become better teachers, because they shift the responsibility for learning more equitably within the classroom, and by so doing, repo-
sition themselves to the subject matter so that they become less authoritative
and more facilitative. When an institution embraces a broad writing-across-the-
curriculum agenda, as ours has, then it also foregrounds the work of those faculty who have chosen to promote it; it has to, since the final success of any
WAC effort lies in the director's ability to transfer responsibility for advancing, promoting, and defining that program to the faculty who have embraced it.
In this case, faculty become responsible for designing and providing their own
professional development, a process of empowerment that models what we
want to have happen in any class where writing instruction takes place. Thus,

a faculty member who produces a scholarly work on writing within her discipline is not only contributing to disciplinary knowledge (the traditional "pure" realm of knowledge that disciplines and departments value), but she is also defining the critical contact zones within the institution, the precise moments and places that the crucial learning of the institution takes place, moments and places that are "sacred" to the teacher and the student. And in an institution that touts itself as a school where teaching takes pride of place among other institutional goals and accomplishments, to suggest that someone working in a WAC program is somehow doing less valuable work than someone advancing the "pure" knowledge of the discipline is misguided and harmful.

Richard Light, in his recent study of college students, *Making the Most of College: Students Speak Their Minds,* asked students about what made certain classes the most engaging and satisfying: "The results are stunning. The relationship between the amount of writing for a course and students' level of engagement—whether engagement is measured by time spent on the course, or the intellectual challenge it presents, or students' level of interest in it—is stronger than the relationship between students' engagement and any other course characteristic" (2001, 55). This finding must have opened a number of eyes and ears when it comes to what students believe best prepares them for professional success; not disciplinary knowledge alone, not mastery of terms and concepts, but constant and sustained writing practice in the use of those terms and concepts, of that disciplinary knowledge. The need for and the value of writing-across-the-curriculum could not have been stated more urgently, and Light's "discovery" goes to the heart of our argument in this essay: a school with a powerful commitment to WAC will not only address the writing skills of its students but will also increase student engagement and understanding of discipline content throughout the undergraduate curriculum. As historian David R. Russell has phrased it, "With WAC, the old battles between access and exclusion, excellence and equity, scientific and humanist world views, liberal and professional education, all come down to very specific questions of responsibility for curriculum and teaching. WAC ultimately asks: in what ways will graduates of our institutions use language, and how shall we teach them to use it in those ways?" (1991, 307). Our institutional system of rewards and valuation needs to mirror what we say we value most in the teaching/learning economy, especially with regards to those faculty who have dedicated themselves to promoting this student-centered learning model.

In her forward to a recent collection of essays devoted to exploring the future of WAC (McLeod, Miraglia, Soven, Thaiss 2001), pioneer Elaine Maimon identified precisely why all the most vexing issues of the composition versus literature [discipline] debate are really irrelevant to the larger question of how WAC is valued and recognized in the professional lives of faculty. Speaking of WAC as a reform movement within the academy, Maimon notes that "WAC has developed within the paradox of the academy, the simultaneous commitment to conservatism (the preservation of knowledge) and to radicalism (the generation of new knowledge). WAC's staying power as an educational reform movement is based on its resilience in resolving this paradox" (vii). This "paradox" describes precisely the divide that has proved to be so destructive in the history of English Studies, between those who have devoted their scholarship to the "pure" discipline of literature and those who have practiced "applications" in the writing classroom. As Maimon correctly formulates it, successful WAC programs have historically flourished on the boundary between these two professional affections, the conservative (discipline) and the radical (constructivism), fostering discussions in various disciplinary classrooms about both how knowledge is made and how writing can be a tool to explore what is presented to students as knowledge within our disciplines. As Gary Olson recently noted in a *Chronicle of Higher Education* feature on "Deconstructing Composition," composition and rhetoric (i.e., writing) form "a discipline about how language works" (McLemee 2003, A16). And so the common distinction within WAC programs between "writing to learn" (WTL) and "writing in the disciplines" (WID) is actually not so much the source of pedagogical and scholarly conflict as it is a revolutionary and complex learning/teaching continuum that engages both faculty and students in the course learning. Faculty learn more about their own teaching and can thus assume greater control over their development and support needs in the classroom; students begin to view writing as a richer experience than the simple production of a term paper or essay that forms the greater part of their final course grade. And the institution benefits from the community-building, which is the inevitable consequence of a broadly conceived and implemented WAC program. We are nearly done reviewing the workshop evaluations of faculty who participated in this summer's WAC workshops (2004), and in response to a question that asked them to name the three most important "take-aways" from the experience, nearly all ninety-seven faculty noted the value and benefit of shared community, especially with faculty from other disciplines. As one participant put it, "I have taught at Quinnipiac for nearly a decade and never appreciated the richness of the faculty community of which I am a part." This experience is part of the solution, we argue, to the endemic conflict between writing and content, both within the English department and in the broader academic community.

Practically, the faculty who devote themselves to the promotion of good undergraduate writing through a WAC program forge these resolutions in a variety of ways, each dependent on developing a different, complementary practice to teaching disciplinarily. As we noted at the beginning of this essay, the faculty who wrote for this volume (and they are mostly representative of their colleagues campuswide) have developed teaching practices that advance both their disciplinary agenda and the university's broader WAC program, which has been in place now for four years. This past summer (2004), we hosted several WAC workshops for faculty from all four undergraduate schools of the university through the generosity of the Davis Educational Foundation, which allowed us to pay each of the participants a small stipend for their time and work. The aim of the workshops was straightforward: to model the learning experience of students in WAC-inspired classrooms, to promote discussion between faculty from different disciplines about common pedagogical problems, and to revise a syllabus for a fall semester course to reflect WAC processes, including the crafting of a first assignment. At the end of the workshops, we asked all participants (nearly one hundred in this first year of a three-year faculty development project) to evaluate their experience. The results were not only overwhelmingly positive, but also instructive in light of Maimon's claim that WAC programs can foster creative resolutions to the traditional (and false) dichotomy between teaching disciplinary content and using writing in the same class to promote thinking and to measure learning. Overall, there are two common threads in these evaluations: the pleasant realization that using writing to learn course material better prepares students to write formally about what they have learned, without compromising the content instruction, and the power and value of cross-disciplinary collaboration that was a key part of all the workshops.

Typical was the comment of one of our chemistry faculty: "The most important aspect of the WAC workshop was the small group and large group work that allowed us to team up with faculty from other disciplines and exchange ideas . . . . We found that we had many common problems in evaluating students and their writing." Another professor in the Interactive Digital Design department noted that "More than simply discussing how writing to learn could be used, we actually did it. As a result, we built a strong community over the course of three days, a process that could be mimicked in the classroom . . . . What has happened, particularly for me, is that I know all the members of my group well enough that I can approach anyone individually about WAC. This is where the true strength of the community lies . . . it is institutional, across the campus." There are dozens of such comments in the evaluations, notable partly because the workshops were mostly led by non-English faculty who had been trained to run these workshops over the past year. As one of our colleagues observed, "This was a workshop for faculty run by faculty. . . . that is an empowering idea." These responses and experiences provide ample evidence for the reforming and reconciling power of WAC, provided that the faculty are themselves invested with the responsibility for faculty and programmatic development. We have learned that the less top-directed the program becomes, the more fully faculty come to identify themselves professionally with the objectives of the WAC program. As one of the faculty trainers (a sociologist) recently wrote, "For me, writing has also become a vehicle for improved teaching—I can no longer see the two as separate enterprises." For us, these are the collaborations and solutions that we have sought for so long within the English department. The good work that all the dedicated faculty who toil on behalf of WAC at Quinnipiac University promises that we will create a diverse and creative community in which the classic separation between good thinking and good writing is no longer found.

Notes

1. Through the generosity of the Davis Educational Foundation, we have received grant monies that will support a three-year faculty development program with a target participation level of 60–70 percent for all faculty, full- and part-time. More on this effort, of which summer 2004 is the first year of implementation, at the end of this essay.

2. See the work on marginalization by bell hooks, especially her contention that these marginal spaces can become important and powerful "sites of resistance" in the broader debate about inclusion within composition studies.

3. There are several good sources that provide detailed examinations of these particular qualities. These are just a few: Terry Eagleton, Frederick Jameson, and Edward Said. *Nationalism, Colonialism, and Literature*. Minneapolis: University of Minnesota Press, 1990. Patrick Brantlinger, *Rule of Darkness: British Literature and Imperialism, 1830–1914*. Ithaca: Cornell University Press, 1988. Spurr, David. *The Rhetoric of Empire: Colonial Discourse in Journalism, Travel Writing*. Durham, NC: Duke University Press, 1993.

4. "If traditional knowledge is oral, then the chances of its practitioners subjecting it to studious critique are presumed to be less likely" (Horner, 369). Bruce Horner, "Traditions and Professionalization: Reconceiving Work in Composition." *College Composition and Communication* 51 (3), Feb. 2000. 366–98.

5. There are, of course, many analyses of this process; typical among them is Robert J. Connor's "Overwork/Underpay: Labor and Status of Composition Teachers Since 1880," *Rhetoric Review* 9 (1), Autumn, 1990: 108–26.

6. At our own institution, for example, we have worked very hard to implicate freshman writing instruction in the broader mandate to address writing instruction in all four years of a student's education. Thanks to the support and involvement of our Freshman Coordinator, Dr. Christine Ross, we have increased the likelihood that the first conversations a student has about good writing in the academy will occur in courses other than English, and a recent Davis Foundation grant for faculty development included many composition teachters—full- and part-time—who were asked to consider how the broader WAC philosophy of the university affects their own instruction.

7. As Toby Fulwiler noted in 1991, these WAC workshops represent a revolution both in terms of pedagogy and as a means of promoting faculty development: "WAC has given new meaning to the concept of faculty development" (181). More locally, one of the participants in our most recent round of WAC workshops noted in his evaluation, "One last, and very significant comment, you [the WAC Director] were not present! I am not sure how many realized this, but I know it was conscious on your part. This was a workshop for faculty run by faculty."

8. See Stephan M. North. 1987. *The Making of Knowledge in Composition: Portrait of an Emerging Field*. Portsmouth, NH: Heinemann. Also David Bartholomae. 1996. "What Is Composition and (if you know what that is) Why Do We Teach It?" In *Composition in the Twenty-First Century: Crisis and Change,* Lynn Z. Bloom, Donald A. Daiker, and Edward M. White, eds. Carbondale: Southern Illinois University Press, 11–28.

9. See Patricia Harkin. 1991. "The Postdisciplinary Politics of Lore." In *Contending With Words: Composition and Rhetoric in a Postmoderm Age,* Patricia Harkin and John Schilb, eds. New York: Modern Language Association, 124–38.

References

Academic Association of Higher Education. *www.aahe.org/newdirections/vision.html*

Arata, Stephen. 1996. *Fictions of Loss in the Victorian Fin de Siècle: Identity and Empire.* Cambridge: Cambridge University Press.

Boyer, Ernest L. 1990. *Scholarship Reconsidered: Priorities of the Professoriate.* Princeton, NJ: Carnegie Foundation for the Advancement of Teaching.

Diamond, Robert, and Bronwyn E. Adam, eds. 1995. *The Disciplines Speak: Rewarding the Scholarly, Professional, and Creative Work of Faculty.* Washington, DC: American Association for Higher Education.

Elbow, Peter. "The Culture of Literature and Composition: What Could Each Learn From the Other?" *College English* 62 (May 2002): 533–46.

Emerson, Lisa. 2004. "The WAC Matrix: Institutional Requirements for Nurturing a Team-Based WAC Program." *Journal of the Council of Writing Program Administrators* 27 (Spring): 53–68.

Fulwiler, Toby. 1991. "The Quiet and Insistent Revolution: Writing Across the Curriculum." In *The Politics of Writing Instruction: Postsecondary.* eds. Richard Bullock and John Trimbur 179–87. Portsmouth, NH: Boynton/Cook, Heinemann.

Leverenz, Carrie. 2000. "Tenure and Promotion in Rhetoric and Composition." *CCCC* 52 (1), September: 143–47.

Light, Richard J. 2001. *Making the Most of College: Students Speak Their Minds.* Cambridge, MA: Harvard University Press.

Loyola University. 1998. English Department Guideline for Promotion and Tenure. *http://www.luc.edu/depts/english/tenure.htm*

McLemee, Scott. 2003. "Deconstructing Composition: The 'New Theory' Wars Break Out in an Unlikely Discipline." In *The Chronicle of Higher Education* 49 (28), March 21: A16.

McLeod, Susan H., Eric Miraglia, Margot Soven, and Christopher Thaiss, eds. 2001. *WAC for the New Millennium.* Urbana, IL: National Council of Teachers of English.

Miraglia, Eric, and Susan H. McLeod. (1997). "Whither WAC? Interpreting the Stories/Histories of Enduring WAC Programs." *Writing Program Administration* 20 (Spring): 46–65.

Russell, David R. 1991. *Writing in the Academic Disciplines, 1870–1990: A Curricular History.* Carbondale: Southern Illinois University Press.

Schuster, Charles, ed. 1998. "Evaluating the Intellectual Work of Writing Administration." *Writing Program Administration* 22 (Fall/Winter): 85–104.

Schuster, Charles I. 1991. "The Politics of Promotion." In *The Politics of Writing Instruction: Postsecondary.* eds. Richard Bullock and John Timbur. 85–95. Portsmouth, NH: Boynton/Cook, Heinemann.

Winterowd, W. Ross. 1987. "The Purification of Literature and Rhetoric." *College English* 49 (3), March: 257–73.

Yood, Jessica. 2003. "Writing the Discipline: A Generic History of English Studies." *College English* 65 (5), May: 526–40.